Faulkner, William (pp. 295–302). "A Rose for Emily," copyright 1930 and renewed 1958 by William Faulkner. Reprinted from _Collected Stories of William Faulkner_ by permission of Random House, Inc., Curtis Brown Ltd., London, Literary Executors of the estate of William Faulkner, and Jonathan Cape Ltd.

Green, Martin (pp. 50 and 118–119). Selections are reprinted from _Re-appraisals: Some Commonsense Readings in American Literature_ by Martin Green with the permission of W. W. Norton & Company, Inc., and Hugh Evelyn Ltd. Copyright © 1965, 1963 by W. W. Norton & Company, Inc.

Hall, Donald (pp. 245–250). "Coping with a Poem" from _The Pleasures of Poetry_ by Donald Hall. Copyright © 1971 by Donald Hall. Reprinted by permission of Harper & Row, Publishers, Inc.

Hardy, Thomas (p. 245). "Transformations" from _The Complete Poems of Thomas Hardy,_ edited by James Gibson (London: Macmillan, 1976, and N.Y.: Macmillan, 1978).

Herbert, Robert L. (pp. 6–7). Robert L. Herbert's essay on Millet's _The Gleaners_ reprinted courtesy of the author and the National Gallery of Canada from the exhibition catalogue _Man and His World: International Fine Arts Exhibition at Expo 67_ (Ottawa: NGC, 1967).

Housman, A. E. (p. 236). "Eight O'Clock" from _The Collected Poems of A. E. Housman._ Copyright 1922 by Holt, Rinehart and Winston. Copyright 1950 by Barclays Bank Ltd. Reprinted by permission of Holt, Rinehart and Winston, Publishers, The Society of Authors as the literary representatives of the Estate of A. E. Housman, and Jonathan Cape Ltd., publishers of A. E. Housman's _Collected Poems._

Jarrell, Randall (p. 204). "The Death of the Ball Turret Gunner" from _The Complete Poems_ by Randall Jarrell. Copyright 1945, 1969 by Mrs. Randall Jarrell. Copyright renewed © 1969 by Mary von Schrader Jarrell. Reprinted with the permission of Farrar, Straus & Giroux, Inc., and Faber and Faber Ltd.

Joyce, James (p. 115). From "Araby" from _Dubliners_ by James Joyce. Originally published by B. W. Heubsch, Inc. in 1916. Copyright © 1967 by the Estate of James Joyce. Reprinted by permission of Viking Penguin Inc., The Society of Authors as the literary representatives of the Estate of James Joyce, and Jonathan Cape Ltd.

Krutch, Joseph Wood (pp. 60–61 and 190–194). From _"Modernism" in the Modern Drama_ by Joseph Wood Krutch. Copyright 1953 by Columbia University Press. Reprinted by permission.

Lodge, David (pp. 145–149). Reprinted from _The Language of Fiction_ by permission of Columbia University Press and Routledge & Kegan Paul Ltd. Copyright 1966, Columbia University Press.

McCarthy, Mary (p. 120). From "Settling the Colonel's Hash" from _On the Contrary_ by Mary McCarthy. Copyright 1951, 1952, 1953, 1954, © 1955, 1958, 1959, 1960, 1961 by Mary McCarthy. Reprinted by permission of Farrar, Straus & Giroux, Inc., and the author.

Morgenstern, Joseph (p. 61). From "On the Road," _Newsweek,_ July 21, 1969. Copyright 1969, by Newsweek, Inc. All Rights Reserved. Reprinted by Permission.

Muir, Kenneth (pp. 188–190). "Hamlet's Foil" from _Shakespeare: Hamlet_ from "Studies in English Literature" series reprinted by permission of Edward Arnold (Publishers) Ltd.

Solomon, Stanley J. (pp. 273–276). From *Beyond Formula: American Film Genres* by Stanley J. Solomon, © 1976 by Harcourt Brace Jovanovich, Inc., and reprinted with their permission.

Van Doren, Mark (pp. 241–245). Excerpt from *Introduction to Poetry* by Mark Van Doren. Copyright 1951 by William Sloan Associates, Inc. Copyright © 1966 by Mark Van Doren. Reprinted by permission of Hill and Wang, a division of Farrar, Straus & Giroux, Inc.

Van Ghent, Dorothy (pp. 118 and 136). From *The English Novel: Form and Function* by Dorothy Van Ghent. Copyright 1953 by Dorothy Van Ghent. Reprinted by permission of Roger Van Ghent, Executor of the Estate of Dorothy Van Ghent.

White, E. B. (pp. 289–292). "Education" — March 1939 — in *One Man's Meat* by E. B. White. Copyright, 1939 by E. B. White. By permission of Harper & Row, Publishers, Inc.

Yeats, William Butler (pp. 11 and 211). "The Balloon of the Mind" and lines from "Sailing to Byzantium" reprinted with permission of Macmillan Publishing Company, Michael B. Yeats, Anne Yeats, and Macmillan, London, Limited from *The Poems* by W. B. Yeats, edited by Richard J. Finneran. "The Balloon of the Mind" copyright 1919 by Macmillan Publishing Co., Inc., renewed 1947 by Bertha Georgie Yeats. "Sailing to Byzantium" copyright 1928 by Macmillan Publishing Co., Inc., renewed 1956 by Georgie Yeats.

Preface

Favorable response to the first four editions has allowed me to revise the book again. There have been many changes throughout, but the most obvious are the addition of a student's analysis of a story, of a student's review of a production of a play, and of the new Modern Language Association form of documentation.

"Types of Writing Assignments," beginning on page xv, following the Contents, lists the chief kinds of assignments, such as essays on character, imagery, style, and so forth, and it indicates the relevant passages in the text along with the illustrative essays. Thus, a student who is going to write about, say, the function of a character — whether in a play or short story or novel — will find, collected under Character, references to the book's chief discussions of the topic and also references to the three essays in the book that concentrate on character. Similarly, the student who is writing a comparison is referred, under Comparison and Contrast, to sample patterns of organization, and to three sample essays.

The first chapter, "Writing about Literature: An Overview," considers the nature of critical writing, treats two kinds of criticism (explication and analysis), and then discusses the problems of choosing a topic and organizing the material. The chapter ends with a brief summary of the process of writing a critical essay.

The second chapter, "Style and Format," is a fairly short and direct approach to the elements of clear writing. It treats such matters as denotation, connotation, subordination, paragraphs, and so forth, and provides a number of specific illustrations taken from good writers. The latter part of the chapter is devoted to manuscript form, quotations, footnotes, and bibliography.

The third chapter, "Practical Applications," discusses reviews, research papers, and essay examinations. It follows Chapter 2 because it continues to deal with more or less mechanical matters, but of course in practice students will not be writing research papers or examinations until after they have become familiar with some or all the matters discussed in the later chapters on literature.

The fourth, fifth, sixth, and seventh chapters introduce the reader to various approaches used in writing about fiction, drama, poetry, and film. These chapters also include sample essays and a number of illustrative paragraphs that should help the reader to see what good writing is and to understand the sorts of problems good writers deal with.

Each of these last four chapters includes, about midway, an essay by a student, and each concludes with two essays by published essayists. The topics and approaches vary widely. Instructors do not want their students to imitate any specific essayist, but again it is useful to have samples of adequate prose and examples of some of the things people do when they write about literature. These essays, along with the earlier material on writing and documentation, may provide students with helpful guides to writing their own readable prose and developing their own approaches to writing about literature and film.

I hope that the preceding remarks tell readers all that they want to know about the scope of the book, but some further words must be added. Dr. Johnson said that "there is not so poor a book in the world that would not be a prodigious effort were it wrought out entirely by a single mind, without the aid of previous investigators." I cannot name all the previous investigators who have helped to shape my ideas, but I must acknowledge my indebtedness to Morton Berman, William Burto, and Marcia Stubbs, who never tire of improving my pages, and (at Little, Brown) to Carolyn Potts, Virginia Pye, Virginia Shine, and Billie Ingram. Others who have offered valuable suggestions include Rebecca Argall, James Blake, Randall Brune, David Cavitch, Warren Chelline, Charles Christensen, William Evans, Shearle Furnish, Bruce Golden, Okey Goode, Patricia Graves, Dean Hall, Gratia Murphy, J. M. Pair, and Virginia Shale.

Contents

Appendixes

Index   *303*

Types of Writing Assignments: A Key to Advice and Examples

The index is the best guide for the student who wants to draw together all references to a given topic, for example on "character" or on "theme," but the following Key may be useful for a student who wants to locate material — especially a sample essay — that will be of assistance in writing a particular kind of essay. Because the topics are not mutually exclusive, most of the sample essays are listed more than once.

A Short Guide
to Writing
about Literature

Part One

1

Writing about Literature: An Overview

WHY WRITE?

People write about literature in order to clarify and to account for their responses to works that interest or excite or frustrate them. In putting words on paper you will have to take a second and a third look at what is in front of you and at what is within you. And so writing is a way of learning. The last word is never said about complex thoughts and feelings, but when we write we hope to make at least a little progress in the difficult but rewarding job of talking about our responses. We learn, and then we hope to interest our reader because we are communicating our responses to material that for one reason or another is worth talking about.

But to resond sensitively to anything and then to communicate responses, one must have some understanding of the thing, and one must have some skill at converting responses into words. This book tries to deepen your understanding of what literature is — what it does and the ways in which it does it — and it tries to help you transform your responses into words that will let your reader share your perceptions, your enthusiasms, and even your doubts. This sharing is, in effect, teaching. Students often think that they are writing for the teacher, but this is a misconception; when you write, *you* are the teacher. An essay on literature is an attempt to help someone to see the work as you see it. If this book had to be boiled down to a single sentence of advice, that sentence would be: Because you are teaching, your essay should embody those qualities which you value in teachers — probably intelligence, open-mindedness, and effort; certainly a desire to offer what help one can.

IMAGINING AN AUDIENCE

If you are not writing for the teacher, for whom are you writing? For yourself, of course, but also for others. Occasionally, in an effort to help you develop an awareness that what you write depends partly on your audience, your instructor may specify an audience, requiring you to write for your school newspaper, or for readers of *The Atlantic* or of *Ms.,* but if an audience is not specified, write for your classmates. If you keep your classmates in mind as your audience, you will not write, "William Shakespeare, England's most famous playwright," because such a remark offensively implies that the reader does not know Shakespeare's nationality or trade. On the other hand, you *will* write, "Sei Sōnagon, a lady of the court in medieval Japan," because you can reasonably assume that your classmates do not know who she is. Similarly, you will not explain that Julius Caesar was a Roman ruler but you probably will explain that Coriolanus (also the subject of one of Shakespeare's tragedies) was a Roman soldier.

THE NATURE OF CRITICAL WRITING

In everyday talk the commonest meaning of **criticism** is something like "finding fault," and to be critical is to be censorious. But a critic can see excellences as well as faults. Because we turn to criticism with the hope that the critic has seen something we have missed, the most valuable criticism is not that which shakes its finger at faults but that which calls our attention to interesting things going on the work of art. Here are two statements, the first by John Dryden (1631–1700), the second by W. H. Auden (1907–1973), suggesting that criticism is most useful when it calls our attention to things worth attending to:

> They wholly mistake the nature of criticism who think its business is principally to find fault. Criticism, as it was first instituted by Aristotle, was meant a standard of judging well; the chiefest part of which is, to observe those excellencies which should delight a reasonable reader.
>
> *Essays,* ed. W. P. Ker (Oxford, 1926), I, p. 179

Now Auden:

> What is the function of a critic? So far as I am concerned, he can do me one or more of the following services:
>
> 1. Introduce me to authors or works of which I was hitherto unaware.
> 2. Convince me that I have undervalued an author or a work because I had not read them carefully enough.
> 3. Show me relations between works of different ages and cultures which I could never have seen for myself because I do not know enough and never shall.
> 4. Give a "reading" of a work which increases my understanding of it.
> 5. Throw light upon the process of artistic "Making."
> 6. Throw light upon the relation of art to life, science, economics, ethics, religion, etc.
>
> *The Dyer's Hand* (New York, 1963), pp. 8–9

Dryden is chiefly concerned with literature as a means of delight, and his criticism aims at increasing the delight we can get from literature; Auden does not neglect this delight, but he extends (especially in his sixth point) the range of criticism to include topics beyond the literary work itself. But in both Dryden and Auden the emphasis on observing, showing, illuminating, suggests that the function of critical writing is not very different from the commonest view of the function of imaginative writing. Here is Joseph Conrad in the preface to one of his novels, *The Nigger of the "Narcissus"*:

> My task which I am trying to achieve is, by the power of the written word, to make you hear, to make you feel — it is, before all, to make you *see*. That — and no more, and it is everything.

This is not far from a comment made by the painter Ben Shahn, who said that in his paintings he wanted to get right the difference between the way a cheap coat and an expensive coat hung.

A Sample Essay

Let's begin with a very brief critical essay, not about literature but about painting. In *The Gleaners* Jean-François Millet tried to show us certain things, and now an essayist tries to show us — tries to make us see — what Millet was doing and how he did it. The following short essay is a note in the catalog issued in conjunction with the art exhibition at the Canadian World's Fair, Expo 67.

Millet's The Gleaners
Robert Herbert

Jean-François Millet, born of well-to-do Norman peasants, began his artistic training in Cherbourg. In 1837 he moved to Paris where he lived until 1849, except for a few extended visits to Normandy. With the sounds of the Revolution of 1848 still rumbling, he moved to Barbizon on the edge of the Forest of Fontainebleau, already noted as a resort of landscape painters, and there he spent the rest of his life. One of the major painters of what came to be called the Barbizon School, Millet began to celebrate the labours of the peasant, granting him a heroic dignity which expressed the aspirations of 1848. Millet's identification with the new social ideals was a result not of overtly radical views, but of his instinctive humanitarianism and his rediscovery in actual peasant life of the eternal rural world of the Bible and of Virgil, his favourite reading since youth. By elevating to a new prominence the life of the common people, the revolutionary era released the stimulus which enabled him to continue this essential pursuit of his art and of his life.

The Gleaners, exhibited in the Salon of 1857, presents the very poorest of the peasants who are fated to bend their backs to gather with clubbed fingers the wisps of overlooked grain. That they seem so entirely wedded to the soil results from the perfect harmony of Millet's fatalistic view of man with the images which he created by a careful disposition of lines, colours and shapes. The three women

Jean-François Millet, *The Gleaners* (1857)
oil, 32⅞ × 43¾ inches
courtesy of Musées Nationaux, Paris

are alone in the bronzed stubble of the foreground, far removed from the bustling activity of the harvesters in the distance, the riches of whose labours have left behind a few gleanings. Millet has weighted his figures ponderously downward, the busy harvest scene is literally above them, and the high horizon line which the taller woman's cap just touches emphasizes their earth-bound role suggesting that the sky is a barrier which presses down upon them, and not a source of release.

The humility of primeval labour is shown, too, in the creation of primitive archetypes rather than of individuals. Introspection such as that seen in Velázquez' *Water Carrier of Seville,* in which the three men are distinct individuals, is denied by suppressing the gleaners' features, and where the precise, fingered gestures of La Tour's *Saint Jerome* bring his intellectual work toward his sensate mind, Millet gives his women club-like hands which reach away from their bent bodies toward the earth.

It was, paradoxically, the urban-industrial revolution in the nineteenth century which prompted a return to images of the preindustrial, ageless labours of man. For all their differences, both Degas and Van Gogh were to share these concerns later, and even Gauguin was to find in the fishermen of the South Seas that humble being, untainted by the modern city, who is given such memorable form in Millet's *Gleaners.*

In this essay there is, of course, **evaluation** or judgment as well as revelation of some of the things that are going on in the painting. First, the writer assumes it is worth his effort to talk about Millet's picture. Second, he explicitly praises some qualities ("perfect harmony," "memorable form"), but mostly the evaluation is implicit in and subordinate to the **description** of what the writer sees. He sees things and calls them to our attention as worthy of note. He points out the earthbound nature of the women, the difference between their hands and those of Saint Jerome (in another picture that was in the exhibition), the influence of the Bible and of Virgil, and so forth. It is clear that he values the picture, and he states some of the reasons he values it; but he is not worried about whether Millet is a better artist than Velázquez, or whether this is Millet's best painting. He is content to help us see what is going on in the picture.

Or, at least he seems to be content to help us see. In fact, of course, he tries to *persuade* us that what he sees is what is going on. And he sees with more than his eyes: memories, emotions, and value systems help him to see, and his skill as a writer helps him to persuade us of the accuracy of his report. If he wants to convince us and to hold our interest, he has to do more than offer random perceptions; he has to present his perceptions coherently.

Let's look for a moment at the **organization** or plan of this essay. In his effort to help us see what is going on, the author keeps his eye on his subject. His opening paragraph includes a few details (among them, that Millet was trained in Cherbourg) that are not strictly relevant to his main point (the vision embodied in the picture), but these must be included because the essay is not only a critical analysis of the picture but an informative headnote in a catalog of an exhibition of works by more than a hundred artists. Even in this preliminary biographical paragraph he moves quickly to the details closely related to the main business: Millet's peasant origin, his early association with landscape painters, his humanitarianism, and his reading of the Bible and Virgil. The second paragraph takes a close look at some aspects of the picture (the women's hands, their position in the foreground, the harvesters above and behind them, the oppressive sky), and the third paragraph makes illuminating comparisons with two other paintings. The last paragraph, like most good concluding paragraphs, while recapitulating the main point (the depiction of ageless labors), enlarges the vision by including references to Millet's younger contemporaries who shared his vision. Notice that this new material does not leave us looking forward to another paragraph but neatly opens up, or enriches, the matter and then turns it back to Millet. (For additional remarks on introductory and concluding paragraphs, see pp. 59–62.)

Some Kinds of Essays

A work of literature, like a painting, is a work of art. It is an object that embodies thoughts and feelings; study of it can increase our understanding of exactly what it is and can deepen our response to it. An enormous body of literature is worth our study, and a wide range of kinds of literary study is designed to bring us to a closer relation with the work. Any writing that helps a reader to understand a literary work can properly be called literary criticism. Sometimes the critic will study the author's sources, seeking to show us — say, by a comparison between Plutarch's *Lives* and Shakespeare's *Julius Caesar* — some of the special qualities in the literary work. Or one may study the author's biography, seeking to show us the degree to which Tennessee Williams's *Glass Menagerie* draws on his childhood experiences. A study of the anthropological and sociological background of the work may show that *A Midsummer Night's Dream* is indebted to May Day customs, or that the film *Dillinger* captures the special qualities that characterized the outlaw during the Depression. A feminist critic (not necessarily a female) may especially wish to compare Shakespeare's treatment of men with his treatment of women in similar circumstances, such as the ways in which they react to suffering.

Although students ordinarily are not required to have familiarity with little-known material, every student knows a good deal about some specialized area (acting in a play, mythology, rock lyrics, Spanish, loneliness, love, the Marx Brothers) and this knowledge may be invaluable in responding to certain texts. The playwright Eugène Ionesco said that the Marx Brothers influenced his first popular play, *The Bald Soprano.*

Essays on literature are not sterile exercises: they are attempts to get on paper — for one's own sake and for the sake of others — a sense of what a reader sees when responding to a literary work of art. Writing such essays ought not to be an activity dispassionately engaged in to please a teacher; it ought to be an activity that educates you and your reader. The job is twofold — seeing and saying — but these two finally are inseparable, for if you don't say it effectively the reader won't see what you have seen, and perhaps you haven't seen it clearly, either. What you say, in short, is a sort of device for helping the reader *and yourself* to see clearly. W. H. Auden's description of a poem can be applied to a good essay: it is a "contraption," but, Auden adds, a "contraption with a guy inside."

TWO COMMON APPROACHES

Explication

A line-by-line or episode-by-episode commentary on what is going on in a text is an **explication** (literally, unfolding or spreading out). It takes some skill to work one's way along without saying, "In line one . . . , in the second line . . . , in the third line. . . ." One must sometimes boldly say something like, "The next stanza begins with . . . and then introduces. . . ." And, of course, one can discuss the second line before the first line if that seems to be the best way of handling the passage.

An explication does not deal with the writer's life or times, and it is not a paraphrase, a rewording — though it may include paraphrase — but a commentary revealing your sense of the meaning of the work. To this end it calls attention, as it proceeds, to the implications of words, the function of rhymes, the shifts in point of view, the development of contrasts, and any other contributions to the meaning.

A Sample Explication

Take, for example, this short poem by William Butler Yeats.

Hands, do what you're bid:
Bring the balloon of the mind
That bellies and drags in the wind
Into its narrow shed.

"The Balloon of the Mind"

Now, it happens that in a prose work, *Reveries over Childhood and Youth,* Yeats already had used the figure of a balloon (dirigible) to represent mental activity: "My thoughts were a great excitement, but when I tried to do anything with them, it was like trying to pack a balloon into a shed in a high wind." But because explication usually confronts the work itself, without relating it to biography, we can pass over this interesting anticipation and confine ourselves to the poem's four lines, thus:

W. B. Yeats's "The Balloon of the Mind"

Yeats's "Balloon of the Mind" is about poetry, specifically about the difficulty of getting one's floating thoughts down in lines on the page. The first line, a short, stern, heavily stressed command to the speaker's hands, perhaps implies by its severe or impatient tone that these hands will be disobedient or inept or careless if not watched closely: the poor bumbling body so often fails to achieve the goals of the mind. The bluntness of the command in the first line is emphasized by the fact that all the subsequent lines have more syllables. Furthermore, the first line is a grammatically complete sentence, whereas the thought of line 2 spills over into the subsequent lines, implying the difficulty of fitting ideas into confining spaces, that is, of getting one's thoughts into order, especially into a coherent poem. Lines 2 and 3 amplify the metaphor already stated in the title (the product of the mind is an airy but unwieldy balloon), and they also contain a second command, "Bring." Alliteration ties this command, "*B*ring," to the earlier "*b*id"; it also ties both of these verbs to their object, "*b*alloon," and to the verb that most effectively describes the balloon, "*b*ellies." In comparison with the peremptory first line of the poem, lines 2 and 3 themselves seem almost swollen, bellying and dragging, an effect aided by using adjacent unstressed syllables ("of the," "[bell]ies and," "in the") and by using an eyerhyme ("mind" and "wind") rather than an exact rhyme. And then comes the short last line: almost before we could expect it, the cumbersome balloon — here, the idea that is to be packed into the stanza — is successfully lodged in its "narrow shed." Aside from the relatively colorless "into," the only words of more than one syllable in the poem are "balloon," "bellies," and "narrow" and all three emphasize the difficulty of the task. But after "narrow"—" the word itself almost looks long and narrow, in this context like a hangar — we get the simplicity of the monosyllable "shed"; and the difficult job is done, the thought is safely packed away, the poem is completed — but again with an off rhyme ("bid" and "shed"), for neatness can go only so far when hands and mind and a balloon are involved.

Because, as we can see from this excellent discussion of Yeats's poem, the language of a literary work is denser (richer in associations or connotations) than the language of discursive prose such as this paragraph, explication is much engaged in bringing to the surface the meanings that are in the words but that may not be immediately apparent. Explication, in short, seeks to make explicit the implicit. Other sample explications, or fragments of explications, appear in Chapters 4, 5, and 6 and Appendix A.

Writing an explication, like almost all other writing, begins not with putting a sheet of paper into a typewriter but with jotting down notes, and the best place for one's preliminary notes is the page in the book with the poem — assuming, of course, that you own the book. (If you don't own the book — or even if you do — it's a good idea to copy out the poem double-spaced, and to jot notes in the margins and between the lines.) As you read, you notice things, and you begin to mark up the text thus:

sounds abrupt

Hands, do what you're bid:

Bring the balloon of the mind

That bellies and drags in the wind *no real rhymes?*

Into its narrow shed.

A pen or pencil will help you to think, and your preliminary jottlings — including questions to yourself such as "meaning?" or "Do these words rhyme?"— will lead you to greater understanding.

Note: The reader of an explication needs to see the text, and because the explicated text is usually short, it is advisable to quote it all. (Remember, your imagined audience consists of your classmates; even if they have already read the work you are explicating, they have not memorized it, and so you helpfully remind them of the work by quoting it.) You can quote the entire text at the outset, or you can quote the first unit (for example, a stanza), then explicate that unit, and then quote the next unit, and so on. And if the poem or passage of prose is longer than, say, six lines, it is advisable to number each line at the right for easy reference.

Analysis

If one has world enough and time, one can set out to explicate all of *Moby-Dick* or *Hamlet;* more likely, one will explicate a page in *Moby-Dick,* or a speech in *Hamlet.* In writing about works longer than a page or two, however, a more common approach than explicating is **analyzing** (literally, separating into parts in order to understand). An analysis may consider only the functions of the setting in *The Adventures of Huckleberry Finn,* or the comedy in *Hamlet,* or the differences and resemblances between Willy Loman and King Lear, or the changes Shakespeare made when he turned his source into *Julius Caesar.*

Analysis, of course, is not a process used only in talking about literature. It is commonly applied in thinking about almost any complex matter. Martina Navratilova plays a deadly game of tennis. What makes it so good? How does her backhand contribute? What does her serve do to her opponent? Another example: a discussion about the morality of condemning killers to death will distinguish at least between those killers whose actions are premeditated and those whose actions are not. And in the first class it might distinguish between professional killers who carefully contrive a death, killers who are irrational except in their ability to contrive a death, and robbers who contrive a property crime and who kill only when they believe that killing is necessary in order to complete the intended crime. One can hardly talk usefully about capital punishment without making some such analysis of killers. And so it makes sense if you are writing about literature — say, about Gatsby's "dream" in Fitzgerald's *Great Gatsby* — to try to see the components of the dream. One critic begins a discussion of it thus:

> Gatsby's dream divides into three basic and related parts: the desire to repeat the past, the desire for money, and the desire for incarnation of "unutterable visions" in the material earth.
>
> Ernest H. Lockridge,
> *Twentieth Century Interpretations of "The Great Gatsby"*
> (Englewood Cliffs, N.J., 1968), p. 11.

And of course the essayist goes on to study these three components in detail.

Although Chapters 4, 5, and 6 contain specimens of analytic criticism, two examples may be useful here.

Suppose you have noticed that singers of blues often sing about traveling. Maybe you recall the lines,

> When a woman takes the blues
> She tucks her head and cries
> But when a man catches the blues,
> He catches a freight and rides,

and you wonder, among other things, "Why all this talk of traveling?" You decide you want to look into something along these lines, and so you search your memory of blues, play whatever records are available, read some anthologies that print blues lyrics, and generally try to set your thoughts in order. You find that blues often talk about traveling, but the travel is not all of the same sort, and you begin to analyze (separate into parts) the blues that use this motif. You begin to jot down words or phrases:

```
disappointed lover

travel to a job

from the South

fantasy travel

back to the South

life is a trip

my first trip out of the state

jail
```

You are making a scratch outline, for you are establishing categories, fiddling with them until you have established categories as nearly coordinate as possible; and you are indicating the order in which you will discuss them. You rearrange them as you refine your thinking, because your essay will not record your thought processes — with all the false steps — as they occurred; the finished essay will record your best thoughts in the order that you judge to be best for a reader. Then perhaps you find it useful to describe your categories a bit more fully:

1. Travel as an escape from unhappy love

2. Travel as an economic necessity when jobs are not available at home

3. Travel as an escape from the South to the North

4. Travel as an escape from the North back to the South

5. Travel as sheer wishful thinking, an image of escape from the unhappiness of life until death releases one

6. Travel as an image of the hard job of living, as in "It's a long old road, but I'm gonna find the end"

7. Enforced travel — to prison

You have now taken the theme of travel and separated it into various parts, not for the fun of inventing complications but for the sake of educating yourself and your reader. Having made these or similar distinctions you can go on to say some interesting things about one or all of these superficially similar but really rather different motifs of travel. You have had to divide "travel" into parts before you can answer the question you began with: "Why all this talk about traveling?" Perhaps your answer — your point or your **thesis** — is that talking about travel is a way of talking about life.

Once you have established your categories and tentatively settled on the order in which you will treat them, your job is half done. You have arrived at a thesis, assembled evidence to persuade the reader to accept the thesis, and begun to organize your essay. Possibly your finished essay will make the following points, in the order given but with convincing detail (perhaps some quotations from blues) to support them:

1. Singers of blues sing of traveling, but the travel is of various sorts. (Note: In your opening paragraph you may want to announce your thesis and indicate the organization your paper will have. Such a paragraph will be a help to both the writer and the reader. But these matters need not be stated formally unless your instructor asks you to do so.)

2. Often people travel because of economic, social, or even physical pressure (to get a job; to get to a more congenial environment in the urban North — or back to the rural South; to go to jail).

3. Most often, however, and perhaps in the most memorable songs, it is for another reason: it is an attempt to reduce the pain of some experiences, especially betrayed love, and the hearer senses that the attempt cannot succeed.

4. In such songs it is usually the men who travel, because they are more mobile than women (women are left to take care of the children), but whether it is the man who has deserted the woman or the woman who has deserted the man, both are pathetic figures because even the deserter will be haunted by the memory of the beloved.

5. But all these variations on the theme of travel overlap, and almost always there is a sense that the trip — whether to the North or the South, to a job or to jail, to a man or to a woman, or to nowhere in particular — is an image or metaphor for the trip through life, the long, painful road that everyone must walk.

A Sample Analysis

In a moment we will look at a student's analysis not of a motif but of a literary work; first, though, read this very short story by Kate Chopin.

The Story of an Hour
Kate Chopin (1851–1904)

Knowing that Mrs. Mallard was afflicted with a heart trouble, great care was taken to break to her as gently as possible the news of her husband's death.

It was her sister Josephine who told her, in broken sentences, veiled hints that revealed in half concealing. Her husband's friend Richards was there, too, near her. It was he who had been in the newspaper office when intelligence of the railroad disaster was received, with Brently Mallard's name leading the list of "killed." He had only taken the time to assure himself of its truth by a second telegram, and had hastened to forestall any less careful, less tender friend in bearing the sad message.

She did not hear the story as many women have heard the same, with a paralyzed inability to accept its significance. She wept at once, with sudden, wild abandonment, in her sister's arms. When the storm of grief had spent itself she went away to her room alone. She would have no one follow her.

There stood, facing the open window, a comfortable, roomy

armchair. Into this she sank, pressed down by a physical exhaustion that haunted her body and seemed to reach into her soul.

She could see in the open square before her house the tops of trees that were all aquiver with the new spring life. The delicious breath of rain was in the air. In the street below a peddler was crying his wares. The notes of a distant song which some one was singing reached her faintly, and countless sparrows were twittering in the eaves.

There were patches of blue sky showing here and there through the clouds that had met and piled above the other in the west facing her window.

She sat with her head thrown back upon the cushion of the chair quite motionless, except when a sob came up into her throat and shook her, as a child who has cried to sleep continues to sob in its dreams.

She was young, with a fair, calm face, whose lines bespoke repression and even a certain strength. But now there was a dull stare in her eyes, whose gaze was fixed away off yonder on one of those patches of blue sky. It was not a glance of reflection, but rather indicated a suspension of intelligent thought.

There was something coming to her and she was waiting for it, fearfully. What was it? She did not know; it was too subtle and elusive to name. But she felt it, creeping out of the sky, reaching toward her through the sounds, the scents, the color that filled the air.

Now her bosom rose and fell tumultuously. She was beginning to recognize this thing that was approaching to possess her, and she was striving to beat it back with her will — as powerless as her two white slender hands would have been.

When she abandoned herself a little whispered word escaped her slightly parted lips. She said it over and over under her breath: "Free, free, free!" The vacant stare and the look of terror that had followed it went from her eyes. They stayed keen and bright. Her pulses beat fast, and the coursing blood warmed and relaxed every inch of her body.

She did not stop to ask if it were not a monstrous joy that held her. A clear and exalted perception enabled her to dismiss the suggestion as trivial.

She knew that she would weep again when she saw the kind, tender hands folded in death; the face that had never looked save with love upon her, fixed and gray and dead. But she saw beyond that bitter moment a long procession of years to come that would belong to her absolutely. And she opened and spread her arms out to them in welcome.

There would be no one to live for during those coming years; she would live for herself. There would be no powerful will bending her in that blind persistence with which men and women believe they have a right to impose a private will upon a fellow-creature. A kind intention or a cruel intention made the act seem no less a crime as she looked upon it in that brief moment of illumination.

And yet she had loved him — sometimes. Often she had not. What did it matter! What could love, the unsolved mystery, count for in face of this possession of self-assertion which she suddenly recognized as the strongest impulse of her being.

"Free! Body and soul free!" she kept whispering.

Josephine was kneeling before the closed door with her lips to the keyhole, imploring for admission. "Louise, open the door! I beg; open the door — you will make yourself ill. What are you doing, Louise? For heaven's sake open the door."

"Go away. I am not making myself ill." No; she was drinking in a very elixir of life through that open window.

Her fancy was running riot along those days ahead of her. Spring days, and summer days, and all sorts of days that would be her own. She breathed a quick prayer that life might be long. It was only yesterday she had thought with a shudder that life might be long.

She arose at length and opened the door to her sister's importunities. There was a feverish triumph in her eyes, and she carried herself unwittingly like a goddess of Victory. She clasped her sister's waist, and together they descended the stairs. Richards stood waiting for them at the bottom.

Some one was opening the front door with a latchkey. It was Brently Mallard who entered, a little travel-stained, composedly carrying his grip-sack and umbrella. He had been far from the scene of accident, and did not even know there had been one. He stood amazed at Josephine's piercing cry; at Richards' quick motion to screen him from the view of his wife.

But Richards was too late.

When the doctors came they said she had died of heart disease — of joy that kills.

Sample Analysis: Ironies of Life in an Hour

Now for the student's analysis, written on an assigned topic: Irony in Kate Chopin's "The Story of an Hour." After thinking about the topic and consulting the jottings (including underlinings and marginal notes) made while reading and rereading, the student found that her underlying thesis — that there are several ironies in the story — broke down into two parts: The chief irony is that Mrs. Mallard dies just as she is beginning to enjoy life, but there are also smaller ironies, such as that the "sad message" turns out (for a while) not to be sad, and that although Richards is "too late" when he tries to save her at the end, if he had been "late" at the beginning the whole mess would not have occurred. The topic ideas of the paragraphs in the essay turned out to be these:

1. The story has an ironic ending, but there are smaller ironies within it.

2. One of these smaller ironies is that the "sad message" turns out, at least for a while, to bring joy.

3. Two other bits of irony are: (a) Richards's well-meaning haste at the beginning is not matched by adequate haste at the end; and (b) the doctors' comments on joy are true in a way that the speakers do not mean.

4. The central irony, however, is that Mrs. Mallard begins to live only after years of marriage, and this new life, which occurs appropriately at springtime, is cut off even as she looks forward not only to summer but to "a long progression of years."

Some such thoughts must have preceded the following essay, but they were arrived at only after reading and rereading, and writing and rewriting. Don't let the excellence of this essay discourage you. You can do as well. Remember, this essay is the product of much work. As the writer wrote, her ideas got better and better, for in her drafts she put down a point and then realized that it needed strengthening (for instance, with a brief quotation) or that — come to think of it — the point couldn't be substantiated and ought to be deleted.

Ironies of Life in an Hour

Kate Chopin's ''Story of an Hour'' — which takes only a few minutes to read — turns out to have an ironic ending, but on rereading it one sees that the irony is not concentrated only in the outcome of the plot — Mrs. Mallard dies just when she is beginning to live — but is also present in many details.

After we know how the story turns out, if we re-read it we find irony at the very start: Mrs. Mallard's friends and relatives all assume, mistakenly, that she was deeply in love with her husband, Brently Mallard, and so they take great care to tell her gently of his death. They mean well, and in fact they *do* well, for they bring her an hour of life, an hour of joyous freedom, but it is ironic that they think their news is sad. True, Mrs. Mallard at first expresses grief when she hears the news, but soon (unknown to her friends) she finds joy in it. And, so Richards's ''sad message,'' though sad in his eyes, is in fact a happy message.

Among the small but significant ironic details is the statement near the end of the story that when Mallard entered the house, Richards tried to conceal him from Mrs. Mallard, but ''Richards was too late.'' This is ironic because almost at the start of the story, in the second paragraph, Richards with the best of motives ''hastened'' to bring his sad message; if he had at the start been ''too late,'' Mallard would have arrived at home first, and Mrs. Mallard's life

would not have ended an hour later but would have gone
on simply as it had been. Yet another irony at the end
of the story is the diagnosis of the doctors. They say
she had died of ''heart disease — of joy that kills.''
In one sense they are right: Mrs. Mallard has for the
last hour experienced a great joy. But of course the
doctors totally misunderstand the joy that kills her.
It is not joy at seeing her husband alive, but her
realization that the great joy she experienced during
the last hour is over.

All these ironic details add richness to the
story, but the central irony resides not in the well-
intentioned but ironic actions of Richards, or in the
unconsciously ironic words of the doctors, but in Mrs.
Mallard's own life. She has for years been alive, and
yet in a way she has been dead, a body subjected to
her husband's will. Now, his apparent death brings her
new life. Appropriately, this new life comes to her at
the season of the year when ''the tops of trees were
all aquiver with the new spring life.'' But, ironi-
cally, her new life will last only an hour. She is
''Free, free, free'' — but only until her husband
walks through the doorway. She looks forward to
''summer days'' but she will not see even the end of
this spring day. If her years of marriage were ironic,
bringing her a sort of living death instead of joy,
her new life is ironic too, not only because it grows
out of her moment of grief for her supposedly dead
husband, but because its vision of ''a long progres—

sion of years'' is cut short within an hour on a
spring day.

The Analysis Analyzed

Let's look at several principles illustrated by this essay.

1. The title of the essay is not merely the title of the work
discussed; rather, it gives the reader a clue, a small idea of the essayist's topic.

2. The opening or introductory paragraph does not begin by
saying "In this story. . . ." Rather, by naming the author and the
title, it lets the reader know exactly what story is being discussed.
It also develops the writer's thesis a bit, so that readers know where
they will be going.

3. The smaller ironies are discussed in the second and third
paragraphs, the central (chief) irony in the last paragraph. That is,
the essay does not dwindle or become anticlimactic; rather, it builds
up.

4. Some brief quotations are used, both to provide evidence
and to let the reader hear — even if fleetingly — Kate Chopin's
writing.

5. The essayist, assuming that the reader has read the work,
does not tell the plot in great detail. But, aware that the reader has
not memorized the story, the essayist gives helpful reminders.

6. The essayist has opinions, but does not keep saying, "In
my opinion" and "I feel that."

7. The present tense is used in narrating the action: "Mrs.
Mallard dies"; "Mrs. Mallard's friends and relatives all assume."

8. Although a concluding paragraph is often useful — if it
does more than merely summarize what has already been clearly
said — it is not essential in a short analysis. In this essay, the last
sentence explains the chief irony and therefore makes an acceptable ending.

Writing as a Process

The essay illustrates yet another principle — but it is invisible. Although the essay is a finished *product,* writing the essay is a *process,* a process of trial and error and success. When we read a lucid textbook, or an editorial in a newspaper, or even another student's paper, we are inclined to think that we cannot do as well, by which we mean that if we sat down at a desk we could not dash off a comparable piece. Of course not; nor did the authors of the effective writing that causes all of us to feel we simply aren't writers.

Perhaps it is best to think of a composition course not as a course in writing but as a course in revising. One revises one's thoughts as one rereads the assigned piece, and one revises further as one jots down notes, begins to arrange the notes, checks the text for supporting detail, fumbles toward a better organization, writes a first draft, rereads the draft, and perhaps starts all over. But the initial efforts are not a waste of time. They are necessary parts of the process, ideas that are modified or even abandoned but that lead a writer to better ideas, or to a more coherent presentation of the same ideas. A cook tastes the soup, and decides it needs a little more salt. The soup, in this stage, we can say, is unsatisfactory (C plus at best) but it is scarcely a failure; it just needs some revising. The process goes on, more salt is added, maybe some parsley too, and the result is at last satisfactory.

The student's essay on Kate Chopin's story went through a fairly long cooking process. You can't see that, because you are being served only the final product, but the fact that the essay flows easily is indeed a sign that the chef did her work well, straining out (in the course of hours) all indigestible lumps. You can do as well, if while you write you remember that the secret ingredient in all good writing is rewriting.

Writing a Summary

One other point: The essay on "The Story of an Hour" does not include a *summary* because the writer knew that all of her readers were thoroughly familiar with Chopin's story. Sometimes, however, it is advisable to summarize the work you are writing about, thus reminding a reader who has not read the work recently, or even informing a reader who may never have read the work. A review of a new work of literature or of a new film, for instance, usually includes a summary, on the assumption that readers are unfamiliar with it.

A summary is a brief restatement or condensation of the plot. Consider this summary of Chopin's "The Story of an Hour."

> A newspaper office reports that Brently Mallard has been killed in a railroad accident. When the news is gently broken to Mrs. Mallard by her sister Josephine, Mrs. Mallard weeps wildly and then shuts herself up in her room, where she sinks into an armchair. Staring dully through the window, she sees the signs of spring, and then an unnameable sensation possesses her. She tries to reject it but finally abandons herself to it. Renewed, she exults in her freedom, in the thought that at last the days will be her own. She finally comes out of the room, embraces her sister, and descends the stairs. A moment later her husband — who in fact had not been in the accident — enters. Mrs. Mallard dies — of the joy that kills, according to the doctors' diagnosis.

Here are a few principles that govern summaries:

1. A summary is much briefer than the original. It is *not* a paraphrase — a word-by-word translation of someone's words into your own. A paraphrase is usually at least as long as the original, whereas a summary is rarely longer than one-fourth of the original and is usually much shorter. A novel may be summarized in a few paragraphs, or even in one paragraph.

2. A summary usually achieves its brevity by omitting almost all of the concrete details of the original and by omitting minor characters and episodes. Notice that the summary of "The Story of an Hour" omits the friend of the family, omits specifying the signs of spring, and omits the business of the sister imploring Mrs. Mallard to open the door.

3. A summary is as accurate as possible, given the limits of space.

4. A summary is normally written in the present tense. Thus, "A newspaper office report*s*. . . . Mrs. Mallard weep*s*. . . ."

5. Because a summary is openly based on someone else's writing and you do not claim that it presents your own ideas or even your own words, you need not use quotation marks around

any words that you take from the original. Thus, after some such lead-in as "Kate Chopin's 'The Story of an Hour' may be summarized thus," you need not say such things as "Chopin then goes onto tell us that Mrs. Mallard. . . ."

6. If the summary is brief (say fewer than 250 words), it may be given as a single paragraph. But if you are summarizing a long work, you may feel that a longer summary is needed. In this case your reader will be grateful to you if you divide the summary into paragraphs. As you draft your summary, you may find natural divisions. For instance, the scene of the story may change midway, providing you with the opportunity to use two paragraphs. Or you may want to summarize a five-act play in five paragraphs.

Summaries have their place in essays, but be sure to remember that a summary is not an analysis; it is only a summary.

FINDING A MANAGEABLE TOPIC

If a topic is assigned, write on it.

If you choose a topic, choose one that can be treated thoroughly within the allotted time and space. Unless you have an enormous amount of time for reflection and revision, you cannot write a meaningful essay of five hundred or even a thousand words on "Character in Nabokov's *Ada*" or on "Symbolism in *Moby-Dick*." And probably you won't really want to write on such topics anyway. Probably *one* character or *one* symbol has caught your interest. Trust your feelings; you are probably on to something interesting, and it will be best to think about this smaller topic for the relatively few hours that you have. A "smaller" topic need not be a dull or trivial one; treated properly, it may illuminate the entire work, or, to change the metaphor, it may serve as a mine shaft that gives entry to the work. "Hamlet's Relationship to Horatio," carefully thought about, will in five hundred or a thousand words tell a reader more (and will have taught its author more) than will "Hamlet as a Tragic Hero." Similarly, "Huck Finn's Imagination" is a better topic than "The Character of Huck Finn," and "The Meanings of 'Economy' in *Walden*" a better topic than "The Meaning of *Walden*."

How do you find a topic, and how do you see it in the light of a thesis? An idea may hit you suddenly; as you are reading you find yourself jotting in the margin, "Contrast with Joyce's treatment of disillusionment," "too heavy irony," or "ugh." If, as you read and reread a work you underline expressions that by their frequency seem especially significant, or you jot notes in the margins, on reviewing your markings you will probably find a topic staring at you. Or an idea may come slowly on rereading. Perhaps you gradually become aware of the frequency of "really" in *The Catcher in the Rye,* and you notice that Holden Caulfield, who is regularly given to saying things such as "if you really want to know" and "I really mean it," at one point explicitly comments on the nature of reality. You work on this and begin to relate it to his abundant discussions of phoneys, and you emerge, perhaps, with the **thesis**, or argument, or proposition, that in Holden's mouth "really" is not merely the filler it seems to be but is a clue to his quest for the real in a world of appearances or phonies.

Think of it in this way: a topic is a subject, and a thesis is a topic with a predicate. "Holden's Use of 'Really' " is a topic, but it can be turned into the thesis mentioned a moment ago: "The word 'really' is a clue to Holden's quest for the real." Of course, some theses are more promising than others: "Holden's Use of 'really' is interesting" is a thesis, but it is vague and provides little help in generating ideas and in shaping your essay. The more precisely you formulate the thesis, the better the paper is going to be. Again, if you review your underlinings and marginal notes, you will probably discover a topic and a thesis. Now is the time to reread and to see if you can find in the text quotations that could probably be used to support your thesis.

If you have thought about the topic, developed a thesis, and stripped it of irrelevancies, you should be able to formulate it in a few words. This formula, or something like it, can be your title. There is nothing wrong with a title as direct as "The Significance of Holden's Use of 'Really' "; although it is scarcely exciting, it is informative. Beware of cute titles, especially those that do not give the reader a good idea of what will follow, such as "Really," or "A Boy's Word." "The Real Holden and Reality" is about as far as one can go. On the other hand, do not simply use the title of the work you are discussing. Create your own title — one that reflects your topic or, better, your thesis. For example, a paper on *Macbeth* should not be called "*Macbeth,*" or even "On *Macbeth*"; rather, it might helpfully be titled "Fate and Free Will in *Macbeth,*" or "*Macbeth's* Failure of Imagination."

One other example of a thesis may be useful here: Mark Van Doren's analysis of Wordsworth's "The Solitary Reaper" (Chapter 6) is held together by his proposition (p. 241) that the poem is admirable "yet each stanza is inferior to the one before it." Van Doren does not simply talk at random about the poem; he has a thesis or argument and he presents it. Notice, too, that Van Doren announces his thesis in his first paragraph. When you are getting ready to write, you may fret for hours, turning your feelings over and over before you perceive them clearly. But when you at last find your thesis, you ought to let the reader know the gist of it early in the essay. The title, the first paragraph, or both are usually appropriate places.

All literary works afford their own topics for analysis, and all essayists must set forth their own theses, but a few useful generalizations may be made. You can often find a thesis by asking one of two questions:

1. *What is this doing?* That is, why is this scene in the novel or play? Why is Beckett's *Waiting for Godot* in two acts, rather than one or three? Why the biblical allusions in *Waiting for Godot?* Why is the clown in *Othello?* Why are these lines unrhymed? Why is this stanza form employed? What is the significance of the parts of the work? (Titles are often highly significant parts of the work: Ibsen explained that he called his play *Hedda Gabler* rather than *Hedda Tesman* because "She is to be regarded rather as her father's daughter than as her husband's wife." Ibsen's *Ghosts,* Kesey's *One Flew over the Cuckoo's Nest,* and Roth's *Great American Novel* would be slightly different things if they had other titles. Beckett's *En attendant Godot* — *Waiting for Godot* — was originally entitled *En attendant,* that is, *Waiting.* Why the change?)

2. *Why do I have this response?* Why do I find this poem clever, or moving, or puzzling? How did the author make this character funny or dignified or pathetic? How did he or she communicate the idea that this character is a bore without boring me?

The first of these questions, "What is this doing?" requires that you identify yourself with the author, wondering, for example, whether this opening scene is the best possible for this story. The second question, "Why do I have this response?" requires that you trust your feelings. If you are amused or bored or puzzled or annoyed, assume that these responses are appropriate and follow them up, at least until a rereading of the work provides other responses.

The chapters on fiction, drama, poetry, and film try to provide the relevant critical vocabulary; they also try to do two other things: suggest the sorts of problems critics write about, and offer paragraphs that can serve as models of critical writing. After reading the chapter on fiction, for example, you should have not only an idea of what plot, symbolism, and setting are but also an idea of how some people write about them. It is primarily from those chapters and from your instructor and, above all, from your own responses to literature that you should get help in developing your sense of appropriate topics, but a few examples are offered here.

Caution: For the sake of clarity, these topics are stated baldly. They are rough beginnings and need to be shaped into theses. Consider the difference between "Hamlet's Relationship to Horatio" (an unshaped topic) and the thesis you might work out: "Although Hamlet admires Horatio's stoic temperament and values his companionship, Hamlet's temperament is more heroic."

Sample Topics in Fiction

PLOT

"Death as a Device to Link Episodes in *Huckleberry Finn*"

"The Appropriateness of the Ending of *Lord of the Flies*"

THEME

"Does the End of *Huckleberry Finn* Violate the Meaning of the Rest of the Work?"

"The 'Phoniness' of Middle-Class Morality in *The Catcher in the Rye*"

"The Female as Victim in Melville's 'The Tartarus of Maids' "

"Absurdity in Camus's *The Plague*"

"Paralysis in Joyce's *Dubliners*"

"Imagery as a Revelation of Theme in . . ."

"Pictures and Sculptures as a Revelation of Theme in Hawthorne's *The Marble Faun*"

"Jazz and Other Popular Music in Fitzgerald's *The Great Gatsby*"

CHARACTER

(Sometimes a mere character sketch may be acceptable; more often one will study character to see how it contributes to the theme or — pp.112–14 — how it helps to define another character.)

"The Distinctive Language of Huck Finn"

"A Comparison between the Widow Douglas in *Tom Sawyer* and in *Huckleberry Finn*"

"What Holden Caulfield is *Really* Like"

"Holden Caulfield: Adolescent Snob or Suffering Saint?"

"Ch'en and Kyo: A Contrast between a Terrorist and a Revolutionary in Malraux's *Man's Fate*"

"Stephen Dedalus: Prig or Artist?"

"The Function of the Three Mates in *Moby-Dick*"

"Dilsey and Joe Christmas: The Poles of Faulkner's Conception of the Role of Black Americans"

"Kesey's Big Nurse Ratched: Victimizer or Victim?"

FORESHADOWING

(Really an aspect of plot and character.)

"Are We Adequately Prepared for Huck's Decision to 'Light Out for the Territory'?"

"Early Tragic Overtones in *Moby-Dick*"

"Suspense and Surprise in . . ."

"The Humor of the Unexpected"

SETTING

"The River vs. Civilization in *Huckleberry Finn*"

"The Function of the Setting in . . ."

"East and West in Fitzgerald's *The Great Gatsby*"

SYMBOLISM

"The River in *Huckleberry Finn*"

"The Meaning of the White Whale"

"Walls in *Bartleby*"

"The Sun in Camus's *The Stranger*"

POINT OF VIEW

"If *Huckleberry Finn* Were Narrated by the Widow Douglas Instead of by Huck . . ."

"Objectivity in 'The Killers' "

"Editorializing in *Tess of the D'Urbervilles*"

"The Unreliable Narrator in . . ."

"The Uses of Schizophrenia: Kesey's Chief Broom as Narrator"

Sample Topics in Drama

When writing about a play, you may find a topic similar to one of those given in the preceding paragraphs. But in addition to those centering on theme, character, foreshadowing, setting, and symbolism, you may find the following examples useful.

IRONY

"Unconscious Irony in *Macbeth*"

"Conscious Irony in *Major Barbara*"

TRAGEDY

"Macbeth: Hero or Villain?"

"A Comparison between King Oedipus and Willy Loman"

"Willy Loman and Arthur Miller's Theory of Tragedy"

"Sartre's *No Exit:* A Tragedy without a Tragic Hero"

"The Black Man as a Tragic Figure in O'Neill"

COMEDY

"The Comic in the Tragic: Beckett's *Waiting for Godot*"

"The Comic Portrayal of Villainy in . . ."

"Tlhe Comc Treatment of a Class Society in Shaw's *Pygmalion*"

"Racist Implications in the Characterization of the Comic Stage Negro"

PLOT

"Surprise vs. Suspense in *Macbeth*"

"Coincidence in *Ghosts*"

"The Turning Point in . . ."

"Flashbacks in *Death of a Salesman*"

GESTURE

"Appropriate Gestures for *Macbeth* in the Banquet Scene"

"Suggestions of Laurel and Hardy and of Chaplin in *Waiting for Godot*"

Sample Topics in Poetry

VOICE

"The Unawareness of Egotism: The Duke in 'My Last Duchess' "

"The New England Voice in Frost's Poems"

"Prufrock's Ironic Self-Depreciation"

"Whitman's 'Barbaric Yawp' "

DICTION

"The Use of Colloquialisms in Frost"

"Shifts in Diction in Allen Ginsberg"

"Patterns of Black Speech in LeRoi Jones"

FIGURATIVE LANGUAGE

"Scientific Imagery as a Vehicle for Passion"

"Metaphors of the Theater in Yeats's 'Lapis Lazuli' "

"Organic Metaphors in a Poem by Whitman"

SYMBOLISM

"Frost's Woods and Stars"

"The City in Robert Lowell's Poetry"

STRUCTURE

"Logic and Illogic in . . ."

"Paradox in . . ."

"The Movement from Anger to Resignation in . . ."

"The Development of the Theme, Stanza by Stanza, in . . ."

IRONY

"Understatement as a Means of Protest in American Folk Ballads"

"The Speaker's Conscious versus Unconscious Irony in Browning's 'My Last Duchess' "

PATTERNS OF SOUND

"Rhyme and Reason in . . ."

"The Not-So-Free Verse of 'When Lilacs Last in the Dooryard Bloom'd' "

"The Influence of the Blues on Some Modern Poets"

Topics for essays on film often resemble those for essays on fiction and drama, but because there are special problems discussion of the matter is postponed until Chapter 7, "Writing about Films."

CONSIDERING THE EVIDENCE

Once your responses have led you to a topic ("The Clown in *Othello*") and then to a thesis ("The clown is relevant"), be certain that you have all the evidence. Usually this means that you should study the context of the material you are discussing. An excerpt from A. E. Housman is a famous instance of failure to keep the context in mind. Housman wrote of a line in Milton's *Arcades*:

> But in these six simple words of Milton —
>
> Nymphs and shepherds, dance no more —
>
> what is it that can draw tears, as I know it can, to the eyes of more readers than one? What in the world is there to cry about? Why have the mere words the physical effect of pathos when the sense of the passage is blithe and gay? I can only say, because they are poetry, and find their way to something in man which is obscure and latent, something older than the present organization of his nature.
>
> *The Name and Nature of Poetry* (New York, 1933), p. 45

This passage tells us something about Housman but nothing about the line in *Arcades;* in its context the line is not a command to stop dancing but only to stop dancing "By sandy Ladon's lillied banks" and to come to "A better soil."

Similarly, before you argue that because Holden distrusts the adult world, "old" is his ultimate word of condemnation, remember that he speaks of "old Phoebe" and of "old Thomas Hardy," both of whom he values greatly. Before you argue that the style of *Romeo and Juliet* is highly formal, remember that it includes such lines as "Where's Potpan, that he helps not to take away? He shift a trencher! He scrape a trencher!" (There *is* a good deal of highly formal writing in the play, and an essay can be written on it, but the essayist should be aware that the play has other styles too.) Before you argue that the imagery in *Romeo and Juliet* associates the lovers with light and death with dark, remember that not every image of light and dark works in this way. At the beginning of the play several extended passages associate the infatuated Romeo with darkness. The discrepancy can be explained; it must be explained.

ORGANIZING THE MATERIAL

" 'Begin at the beginning,' the King said very gravely, 'and go on till you come to the end: then stop.' " This is how your paper should seem to the reader, but it need not have been drafted thus. In fact, unless you are supremely gifted, you will (like the rest of us) have to work very hard to make things easy for the reader.

After locating a topic, converting it into a thesis, and weighing the evidence, a writer has the job of organizing the material into a coherent whole, a sequence of paragraphs that holds the reader's interest (partly because it sets forth material clearly) and that steadily builds up an effective argument. Notice that in the essay on irony (pp. 21–23) in Kate Chopin's "The Story of an Hour," the student wisely moves from the lesser ironies to the chief irony. To begin with the chief irony and end with the lesser ironies would almost surely be anticlimactic.

The organization of an essay will of course depend on the nature of the essay: an essay on foreshadowing in *Macbeth* will probably be organized chronologically (material in the first act will be discussed before material in the second act), but an essay on the character of Macbeth may conceivably begin with the end of the play, discussing Macbeth as he is in the fifth act, and then may work backward through the play, arriving at last at the original Macbeth, so to speak, of the beginning of the play. (This is not to suggest that such an organization be regularly employed in writing about a character — only that it might be effectively employed.) Or suppose one is writing about whether or not Macbeth is a victim of fate. The problem might be stated, and the essayist might go on to take up one view and then the other. But which view should be set forth first? Probably it will be best to let the reader first hear the view that will be refuted, so that you can build to a climax.

The important point is not that there is only one way to organize an essay, but that an essayist find the way that seems best for the particular topic and argument. Once you think you know more or less what you want to say, you will usually, after trial and error, find what seems the best way of communicating it to a reader. A scratch outline (see p. 15) will help you to find your way, but don't assume that once you have settled on an outline the organization of your essay is finally established. After you read the draft that you base on your outline, you may realize that a more effective organization will be more helpful to your reader — which means that you must move paragraphs around, revise your transitions, and, in short, produce another draft.

COMPARISON: AN ANALYTIC TOOL

Analysis frequently involves comparing: things are examined for their resemblances to and differences from other things. Strictly speaking, if one emphasizes the differences rather than the similarities, one is contrasting rather than comparing, but we need not preserve this distinction: we can call both processes *comparing*.

Although your instructor may ask you to write a comparison of two works of literature, you should understand that the *subject* of the essay is the works and that the comparison is simply an effective analytic technique to show some of the qualities in the works. You might compare Chopin's use of nature in "The Story of an Hour" (page 23) with the use of nature in another story, in order to reveal the subtle differences between the stories, but a comparison of works utterly unlike can hardly tell the reader or the writer anything.

Something should be said about organizing a comparison, say between the settings in two stories, between two characters in a novel (or even between a character at the end of a novel and the same character at the beginning), or between the symbolism of two poems.★ Probably a student's first thought, after making some jottings, is to discuss one half of the comparison and then go on to the second half. Instructors and textbooks (though not this one) usually condemn such an organization, arguing that the essay breaks into two parts and that the second part involves a good deal of repetition of categories set up in the first part. Usually they recommend that the students organize their thoughts differently, somewhat along these lines:

1. First similarity
    a. first work (or character, or characteristic)
    b. second work
2. Second similarity
    a. first work
    b. second work

★Two essays that make comparisons are printed in this book, Kenneth Muir's on Hamlet and Laertes (p. 188) and Joseph Wood Krutch's on Tennessee Williams and Arthur Miller (p. 190).

3. First difference
   a. first work
   b. second work
4. Second difference
   a. first work
   b. second work

and so on, for as many additional differences as seem relevant. If one wishes to compare *Huckleberry Finn* with *The Catcher in the Rye*, one may organize the material thus:

1. First similarity: the narrator and his quest
   a. Huck
   b. Holden
2. Second similarity: the corrupt world surrounding the narrator
   a. society in *Huck*
   b. society in *Catcher*
3. First difference: degree to which the narrator fulfills his quest and escapes from society
   a. Huck's plan to "light out" to the frontier
   b. Holden's breakdown

Here is another way of organizing a comparison and contrast:

1. First point: the narrator and his quest
   a. similarities between Huck and Holden
   b. differences between Huck and Holden
2. Second point: the corrupt world
   a. similarities between the worlds in *Huck* and *Catcher*
   b. differences between the worlds in *Huck* and *Catcher*
3. Third point: degree of success
   a. similarities between Huck and Holden
   b. differences between Huck and Holden

But a comparison need not employ either of these structures. There is even the danger that an essay employing either of them may not come into focus until the essayist stands back from the seven-layer cake and announces, in the concluding paragraph, that the odd layers taste better. In one's preparatory thinking, one may want to make comparisons in pairs (good-natured humor: the clown in *Othello,* the clownish grave-digger in *Hamlet;* social satire: the clown in *Othello,* the grave-digger in *Hamlet;* relevance to main theme: . . . ; length of role: . . . ; comments by other characters: . . .), but one must come to some conclusions about what these add up to before writing the final version. This final version should not duplicate the thought processes; rather, it should be organized so as to make the point — the thesis — clearly and effectively. After reflection, one may believe that although there are superficial similarities between the clown in *Othello* and the clownish grave-digger in *Hamlet,* there are essential differences; then in the finished essay one probably will not wish to obscure the main point by jumping back and forth from play to play, working through a series of similarities and differences. It may be better to discuss the clown in *Othello* and then to point out that, although the grave-digger in *Hamlet* resembles him in A, B, and C, the grave-digger also has other functions (D, E, and F) and is of greater consequence to *Hamlet* than the clown is to *Othello.* Some repetition in the second half of the essay ("The grave-digger's puns come even faster than the clown's. . . .") will bind the two halves into a meaningful whole, making clear the degree of similarity or difference. The point of the essay presumably is not to list pairs of similarities or differences but to illuminate a work, or works, by making thoughtful comparisons.

Although in a long essay one cannot postpone until page 30 a discussion of the second half of the comparison, in an essay of, say, fewer than ten pages nothing is wrong with setting forth one half of the comparison and then, in light of it, the second half. The essay will break into two unrelated parts if the second half makes no use of the first, or if it fails to modify the first half, but not if the second half looks back to the first half and calls attention to differences that the new material reveals. Students ought to learn how to write an essay with interwoven comparisons, but they ought also to know that there is another, simpler and clearer way to write a comparison.

The following summary, paragraph by paragraph, of Stanley Kauffmann's comparison of film versions of Joyce's *Ulysses* and *Finnegans Wake* gives an idea of how a comparison can be treated. Kauffmann's essay, published in the *New American Review #2,* is, of course, filled with concrete details that here are omitted, but the gist of the eleven paragraphs is as follows:

1. Because subjectivity fascinates film-makers, it is natural that Joyce's two great novels of subjectivity would be filmed. One film is good, the other poor.

2. The poor film is *Ulysses,* a book that summarizes a vast amount of life.

3. The film of *Ulysses* has two motifs: tolerance and sexual candor. But these are only minor parts of the novel.

4. The film cannot be said to be faithful to the novel. True, it adds almost nothing; but it omits an enormous amount.

5. Some things of course simply cannot be filmed, and so let us look at what is present rather than what is absent in the film. The opening is good, but . . . , and . . . , and . . . are poor.

6. In general, the acting is poor.

7. On the other hand, the film of *Finnegans Wake* is pretty successful, capturing the effect of a dream.

8. Though a bit long, and with some of the faults of the film of *Ulysses,* the film of *Finnegans Wake* is interesting, imaginative, and inventive.

9. The director uses subtitles, an effective device because Joyce's words (often puns) are "visual objects."

10. The actors effectively convey in their lines the sense of a dream.

11. The film of *Finnegans Wake* captures the mythical quality that the film of *Ulysses* fails to capture.

As this skeleton of the essay shows, Kauffmann introduces both halves of the comparison in his opening paragraph; paragraphs 2–6 concentrate on one half (the film of *Ulysses*); paragraphs 7 and 8 concentrate on the second half of the comparison — but they remind the reader of the first half; paragraphs 9 and 10 discuss more fully the second — more important — film; and paragraph 11, the conclusion, offers a final judgment on both films.

Finally, a reminder: the purpose of a comparison is to call attention to the unique features of something by holding it up against something similar but significantly different. You can compare Macbeth with Banquo (two men who hear a prophecy, but who respond differently), or Macbeth with Lady Macbeth (a husband and wife, both eager to be monarchs but differing in their sense of the consequences), or Hamlet and Holden Caulfield (two people who see themselves as surrounded by a corrupt world), but you can hardly compare Holden with Macbeth or with Lady Macbeth — there simply aren't enough points of resemblance to make it worth your effort to call attention to subtle differences. If the differences are great and apparent, a comparison is a waste of effort. ("Blueberries are different from elephants. Blueberries do not have trunks. And elephants do not grow on bushes.") Indeed, a comparison between essentially and evidently unlike things can only obscure, for by making the comparison the writer implies that there are significant similarities, and readers can only wonder why they do not see them. The essays that do break into two halves are essays that make uninstructive comparisons: the first half tells the reader about five qualities in Dickens, the second half tells the reader about five different qualities in Dylan Thomas.

COMMUNICATING JUDGMENTS

Because a critical essay is a judicious attempt to help a reader see what is going on in a work or in a part of a work, the voice of the critic usually sounds, on first hearing, impartial; but good criticism includes — at least implicitly — evaluation. The critic may say not only that the setting changes (a neutral expression) but also that "the novelist aptly shifts the setting" or "unconvincingly describes . . ." or "effectively juxtaposes. . . ." These evaluations are supported with evidence. The critic has feelings about the work under discussion and reveals them, not by continually saying "I feel" and "this moves me," but by calling attention to the degree of success or failure perceived. Nothing is wrong with occasionally using "I," and noticeable avoidances of it — "it is seen that," "this writer," "we," and the like — suggest an offensive sham modesty; but too much talk of "I" makes a writer sound like an egomaniac. Here is a sentence from the opening paragraph in a review of George Orwell's *1984:* "I do not think I have ever read a novel more frightening and depressing; and yet, such are the originality, the suspense, the speed of writing and withering indignation that it is impossible to put the book down." Fine —provided that the reviewer goes on to offer evidence that enables us to share his or her evaluations of *1984*.

One final remark on communicating judgments: Write sincerely. Any attempt to neglect your own thoughtful responses and replace them with fabrications designed to please an instructor will surely fail. It is hard enough to find the words that clearly communicate your responses; it is almost impossible to find the words that express your hunch about what your instructor expects your responses to be. George Orwell shrewdly commented on the obvious signs of insincere writing: "When there is a gap between one's real and one's declared aims, one turns as it were instinctively to long words and exhausted idioms, like a cuttlefish squirting out ink."

REVIEW: HOW TO WRITE AN EFFECTIVE ESSAY

All writers must work out their own procedures and rituals (John C. Calhoun liked to plough his farm before writing), but the following suggestions may provide some help:

1. Read the work carefully.

2. Choose a worthwhile and compassable subject, something that interests you and is not so big that your handling of it must be superficial. As you work, shape your topic, narrowing it from, say, "The Character of Hester Prynne" to "The Effects of Alienation on Hester Prynne."

3. Reread the work, jotting down notes on all relevant matters. As you read, reflect on your reading and record your reflections. If you have a feeling or an idea, jot it down; don't assume that you will remember it when you get around to writing your essay. The margins of the book are a good place for initial jottings, but many people find that in the long run it is easiest to transfer these notes to three- by five-inch cards, writing on one side only.

4. Sort your cards into some kind of reasonable divisions, and reject cards irrelevant to your topic. As you work you may discover a better way to group your notes. If so, start reorganiz-

ing. If you are writing an explication, the order probably is essentially the order of the lines or of the episodes, but if you are writing an analysis you may wish to organize your essay from the lesser material to the greater (to avoid anticlimax) or from the simple to the complex (to ensure intelligibility). If you are discussing the roles of three characters in a story, it may be best to build up to the one of the three that you think the most important. If you are comparing two characters, it may be best to move from the most obvious contrasts to the least obvious. When you have arranged your notes into a meaningful sequence of packets, you have approximately divided your material into paragraphs.

5. Get it down on paper. Perhaps begin by jotting down your thesis and under it a tentative outline. Most essayists find it useful to jot down some sort of outline, indicating the main idea of each paragraph and, under each main idea, supporting details that give it substance. An outline — not necessarily anything highly formal with capital and lower-case letters and roman and arabic numerals but merely key phrases in some sort of order — will help you to overcome the paralysis called "writer's block" that commonly afflicts professionals as well as students. A page of paper with ideas in some sort of sequence, however rough, ought to encourage you that you do have something to say. And so, despite the temptation to sharpen another pencil or to put a new ribbon into the typewriter, the best thing to do at this point is to follow the advice of Isaac Asimov, author of one hundred and fifty books in thirty years: "Sit down and start writing." If you don't feel that you can work from note cards and a rough outline, try another method: get something down on paper, writing freely, sloppily, automatically, or whatever, but allow your ideas about what the work means to you and how it conveys its meaning — rough as your ideas may be — to begin to take visible form. If you are like most people you can't do much precise thinking until you have committed to paper at least a rough sketch of your initial ideas. Later you can push and polish your ideas into shape, perhaps even deleting all of them and starting over, but it's a lot easier to improve your ideas once you see them in front of you than it is to do the job in your head. On paper one word leads to another; in your head one word often blocks another.

Just keep going; you may realize, as you near the end of a sentence, that you no longer believe it. Okay; be glad that your first idea led you to a better one, and pick up your better one and keep going with it. What you are doing is, in a sense, by trial and error pushing your way not only toward clear expression but toward sharper ideas and richer responses.

6. If there is time, reread the work, looking for additional material that strengthens or weakens your main point; take account of it in your outline or draft.

7. With your outline or draft in front of you, write a more lucid version, checking your notes for fuller details, such as supporting quotations. If, as you work, you find that some of the points in your earlier jottings are no longer relevant, eliminate them; but make sure that the argument flows from one point to the next. As you write, your ideas will doubtless become clearer; some may prove to be poor ideas, but you probably will also find that you have good ideas that you were unaware of before you put pen to paper. And once you put them on paper, you can improve them. In "To Autumn," John Keats in his draft first described Autumn as "dosed with the fume of poppies." This wording must have immediately struck him as vulgar, and he altered it to "dazed with the fume of poppies," but he continued to feel that something was not right, and he changed it yet again, to "drowsed with the fume of poppies." But without his first effort, "dosed," he could not have reached "drowsed." (What was true of Keats is true of all of us. We rarely know exactly what our ideas are until we have them set down on paper. As the little girl said, replying to the suggestion that she should think before she spoke, "How do I know what I think until I say it?") Not until you have written a draft do you really have a strong sense of how good your essay may be.

8. After a suitable interval, preferably a few days, read the draft with a view toward revising it, not with a view toward congratulating yourself. A revision, after all, is a re-vision, a second (and presumably sharper) view. When you revise, you will be in the company of Picasso, who said that in painting a picture he advanced by a series of destructions. A revision — say, the substitution of a precise word for an imprecise one — is not a matter of prettifying but of thinking. As you read, correct things that dis-

turb you (awkward repetitions that bore, inflated utterances that grate), add supporting detail where the argument is undeveloped (a paragraph of only one or two sentences is usually an undeveloped paragraph), and ruthlessly delete irrelevancies however well written they may be. But remember that a deletion probably requires some adjustment in the preceding and subsequent material. Make sure that the opening and concluding paragraphs are effective (more on this, pp. 59–62), and that between these paragraphs the argument, aided by transitions, runs smoothly. The details should be relevant, the organization reasonable, the argument clear. Check all quotations for accuracy. Quotations are evidence, usually intended to support your assertions, and it is not nice to alter the evidence, even unintentionally. If there is time (there almost never is), put the revision aside, reread it in a day or two, and revise it again, especially with a view toward shortening it.

9. Type or write a clean copy, following the principles concerning margins, pagination, footnotes, and so on set forth in Chapter 2. If you have borrowed any ideas, be sure to give credit to your sources. Remember that plagiarism is not limited to unacknowledged borrowing of words; a borrowed idea, even when put into your own words, requires acknowledgment. (On giving credit to sources, see pp. 73–86.)

10. Proofread and make corrections as explained on pages 66–72.

In short, (a) is the writing true (do you have a point that you state accurately), and (b) is the writing good (do your words and your organization clearly and effectively convey your meaning)? All of this adds up to Mrs. Beeton's famous recipe: "First catch your hare, then cook it."

2
Style and Format

PRINCIPLES OF STYLE

Writing is hard work (Lewis Carroll's school in *Alice's Adventures in Wonderland* taught reeling and writhing), and there is no point fooling ourselves into believing that it is all a matter of inspiration. There is ample evidence that many of the poems, stories, plays, and essays that seem, as we read them to flow so effortlessly were in fact the product of innumerable revisions. "Hard labor for life" was Conrad's view of his career as a writer. This labor, for the most part, is directed not to prettifying language but to improving one's thoughts and then getting the words that communicate these thoughts exactly. There is no guarantee that effort will pay off, but failure to expend effort is sure to result in writing that will strike the reader as confused. It won't do to comfort yourself with the thought that you have been misunderstood. You may know what you *meant to say,* but your reader is the judge of what indeed you *have said.* As Coleridge puts it, writers must not only know what they mean but must know "what the words mean by which they attempt to convey their meaning."

Big books have been written on the elements of good writing, but the best way to learn to write is to do your best, revise it a few days later, hand it in, and then study the annotations an experienced reader puts on your essay. In revising the annotated passages, you will learn what your weaknesses are. After drafting your next essay, put it aside for a day or so; when you reread it, preferably aloud, you may find much that bothers you. If the argument does not flow, check to see whether your organization is reasonable and whether you have made adequate transitions. Do not hesitate to delete interesting but irrelevant material that obscures the argument. Make the necessary revisions again and again if there is time. Revision is indispensable if you wish to avoid (in Maugham's words) "the impression of writing with the stub of a blunt pencil."

Still, a few principles can be briefly set forth here. On Dr. Johnson's belief that we do not so much need to be taught as to be reminded, these principles are brief imperatives rather than detailed instructions. They will not suppress your particular voice. Rather, they will get rid of static, enabling your voice to come through effectively. You have something to say, but you can only say it after your throat is cleared of "Well, what I meant was," and "It's sort of, well, you know." Your readers do *not* know; they are reading in order to know. The paragraphs that follow are attempts to help you let your individuality speak clearly.

Get the Right Word

DENOTATION

Be sure the word you choose has the right explicit meaning, or **denotation.** Don't say "tragic" when you mean "pathetic," "sarcastic" when you mean "ironic," "free verse" when you mean "blank verse," "disinterested" when you mean "uninterested."

CONNOTATION

Be sure the word you choose has the right association or implication — that is, the right **connotation.** Here are three examples of words with the wrong connotations for their contexts: "The heroic spirit is not dead. It still *lurks* in the hearts of men." ("Lurks" suggests a furtiveness inappropriate to the heroic spirit. Something like "lives" or "dwells" is needed.) "Close study will *expose* the strength of Albee's style." ("Reveal" would be better than "expose" here; "expose" suggests that some weakness will be brought to light, as in "Close study will expose the flimsiness of the motivation.") "Although Creon suffers, his suffering is not great enough to *relegate* him to the role of tragic hero." (In place of "relegate," we need something like "elevate" or "exalt.")

CONCRETENESS

Catch the richness, complexity, and uniqueness of things. Do not write "Here one sees his lack of emotion" if you really mean "Here one sees his indifference" or "his iciness" or "his impartiality" or whatever the exact condition is. Instead of "The clown's part in *Othello* is very small," write "The clown appears in only two scenes in *Othello*" or "The clown in *Othello* speaks only thirty lines." ("Very," as in "very small" or "very big," is almost never the right word. A role is rarely "very big"; it "dominates" or "overshadows" or "is second only to. . . .")

In addition to using the concrete word and the appropriate detail, use illustrative **examples.** Northrop Frye, writing about the perception of rhythm, illustrates his point.

> Ideally, our literary education should begin, not with prose, but with such things as "this little pig went to market" — with verse rhythm reinforced by physical assault. The infant who gets bounced on somebody's knee to the rhythm of "Ride a cock horse" does not need a footnote telling him that Banbury Cross is twenty miles northeast of Oxford. He does not need the information that "cross" and "horse" make (at least in the pronunciation he is most likely to hear) not a rhyme but an assonance. . . . All he needs is to get bounced.
>
> *The Well-tempered Critic* (Bloomington, Ind., 1963), p. 25

Frye does not say our literary education should begin with "simple rhymes" or with "verse popular with children." He says "with such things as 'this little pig went to market,' " and then he goes on to add "Ride a cock horse." We know exactly what he means. Notice, too, that we do not need a third example. Be detailed, but know when to stop.

Your reader is likely to be brighter and more demanding than Lady Pliant, who in a seventeenth-century play says to a would-be seducer, "You are very alluring — and say so many fine Things, and nothing is so moving to me as a fine Thing." "Fine Things," of course, are what is wanted, but only exact words and apt illustrations will convince intelligent readers that they are hearing fine things.

LEVELS OF USAGE

Although the dividing lines cannot always be drawn easily, tradition recognizes three levels: formal, informal, and vulgar or popular, though sometimes "popular" is used to designate a level between informal and vulgar. **Formal writing** — at its highest or most formal — presumes considerable importance in the writer, the audience, and the topic. A noted figure, say a respected literary critic, examining an influential book and addressing the world of thoughtful readers, may use a formal style, as Lionel Trilling does here in a criticism of V. L. Parrington's *Main Currents in American Literature.*

> To throw out Poe because he cannot be conveniently fitted into a theory of American culture, to speak of him as a biological sport and as a mind apart from the main current, to find his gloom to be merely personal and eccentric, "only the atrabilious wretchedness of a dipsomaniac," as Hawthorne's was "no more than the skeptical questioning of life by a nature that knew no fierce storms," to judge Melville's response to American life to be less noble than that of Bryant or of Greeley, to speak of Henry James as an escapist, as an artist similar to Whistler, a man characteristically afraid of stress — this is not merely to be mistaken in aesthetic judgment; rather it is to examine without attention and from the point of view of a limited and essentially arrogant conception of reality the documents which are in some respects the most suggestive testimony to what America was and is, and of course to get no answer from them.
>
> *The Liberal Imagination* (New York, 1950), p. 21

Notice that in Trilling's sentence the structure is this: "To throw . . . , to speak . . . , to find . . . , to judge . . . , to speak . . . ," and we still do not have an independent clause. Two-thirds of the way through, with "this is not merely to be mistaken," the previous words come into focus, but the meaning is still incomplete. To do such-and-such "is not merely to be mistaken," but what *is* it to be? At last we are told: "It is to examine without attention . . . and . . . to get no answer. . . ."

Consider also the beginning of the Gettysburg Address. Unless you are the president of the United States dedicating a national cemetery during a civil war, it is best not to speak of "Four score and seven years." "Eighty-seven" will have to do. Of course, formal English includes many simple words ("four," "and," "seven"), but it is notable for its use of relatively uncommon words, such as "score" and "hallow," and its long sentences, balanced or antithetical, which suspend their meaning until the end.

A formal sentence need not be long. Here is a fairly short formal sentence by W. H. Auden: "Owing to its superior power as a mnemonic, verse is superior to prose as a medium for didactic instruction." In another frame of mind Auden might have written something less formal, along these lines: "Because it stays more easily in the memory, verse is better than prose for teaching." This revision of Auden's sentence can be called **informal,** but it is high on the scale, the language of an educated person writing courteously to an audience he conceives of as his peers. It is the level of almost all serious writing about literature. A low informal version might be: "Poetry sticks in your head better than prose; so if you want to teach something, poetry is better." This is the language any of us might use in our most casual moments; it is almost never the language used in writing about literature.

Below low informal is the **vulgar** language of near-illiterates who do not write about literature: "Poems stays in me head like words don't. Poems teach good." People who do write about literature should not treat their subjects and their readers as though they were members of the family they can horse around with. (This last sentence, already pretty informal, can be made even more annoyingly informal: "They shouldn't fool around with what they're talking about and with their readers like they're horsing around with the kids.")

Remember, when you are writing *you* are the teacher: you are trying to help someone to see things as you see them, and it is unlikely that either solemnity or heartiness will help anyone see anything your way. There is rarely a need to write that some of the best folk singers have been "incarcerated" or (at the other extreme) have been "thrown in the clink." "Imprisoned" or "put into prison" will probably do the job best. Nor will it do to "finagle" with an inappropriate expression by putting it in "quotes." As the previous sentence indicates, the apologetic quotation marks do not make such expressions acceptable, only more obvious and more offensive. The quotation marks tell the reader that the writer knows he or she is using the wrong word but is unwilling to find the right word. If for some reason a relatively low word is the right one, use it and don't apologize with quotation marks (for instance, the use of "fiddle-faddle" without quotation marks on p. 162).

In short, in "every phrase / And sentence that is right," as T. S. Eliot says in *Four Quartets,*

> every word is at home,
> Taking its place to support the others,
> The word neither diffident nor ostentatious,
> An easy commerce of the old and the new,
> The common word exact without vulgarity,
> The formal word precise but not pedantic,
> The complete consort dancing together.

REPETITION AND VARIATION

Although some repetitions — say, of words like "surely" or "it is noteworthy" — reveal a tic that ought to be cured by revision, don't be afraid to repeat a word if it is the best word. The following paragraph repeats "interesting," "paradox," "Salinger," "what makes," and "book"; notice also "feel" and "feeling."

> The reception given to *Franny and Zooey* in America has illustrated again the interesting paradox of Salinger's reputation there; great public enthusiasm, of the *Time* magazine and Best Seller List kind, accompanied by a repressive coolness in the critical journals. What makes this a paradox is that the book's themes are among the most ambitiously highbrow, and its craftsmanship most uncompromisingly virtuoso. What makes it an interesting one is that those who are most patronising about the book are those who most resemble its characters; people whose ideas and language in their best moments resemble Zooey's. But they feel they ought not to enjoy the book. There is a very strong feeling in American literary circles that Salinger and love of Salinger must be discouraged.
>
> Martin Green, *Re-appraisals* (New York, 1965), p. 197

Repetition, a device necessary for continuity and clarity, holds the paragraph together. There are, of course, variations: "*Franny and Zooey*" becomes "the book," and then instead of "the book's" we get "its." Similarly "those who" becomes "people," which in turn becomes "they." Such substitutions, which neither confuse nor distract, keep the paragraph from sounding like a broken phonograph record.

Pronouns are handy substitutes, and they ought to be used, but other substitutes need not always be sought. An ungrounded fear of repetition often produces a vice known as *elegant variation:* having mentioned *Franny and Zooey,* an essayist next speaks of "the previously mentioned work," then of "the tale," and finally of "this work of our author." This is far worse than repetition; it strikes the reader as silly. Pointless variation of this sort, however, is not be be confused with a variation that communicates additional useful information, such as "these two stories about the Glass family"; this variation is entirely legitimate, indeed necessary, for it furthers the discussion. But elegant variation can be worse than silly; it can be confusing, as in "My first *theme* dealt with plot, but this *essay* deals with character." The reader wonders if the writer means to suggest that an essay is different from a theme.·

Notice in these lucid sentences by Helen Gardner the effective repetition of "end" and "beginning."

> *Othello* has this in common with the tragedy of fortune, that the end in no way blots out from the imagination the glory of the beginning. But the end here does not merely by its darkness throw up into relief the brightness that was. On the contrary, beginning and end chime against each other. In both the value of life and love is affirmed.
>
> *The Noble Moor* (Oxford, 1956), p. 203

The substitution of "conclusion" or "last scene" for the second "end" would be worse than pointless; it would destroy Gardner's point that there is *identity* or correspondence between beginning and end.

But do not repeat a word if it is being used in a different sense. Get a different word. Here are two examples of the fault: "This *theme* deals with the *theme* of the novel." (The first "theme" means "essay"; the second means "underlying idea," "motif.") "Caesar's *character* is complex. The comic *characters* too have some complexity." (The first "character" means "personality"; the second means "persons," "figures in the play.")

THE SOUND OF SENSE

Avoid awkward repetitions of sound, as in "The story is marked by a remarkable mystery," "The reason the season is Spring . . . ," "Circe certainly . . . ," "This is seen in the scene in which

. . ." These irrelevant echoes call undue attention to the words and thus get in the way of the points you are making. But word-play can be effective when it contributes to meaning. Gardner's statement that in the beginning and the end of *Othello* "the value of life and love is affirmed," makes effective use of the similarity in sound between "life" and "love." Her implication is that these two things that sound alike are indeed closely related, an idea that reinforces her contention that the beginning and the end of the play are in a way identical.

Write Effective Sentences

ECONOMY

Say everything relevant, but say it in the fewest words possible. The wordy sentence, "There are a few vague parts in the story that give it a mysterious quality," can be written more economically as "A few vague parts in the story give it a mysterious quality." (Nothing has been lost by deleting "There are" and "that.") Even more economical is: "A few vague parts add mystery to the story." The original version says nothing that the second version does not say, and says nothing that the third version — nine words against fifteen — does not say. If you find the right nouns and verbs, you can often delete adjectives and adverbs. (Compare "a mysterious quality" with "mystery.") Another example of wordiness is: "Sophocles' tragic play *Antigone* is mistitled because Creon is the tragic hero, and the play should be named for him." These twenty words can be reduced, with no loss of meaning, to nine words: "Sophocles' *Antigone* is mistitled; Creon is the tragic hero."

Something is wrong with a sentence if you can delete words and not sense the loss. A chapter in a recent book on contemporary theater begins:

> One of the principal and most persistent sources of error that tends to bedevil a considerable proportion of contemporary literary analysis is the assumption that the writer's creative process is a wholly conscious and purposive type of activity.

Well, there is something of interest here, but it comes along with a lot of hot air. Why that weaseling ("*tends to* bedevil," "a *consid-*

erable proportion"), and why "type of activity" instead of "activity"? Those spluttering *p*'s ("principal and most persistent," "proportion," "process," "purposive") are a giveaway; the writer is letting off steam, not thinking. Pruned of the verbiage, what he says adds up to this:

> One of the chief errors bedeviling much contemporary criticism is the assumption that the writer's creative process is wholly conscious and purposive.

If he were to complain that this revision deprives him of his style, might we not fairly reply that what he calls his style is the display of insufficient thinking, a tangle of deadwood?

Cut out all the deadwood, but in cutting it out, do not cut out supporting detail. Supporting detail is wordiness only when the details are so numerous and obvious that they offend the reader's intelligence.

The **passive voice** (wherein the subject is the object of the action) is a common source of wordiness. Do not say "This story was written by Melville"; instead, say "Melville wrote this story." The revision is one-third shorter, and it says everything that the longer version says. Sometimes, of course, the passive voice, although less vigorous, may be preferable to the active voice. Changing "The novel was received in silence" to "Readers neglected the novel" makes the readers' response more active than it was. The passive catches the passivity of the response. Furthermore, the revision makes "readers" the subject, but the true subject is (as in the original) the novel.

PARALLELS

Use parallels to clarify relationships. Few of us are likely to compose such deathless parallels as "I came, I saw, I conquered," or "of the people, by the people, for the people," but we can see to it that coordinate expressions correspond in their grammatical form. A parallel such as "He liked to read and to write" (instead of "He liked reading and to write") makes its point neatly. No such neatness appears in "Virginia Woolf wrote novels, delightful letters, and penetrating stories." The reader is left wondering what value the novels have. If one of the items has a modifier, usually all should have modifiers. Notice how the omission of "the noble" in the following sentence would leave a distracting gap: "If the wicked Shylock cannot enter the fairy story world of Belmont, neither can the noble Antony." Other examples of parallels are: "Mendoza longs to be an Englishman and to marry the girl he loves" (*not* "Mendoza longs to be an Englishman and for the girl he loves"); "He talked about metaphors, similes, and symbols" (*not* "He talked about metaphors, similes, and about symbols"). If one wishes to emphasize the leisureliness of the talk, one might put it thus: "He talked about metaphors, about similes, and about symbols." The repetition of "about" in this version is not wordiness; because it emphasizes the leisureliness, it does some work in the sentence. Notice, in the next example, how Gardner's parallels ("in the," "in his," "in his," "in the") lend conviction:

> The significance of *Othello* is not to be found in the hero's nobility alone, in his capacity to know ecstasy, in his vision of the world, and in the terrible act to which he is driven by his anguish at the loss of that vision. It lies also in the fact that the vision was true.
>
> *The Noble Moor,* p. 205

SUBORDINATION

Make sure that the less important element is subordinate to the more important. In the following example the first clause, summarizing the writer's previous sentences, is a subordinate or dependent clause; the new material is made emphatic by being put into two independent clauses:

> As soon as the Irish Literary Theatre was assured of a nationalist backing, it started to dissociate itself from any political aim, and the long struggle with the public began.

The second and third clauses in this sentence, linked by "and," are coordinate — that is, of equal importance.

We have already discussed parallels ("I came, I saw, I conquered") and pointed out that parallel or coordinate elements should appear so in the sentence. The following line gives time and eternity equal treatment: "Time was against him; eternity was for him." The quotation is a **compound sentence** — composed of two or more clauses that can stand as independent sentences but that are connected with a coordinating conjunction such as *and, but, for, nor, yet,* and *if;* or with a correlative conjunction such as *not only*

. . . *but also;* or with a conjunctive adverb such as *also,* or *however;* or with a colon, semicolon or (rarely) a comma. But a **complex sentence** (an independent clause and one or more subordinate clauses) does not give equal treatment to each clause; whatever is outside the independent clause is subordinate, less important. Consider this sentence:

> Aided by Miss Horniman's money, Yeats dreamed of a poetic drama.

The writer puts Yeats's dream in the independent clause, subordinating the relatively unimportant Miss Horniman. (Notice, by the way, that emphasis by subordination often works along with emphasis by position. Here the independent clause comes *after* the subordinate clause; the writer appropriately put the more important material in the more emphatic position.)

Had the writer wished to give Miss Horniman more prominence, the passage might have run:

> Yeats dreamed of a poetic drama, and Miss Horniman subsidized that dream.

Here Miss Horniman at least stands in an independent clause, linked to the previous independent clause by "and." The two clauses, and the two people, are now of approximately equal importance.

If the writer had wanted to emphasize Miss Horniman and to deemphasize Yeats, he might have written:

> While Yeats dreamed of a poetic drama, Miss Horniman provided the money.

Here Yeats is reduced to the subordinate clause, and Miss Horniman is given the dignity of the only independent clause. (And again notice that the important point is also in the emphatic position, near the end of the sentence. A sentence is likely to sprawl if an independent clause comes first, followed by a long subordinate clause of lesser importance, such as the sentence you are now reading.)

In short, though simple sentences and compound sentences have their place, they make everything of equal importance. Since everything is not of equal importance, you must often write complex and compound-complex sentences, subordinating some things to other things.

Write Unified and Coherent Paragraphs

UNITY

A unified paragraph is a group of sentences (rarely a single sentence) on a single idea. The idea may have several twists or subdivisions, but all the parts — the sentences — should form a whole that can be summarized in one sentence. A paragraph is, to put the matter a little differently, one of the major points supporting your thesis. If your essay is some five hundred words long — about two double-spaced typewritten pages — you probably will not break it down into more than four or five parts or paragraphs. (But you *should* break your essay down into paragraphs, that is, coherent blocks that give the reader a rest between them. One page of typing is about as long as you can go before the reader needs a slight break.) A paper of five hundred words with a dozen paragraphs is probably faulty not becuase it has too many ideas but becuase it has too few *developed* ideas. A short paragraph — especially one consisting of a single sentence — is usually anemic; such a paragraph may be acceptable when it summarizes a highly detailed previous paragraph or group of paragraphs, or when it serves as a transition between two complicated paragraphs, but usually summaries and transitions can begin the next paragraph.

Each paragraph has a unifying idea, which may appear as a **topic sentence.** Most commonly, the topic sentence is the first sentence, forecasting what is to come in the rest of the paragraph; or it may be the second sentence, following a transitional sentence. Less commonly, it is the last sentence, summarizing the points that the paragraph's earlier sentences have made. Least commonly — but thoroughly acceptable — the topic sentence may appear nowhere in the paragraph, in which case the paragraph has a **topic idea** — an idea that holds the sentences together although it has not been explicitly stated. Whether explicit or implicit, an idea must unite the sentences of the paragraph. If your paragraph has only one or two sentences, the chances are that you have not adequately developed its idea. You probably have not provided sufficient details — perhaps including brief quotations — to support your topic sentence or your topic idea.

A paragraph can make several points, but the points must be related, and the nature of the relationship must be indicated so that there is, in effect, a single unifying point. Here is a paragraph, unusually brief, that may seem to make two points but that, in fact, holds them together with a topic idea. The author is Edmund Wilson.

> James Joyce's *Ulysses* was an attempt to present directly the thoughts and feelings of a group of Dubliners through the whole course of a summer day. *Finnegans Wake* is a complementary attempt to render the dream fantasies and the half-unconscious sensations experienced by a single person in the course of a night's sleep.
>
> *The Wound and The Bow* (New York, 1947), p. 243

Wilson's topic idea is that *Finnegans Wake* complements *Ulysses*. Notice, by the way, that the sentence about *Finnegans Wake* concludes the paragraph. Not surprisingly, Wilson's essay is about this book, and the structure of the paragraph allows him to get into his subject.

The next example may seem to have more than one subject (Richardson and Fielding were contemporaries; they were alike in some ways; they were different in others), but again the paragraph is unified by a topic idea (although Richardson and Fielding were contemporaries and were alike in some ways, they differed in important ways).

> The names of Richardson and Fielding are always coupled in any discussion of the novel, and with good reason. They were contemporaries, writing in the same cultural climate (*Tom Jones* was published in 1749, a year after *Clarissa*). Both had genius and both were widely recognized immediately. Yet they are utterly different in their tastes and temperaments, and therefore in their visions of city and country, of men and women, and even of good and evil.
>
> Elizabeth Drew, *The Novel* (New York, 1963), p. 59

This paragraph, like Edmund Wilson's, closes in on its subject.

The beginning and especially the end of a paragraph are usually the most emphatic parts. A beginning may offer a generalization that the rest of the paragraph supports. Or the early part may offer details, preparing for the generalization in the later part. Or the paragraph may move from cause to effect. Although no rule can cover all paragraphs (except that all must make a point in an orderly way), one can hardly go wrong in making the first sentence either a transition from the previous paragraph or a statement of the paragraph's topic. Here is a sentence that makes a transition and also states the topic: "Not only narrative poems but also meditative poems may have a kind of plot." This sentence gets the reader from plot in narrative poetry (which the writer has been talking about) to plot in meditative poetry (which the writer goes on to talk about).

COHERENCE

If a paragraph has not only unity but also a structure, then it has coherence, its parts fit together. Make sure that each sentence is properly related to the preceding and the following sentences. Nothing is wrong with such obvious transitions as "moreover," "however," "but," "for example," "this tendency," "in the next chapter," and so on; but of course (1) these transitions should not start every sentence (they can be buried thus: "Creeley, moreover, . . ."), and (2) they need not appear anywhere in the sentence. The point is not that transitions must be explicit, but that the argument must proceed clearly. The gist of a paragraph might run thus: "Speaking broadly, there were in the Renaissance two comic traditions. . . . The first. . . . The second. . . . The chief difference. . . . But both traditions. . . ."

Here is a paragraph by Elizabeth Drew discussing one aspect of *Great Expectations*. The structure is basically chronological, but notice too the effective use of a parallel as a linking device within the last sentence. (The links are italicized.)

> Some of the most poignant scenes in the book are the *opening ones,* which describe the atmosphere in which Pip grows up. *He is introduced* as "a small bundle of shivers" alone in the graveyard, *which is followed* by the terrifying intrusion of the world of active violence and fear as the convict seizes him. *Then we see* the household at the forge, where he is made to feel guilty and ashamed of his very existence; the Christmas party at which he is baited and bullied by his elders; his treatment at the hands of the hypocritical Pumblechook; his introcution to Estella, who reveals to him that he is coarse and common. *Dickens knows* that in children "there is nothing so finely perceived and so finely felt, as injustice," and looking back on his

childhood, *Pip too knows* that truth: "Within myself, I had sustained, from my babyhood, a perpetual conflict with injustice."

The Novel, p. 197

INTRODUCTORY PARAGRAPHS

Beginning a long part of one of his long poems, Byron aptly wrote, "Nothing so difficult as a beginning." Almost all writers — professionals as well as amateurs — find that the beginning paragraphs in their drafts are false starts. Don't worry too much about the opening paragraphs of your draft; you'll almost surely want to revise your opening later anyway, and when writing a first draft you merely need something — almost anything may do — to get you going. Though on rereading you will probably find that the first paragraph or two should be replaced, those opening words at least helped you to break the ice.

In your finished paper the opening cannot be mere throat-clearing. It should be interesting and informative. Don't paraphrase your title ("Sex in *1984*") in your first sentence: "This theme will study the topic of sex in *1984*." There is no information about the topic here, at least none beyond what the title already gave, and there is no information about you, either, that is, no sense of your response to the topic, such as might be present in, say, "In George Orwell's *1984* the rulers put a lot of energy into producing antisexual propaganda, but Orwell never convinces us of the plausibility of all of this activity."

Often you can make use of a quotation, either from the work or from a critic. After all, if a short passage from the work caught your attention and set you thinking and stimulated you to develop a thesis, it may well provide a good beginning for your essay.

Here is a nice opening from a chapter on Norman Mailer, by Richard Poirier: "Mailer is an unusually repetitious writer. Nearly all writers of any lasting interest are repetitious." The first sentence, simple though it is, catches our attention; the second gives the first a richer meaning than we had attributed to it. Poirier then goes on to give examples of major writers who are obsessed with certain topics, and he concludes the paragraph with a list of Mailer's obsessions. Such an opening paragraph is a slight variant on a surefire method: *you cannot go wrong in suggesting your thesis* in your opening paragraph, moving from a rather broad view to a narrower one. If you look at the sample essays in this book — those by students as well as those by published critics — you will see that most good opening paragraphs clearly indicate the writer's thesis. Here is an introductory paragraph, written by a student, on the ways in which Shakespeare manages, in some degree, to present Macbeth sympathetically.

> Near the end of <u>Macbeth</u>, Malcolm speaks of Macbeth as a ''dead butcher'' (5.8.69), and there is some — perhaps much — truth in this characterization. Macbeth is the hero of the play, but he is also the villain. And yet to call him a villain is too simple. Despite the fact that he murders his king, his friend Banquo, and even the utterly innocent Lady Macduff and her children, he engages our sympathy, largely because Shakespeare continually reminds us that Macbeth never(despite appearances) becomes a cold-blooded murderer. Macbeth's violence is felt not only by his victims but by Macbeth himself; his deeds torture him, plaguing his mind. Despite all his villainy, he is a man with a conscience.

One other kind of introduction is tricky and should be used cautiously. Sometimes an introductory paragraph delicately misleads the audience; the second paragraph reverses the train of thought and leads into the main issue. Here is an example by Joseph Wood Krutch, from *"Modernism" in Modern Drama*. Only the first part of the second paragraph is given, but from it you can see what direction Krutch is taking.

> One evening in 1892, the first of Oscar Wilde's four successful comedies had in London its first performance. It is said that after the last curtain the audience rose to cheer — and it had good reason to do so. Not in several generations had a new play so sparkled with fresh and copious wit of a curiously original kind.

By now the play itself, *Lady Windermere's Fan,* seems thin and faded. To be successfully revived, as it was a few seasons ago in the United States, it has to be presented as "a period piece" — which means that the audience is invited to laugh at as well as with it. . . .

(Ithaca, N.Y., 1953), p. 43

Here is another example, this one containing the reversal at the end of the opening paragraph.

Time and again I wanted to reach out and shake Peter Fonda and Dennis Hopper, the two motorcyclist heroes of *Easy Rider,* until they stopped their damned-fool pompous poeticizing on the subject of doing your own thing and being your own man. I dislike Fonda as an actor; he lacks humor, affects insufferable sensitivity and always seems to be fulfilling a solemn mission instead of playing a part. I didn't believe in these Honda hoboes as intuitive balladeers of the interstate highways, and I had no intention of accepting them as protagonists in a modern myth about the destruction of innocence. To my astonishment, then, the movie reached out and profoundly shook me.

Joseph Morgenstern, "On the Road," *Newsweek,* July 21, 1969, p. 95

CONCLUDING PARAGRAPHS

With conclusions, as with introductions, try to say something interesting. It is not of the slightest interest to say "Thus we see . . . [here the writer echoes the title and the first paragraph]." There is some justification for a summary at the end of a long paper because the reader may have half forgotten some of the ideas presented thirty pages earlier, but a paper that can easily be held in the mind needs something different. A good concluding paragraph does more than provide an echo of what the writer has already said. It rounds out the previous discussion, normally with a few sentences that summarize (without the obviousness of "We may now summarize"), but it also may draw an inference that has not previously been expressed. To draw such an inference is not to introduce a new idea — a concluding paragraph is hardly the place for a new idea — but is to see the previous material in a fresh perspective. A good concluding paragraph closes the issue while enriching it. Notice how the two examples that follow all wrap things up and, at the same time, open out by suggesting a larger frame of reference.

The first example is the conclusion to Norman Friedman's "Point of View in Fiction." In this fairly long discussion of the development of a critical concept, Friedman catalogs various points of view and then spends several pages arguing that the choice of a point of view is crucial if certain effects are to be attained. The omniscient narrator of a novel who comments on all that happens, Friedman suggests, is a sort of free verse of fiction, and an author may willingly sacrifice this freedom for a narrower point of view if he or she wishes to make certain effects. Friedman concludes:

> All this is merely to say, in effect, that when an author surrenders in fiction, he does so in order to conquer; he give up certain privileges and imposes certain limits in order the more effectively to render his story-illusion, which constitutes artistic truth in fiction. And it is in the service of this truth that he spends his creative life.
>
> *PMLA, 70* (1955), 1160–1184

Notice that Friedman devotes the early part of his paragraph to a summary of what has preceded, and then in the latter part he puts his argument in a new perspective.

A second example of a concluding paragraph that restates the old and looks toward the new comes from Richard B. Sewall's discussion of *The Scarlet Letter.*

> Henry James siad that Hawthorne had "a cat-like faculty of seeing in the dark"; but he never saw through the dark to radiant light. What light his vision reveals is like the fitful sunshine of Hester's and Dimmesdale's meeting in the forest — the tragic opposite of Emerson's triumphant gleaming sun that "shines also today."
>
> *The Vision of Tragedy* (New Haven, 1959), p. 91

Finally, don't feel that you must always offer a conclusion in your last paragraph. Especially if your paper is fairly short — let's say fewer than five pages — when you have finished your analysis or explication it may be enough to stop. If, for example, you have been demonstrating throughout your paper that in *Julius Caesar* Shakespeare condensed the time (compared to his historical source) and thus gave the happenings in the play an added sense of urgency, you scarcely need to reaffirm this point in your last paragraph. Probably it will be conclusion enough if you just offer your final evidence, in a well-written sentence, and then stop.

Write Emphatically

All that has been said about getting the right word, about effective sentences, and about paragraphs is related to the matter of **emphasis.** But we can add a few points here. The first rule (it will be modified in a moment) is: Be emphatic. But do not attempt to achieve emphasis, as Queen Victoria did, by a *style* consisting *chiefly* of *italics* and *exclamation* marks!!! Nor can you rely on expressions such as "very important," "definitely significant," and "really beautiful." The proper way to be emphatic is to find the right word, to use appropriate detail, to subordinate the lesser points, and to develop your ideas reasonably. The beginning and the end of a sentence (and of a paragraph) are emphatic positions; of these two positions, the end is usually the more emphatic. Here is a sentence that properly moves to an emphatic end:

> Having been ill-treated by Hamlet and having lost her father, Ophelia goes mad.

If the halves are reversed, the sentence peters out:

> Ophelia goes mad because she has been ill-treated by Hamlet and she has lost her father.

Still, even this version is better than the shapeless

> Having been ill-treated by Hamlet, Ophelia goes mad, partly too because she has lost her father.

The important point, that she goes mad, is dissipated by the lame addition of words about her father. In short, avoid anticlimaxes such as "Macbeth's deed is reprehensible and serious."

But the usual advice, build to emphatic ends, needs modification. Don't write something that sounds like an advertisement for *The Blood of Dracula:* "In her eyes DESIRE! In her veins — the blood of a MONSTER!!!" Be emphatic but courteous; do not shout.

One further caution: It is all very well to speak in a courteously low voice, but do not be so timid that you whisper assertions in a negative form. Think twice before you let something like this remain in your manuscript: "Melville is not unsuccessful in his depiction of the pathos of madness." The writer seems reluctant to come out and say "Melville succeds in depicting the pathos of madness." If this statement needs qualification (for example, Melville succeeds only in such-and-such a chapter or only intermittently), give the qualifications, but do not think that the weaseling "not unsuccessful" is adequate. It is not unlikely that the readers will not be pleased, which means that it is likely they will be displeased.

A Note on Authors' Names and Other Troublesome Matters

A good many rules, thinly disguised as pleasant suggestions, have been offered. The succeeding pages will offer more, but a few common difficulties don't lend themselves to discussion under any of the previous or the succeeding topics, and so they are simply grouped here.

1. If the author you are writing about is male, it is usually best to give his full name when you first mention him ("Most readers of Ken Kesey's *One Flew Over the Cuckoo's Nest* will remember . . ."); but if he is so well known that his last name is a household word (for example, Dickens, Shakespeare, Thoreau), it is common to omit the first name even in the first reference. To say "In William Shakespeare's *Hamlet*" is almost to imply that the reader needs help in identifying Shakespeare. In subsequent references to a living male author, it is enough to give only his last name ("Moreover, Kesey . . ."), unless your sense of courtesy compels you to preface it with "Mr." No really comfortable convention exists; one feels a bit disrespectful in speaking of "Kesey," a bit stuffy in speaking of "Mr. Kesey," and very phony in speaking of "Ken." Never — not even in an attempt at whimsy — use "Mr." before the name of a dead author.

Things are even more uncomfortable in speaking of women. Male chauvinism is perhaps responsible for the convention of repeatedly using the full name for women ("Jane Austen," for the tenth time in the essay), or for repeatedly prefacing the last name with "Miss" or "Mrs." or "Ms." even though males may get no such courteous treatment. But these ostentatiously polite conventions are disappearing, and it is now acceptable to give women and men the same treatment.

2. Don't write "e.g." when you mean "i.e." — a common confusion. I.e. (Latin, *id est*), meaning "that is," should be distin-

guished from e.g. (*exempli gratia*), meaning "for example." Thus: "Modern poets, i.e., poets who wrote after World War II. . . ." And: "Modern poets, e.g., Creeley and Sexton, unlike poets who wrote before World War II. . . .

3. If you write "such as," it is advisable to follow it with more than one example. A reader probably cannot gather from a single example the quality you have in mind. After all, "Dogs such as German shepherds make good seeing-eye dogs" does not really allow the reader to know which quality in a dog you have in mind. Bigness? Aggressiveness? Short hair? And so, "Dramatists such as Albee and Beckett" is far clearer than "Dramatists such as Albee."

4. To indicate a dash, type two hyphens without hitting the space-bar before, between, or after them.

5. Hyphenate "century" when it is used as an adjective. "Nineteenth-century authors often held that. . . ." But: "Eliot, born in the nineteenth century, often held that. . . ." The principle is: Use a hyphen to join words that are used as a single adjective, for example, a "six-volume work," "an out-of-date theory," and so "a nineteenth-century author." Notice that the hyphen is neither preceded nor followed by a space.

REMARKS ABOUT MANUSCRIPT FORM

Basic Manuscript Form

Much of what follows is nothing more than common sense. Unless your instructor specifies something different, you can adopt these principles as a guide.

1. Use 8½ by 11-inch paper of good weight. Keep as lightweight a carbon copy as you wish, or make a photocopy, but hand in a sturdy original.

2. Write on one side of the page only. If you typewrite, double-space, typing with a reasonably fresh ribbon. If you submit a handwritten copy, use lined paper and write, in dark blue or black ink, on every other line if the lines are closely spaced.

3. Put your name and class or course number in the upper right-hand corner of the first page, one inch from the top and flush

with the left margin. It is a good idea to put your last name before the page number in the upper corner of each subsequent page so that the instructor can easily reassemble your essay if somehow a page gets mixed in with other papers.

4. Double-space after the name or number of the course, and then center the title of your essay. Capitalize the first letter of the first and last words of your title, and capitalize the first letter of all the other words except articles, conjunctions, and prepositions, thus:

```
The Diabolic and Celestial Images in The Scarlet Letter
```

Notice that your title is neither underlined (indicating italics) nor enclosed in quotation marks (though of course if, as here, it includes material that normally would be italicized or in quotation marks, that material continues to be so written). If the title runs more than one line, double-space between the lines.

5. Begin the essay by double-spacing *twice* below the title. If your instructor prefers a title page, begin the essay on the next page.

6. Except for page numbers, leave an adequate margin at top, bottom, and sides.

7. Number the pages consecutively, using arabic numerals in the upper right-hand corner half an inch from the top. Do not put a period or a hyphen after the number, and do not precede it with "p." or "page." If you give the title on a separate page, do not number the page; the page that follows it is page 1.

8. Fasten the pages of your paper with a paper clip in the upper left-hand corner. Stiff binders are unnecessary; indeed, they are a nuisance to the instructor, adding bulk and making it awkward to write annotations.

Corrections in the Final Copy

Your extensive revisions should have been made in your drafts, but minor last-minute revisions may be made on the finished copy. Proofreading may catch some typographical errors, and you may want to change a word here and there. You need not retype the page, or even erase. You can make corrections with the following proofreader's symbols:

Changes in wording may be made by crossing through words and rewriting just above them either on the typewriter or by hand in pen:

```
                          toward
Orwell is sympathetic for most of the animals in Ani-
mal Farm, but he seems to have special affection for
the work-horse.
```

Additions should be made above the line, with a caret (∧) below the line at the appropriate place:

```
                              of
Orwell is sympathetic toward most∧the animals in Ani-
mal Farm, but he seems to have special affection for
the work-horse.
```

Transpositions of letters may be made thus:

```
Orwell is sympathetic toward most the animals in Ani-
mal Farm, but he seems to have special affection for
the work-horse.
```

Deletions are indicated by a horizontal line through the word or words to be deleted. Delte a single letter by drawing a vertical or diagonal line through it.

```
Orwell is sympathetic toward most most of the animals
in Animal Farm, but he seems to have special afffec-
tion for the work-horse.
```

Separation of words accidentally run together in indicated by a vertical line, *closure* by a curved line connecting the things to be closed up.

```
Orwell is sympathetic toward most|of the a⌢nimals in

Animal Farm, but he seems to have special affection

for the work-horse.
```

Paragraphing may be indicated by the symbol 𝓟 before the word that is to begin a new paragraph.

```
Orwell is sympathetic toward most of the animals in

Animal Farm, but he seems to have special affection

for the work-horse. 𝓟 Only the pigs seem to be pictured

unsympathetically.
```

Quotations and Quotation Marks

Excerpts from the literature you are writing about are indispensable. Such quotations (not to be called "quotes") not only let your readers know what you are talking about; they give your readers the material you are responding to, thus letting them share your responses.

Here are some mechanical matters:

1. Distinguish between short and long quotations, and treat each appropriately. Short quotations (usually defined as not more than two three lines of poetry or four lines of typed prose) are enclosed within quotation marks and run into the text (rather than set off, without quotation marks). Examples:

```
LeRoi Jones's ''Preface to a Twenty Volume Suicide

Note'' ends with a glimpse of the speaker's daughter

peeking into her ''clasped hands,'' either playfully

or madly.
```

```
Pope's Essay on Criticism begins informally with a

contraction, but the couplets nevertheless have an

authoritative ring: '' 'Tis hard to say, if greater

want of skill / Appear in writing or in judging ill.''
```

Notice that in the second example a slash (diagonal line, virgule) is used to indicate the end of a line of verse other than the last line quoted. The slash is, of course, not used if the poetry is set off, indented, and printed as verse, thus:

```
Pope's Essay on Criticism begins informally with a

contraction, but the couplets nevertheless have an

authoritative ring:

        'Tis hard to say, if greater want of skill
        Appear in writing or in judging ill;
        But of the two less dangerous is the offense
        To tire our patience than mislead our sense.
```

Material that is set off (usually four or more lines of verse, five or more lines of prose) is not enclosed within quotation marks. To set it off, begin a new line, indent ten spaces from the left margin, and type it double-spaced. If you are quoting two or more paragraphs of prose, indent the first line of each paragraph an additional three spaces — but do not add these spaces to the first passage if it did not begin the paragraph in your source.

If you are quoting very short lines of poetry, you may center them so that the page does not look unbalanced.

Notice that long quotations, whether prose or poetry are usually introduced by a sentence ending with a colon. Although recent standard practice is to indent and double-space long quotations, some manuals of style call for single-spacing them. But whichever procedure you adopt, be consistent. Be sparing in your use of long quotations. Use quotations as evidence, not as padding. Do not bore the reader with material that can be effectively reduced either by paraphrase or by cutting. If you cut, indicate ellipses as explained below under 3.

2. The quotation must fit grammatically into your sentence. *Not:*

```
Near the end of the play Othello says that he ''have
done the state some service.''
```

Corrected:

```
Near the end of the play Othello says that he has
''done the state some service.''
```

Or, of course, you can say:

```
Near the end of the play Othello says, ''I have done
the state some service.''
```

3. The quotation must be exact. Any material that you add must be in brackets, thus:

```
When Pope says that Belinda is ''the rival of his
[that is, the sun's] beams,'' he uses comic hyperbole.

Stephen Dedalus sees the ball as a ''greasy leather
orb [that] flew like a heavy bird through the grey
light.''
```

If you wish to omit material from within a quotation, indicate the ellipsis by three periods with a space before and after each period. If a sentence ends in an omission, add a closed-up period and then three spaced periods to indicate the omission. The following example is based on a quotation from the sentences immediately before this one:

```
The manual says that ''if you . . . omit material from

within a quotation, [you must] indicate the ellipsis.

 . . . If a sentence ends in an omission, add a closed-

up period and then three spaced periods. . . .''
```

Notice that although material preceded "if you," periods are not needed to indicate the omission because "If you" began a sentence in the original. Customarily initial and terminal omissions are indicated only when they are part of the sentence you are quoting. Even such omissions need not be indicated when the quoted material is obviously incomplete — when, for instance, it is a word or phrase. (See the first example in this item, which quotes Pope's phrase "the rival of his beams.")

When a line or more of verse is omitted from a passage that is set off, the three spaced periods are printed on a separate line.

```
'Tis hard to say, if greater want of skill

Appear in writing or in judging ill.



          . . .



A fool might once himself alone expose,

Now one in verse makes many more in prose.
```

4. Identify the speaker or writer of the quotation, so that readers are not left with a sense of uncertainty, Usually this identification precedes the quoted material (for example, "Smith says . . .") in accordance with the principle of letting readers know where they are going, but occasionally it may follow the quotation, especially if it will provide something of a pleasant surprise. For instance, in a discussion of T. S. Eliot's poetry, you might quote a hostile comment on one of the poems and then reveal that Eliot himself was the speaker.

5. Commas and periods go inside the quotation marks. (*Exception:* If the quotation is immediately followed by material in parentheses or in brackets, close the quotation, then give the parenthetic or bracketed material, and then — after the closing parenthesis or bracket — put the comma or period.) Marks of punctuation other than periods and commas (that is, semicolons, colons, and dashes) go outside. Question marks and exclamation points go inside if they are part of the quotation, outside if they are your own.

```
Amanda ironically says to her daughter, ''How old are

you, Laura?'' Is it possible to fail to hear Laura's

weariness in her reply, ''Mother, you know my age''?
```

6. Use *single* quotation marks for material contained within a quotation that itself is within quotation marks, thus:

```
T. S. Eliot says, ''Mr. Richards observes that 'poetry

is capable of saving us.' ''
```

7. Use quotation marks around titles of short works; that is, for titles of chapters in books, and for stories, essays, and poems that might not be published by themselves, songs, speeches, and lectures. Unpublished works, even book–length dissertations, are also enclosed in quotation marks.

When does one *not* use quotation marks around a title? (1) Use *italics* (indicated by underlining) for titles of books, for example, for novels, periodicals, pamphlets, collections of stories or essays, plays, and long poems such as *Paradise Lost* and *The Rime of the Ancient Mariner.* (2) Titles of sacred works (for example, the Bible, the Old Testament, Genesis, the Gospel according to St. John, the Koran) are neither underlined nor enclosed within quotation marks.

Footnotes and Documentation

KINDS OF FOOTNOTES

If you have read any scholarly books, or articles in journals — for example while doing research for a paper — you have probably noticed that footnotes are of two sorts: (1) they may give documentation — that is, they may cite the sources of quotations, facts, and opinions used; or (2) they may give additional comments that would interrupt the flow of the argument in the body of the paper. This second type perhaps requires comment. In an essay you may wish to indicate that you are familiar with an opinion contrary to the one you are offering, but you may not wish to digress upon it during your argument. A footnote lets you refer to it and indicate why you are not considering it. Or a footnote may contain full statistical data that support the point but that would seem unnecessarily detailed and even tedious in the body of the paper. Footnotes of this sort, giving additional commentary, should be used sparingly. There are times when digressions or supporting details may be appropriately relegated to a footnote, but if the thing is worth saying, it is usually worth saying in the body of the paper. Don't get into the habit of affixing either trivia or miniature essays to the bottom of each page of your essay.

The other kind of footnote, merely giving documentation, is now out of fashion, chiefly because it is expensive to print. High costs have forced publishers of journals and books to devise a cheaper system for giving documentation, that is, for giving credit to one's source. This system will be explained in a moment, but first we should look at this whole topic of what sort of thing requires documentation.

WHAT TO DOCUMENT: AVOIDING PLAGIARISM

Honesty requires that you acknowledge your indebtedness for material, not only when you quote directly from a work, but also when you appropriate an idea that is not common knowledge. Not to acknowledge such borrowing is plagiarism. If in doubt as to whether or not to give credit, give credit. But you ought to develop a sense of what is considered common knowledge. Definitions in a dictionary can be considered common knowledge, and

so there is no need to say, "According to Webster, a novel is . . ."
(Weak in three ways: It's unnecessary, it's uninteresting, and it's
unclear since "Webster" appears in the titles of several dictionar-
ies, some good and some bad.) Similarly, the date of first publication of *The Scarlet Letter* can be considered common knowledge.
Few can give it when asked, but it can be found out from innumerable sources, and no one need get the credit for providing you
with the date. The idea that Hamlet delays is also a matter of
common knowledge. But if you are impressed by So-and-so's argument that Claudius has been much maligned, you should give
credit to So-and-so. Similarly, if you simply *know*, from your
reading of J. D. Salinger and perhaps from your reading of Zen
philosophy, that Salinger was influenced by Zen thinking, you need
not cite a specific source for an assertion to that effect; but if you
cannot think of an example of the influence, and if you have not
read any Zen philosophy, you should give credit to the source that
gave you the information.

Suppose that you happen to come across Frederick R. Karl's
statement, in *A Reader's Guide to the Contemporary English Novel,*
that George Orwell was "better as a man than as a novelist." This
is an interesting and an effectively worded idea. You cannot use
these words without giving credit to Karl. Nor can you retain the
idea but alter the words, for example, to "Orwell was a better human being than he was a writer of fiction," presenting the idea as
your own, for here you are simply lifting Karl's idea — and putting it less effectively. If you want to use Karl's point, give him
credit and — since you can hardly summarize so brief a statement — use his exact words and put them within quotation marks.

But what about a longer passage that strikes you favorably?
Let's assume that in reading Alex Zwerdling's *Orwell and the Left*
you find the following passage interesting:

> *Nineteen Eighty-Four* might be said to have a predominantly nega-
> tive goal, since it is much more concerned to fight *against* a possible
> future society than *for* one. Its tactics are primarily defensive. Win-
> ston Smith is much less concerned with the future than with the
> past — which is of course the reader's present.

You certainly *cannot* say:

> The goal of *Nineteen Eighty-Four* can be said to be chiefly negative,
> because it is devoted more to opposing some future society than it

is to fighting for a future society. Smith is more concerned with the past (our present) than he is with the future.

This passage is simply a theft of Zwerdling's property; the writer has stolen Zwerdling's automobile and put a different color of paint on it. How, then, can a writer use Zwerdling's idea? (1) Give Zwerdling credit and quote directly, or (2) give Zwerdling credit and summarize his point in perhaps one-third of the length, or (3) give Zwerdling credit and summarize the point but include —within quotation marks — some phrase you think is especially quotable. Thus:

1. *Direct quotation:* In a study of Orwell's politics, Alex Zwerdling says, "*Nineteen Eighty-Four* might be said to . . ."

2. *Summary:* The goal of *Nineteen Eighty-Four,* Zwerdling points out, is chiefly opposition to, rather than advocacy of, a certain kind of future society.

3. *Summary with selected quotation:* Zwerdling points out that the goal of *Nineteen Eighty-Four* is "predominantly negative," opposition to, rather than advocacy of, a certain kind of future society.

DOCUMENTATION

The use of footnotes to cite sources is illustrated in this book on pages 121 and 174, but documentation now is often given in a different way. We'll begin at the end: a list headed Works Cited is included at the end of the essay. (As will be explained on page 83, within your essay you will make references to pages in these works.) Below is a sample of such a list, in the form established by the Modern Language Association in 1983. This sample covers the kinds of writings you will chiefly draw on, but it is not exhaustive. For thorough coverage, consult Joseph Gibaldi and Walter S. Achtert *MLA Handbook for Writers of Research Papers,* 2nd ed. (New York: Modern Language Association of America, 1984). Notice that the list is alphabetical (Abrams, Chaucer, Churchill, Coleridge, Douglas, Frye, and so on), with the author's *last name given first,* but if a work is by two authors, the second author's name is given in the usual order, first name first, as in the example of Wimsatt and Brooks. Do not abbreviate names unless that is the way they appear in the source. If a work is anonymous, alphabetize it under the first word of its title, or under the second word if the first word is *A, An,* or *The.* Thus, an anonymous book entitled *The New Classical Dictionary* would be alphabetized under *New.*

    The form or style of the list, which at first glance seems inconsistent, will be clarified in a moment. The words Works Cited are typed, centered, one inch from the top of a new page. The page numbers on your typed list continue those of your essay. If the last page of your essay is 9, the first page of the list is 10.

Works Cited

Abrams, M. H., et al., eds. <u>The Norton Anthology of English Literature</u>. 4th ed. 2 vols. New York: Norton, 1979.

Chaucer, Geoffrey. <u>The Works of Geoffrey Chaucer</u>. Ed. F. N. Robinson. 2nd ed. Boston: Houghton, 1957.

Churchill, Winston. <u>The Age of Revolution</u>. Vol. 3 of <u>A History of the English-Speaking Peoples</u>. New York: Dodd, 1957.

Coleridge, Samuel Taylor. ''Kubla Khan.'' <u>Norton Anthology of English Literature</u>. Ed. M. H. Abrams et al. 4th ed. 2 vols. New York: Norton, 1979. 2:353–55.

Douglas, Ann. <u>The Feminization of American Culture</u>. New York: Knopf, 1977.

Frye, Northrop. <u>Fables of Identity: Studies in Poetic Mythology</u>. New York: Harcourt, 1963.

———. <u>Fools of Time: Studies in Shakespearian Tragedy</u>. Toronto: U of Toronto, 1967.

Gogol, Nikolai. <u>Dead Souls</u>. Trans. Andrew McAndrew. New York: New American Library, 1961.

Houghton, Walter E., and G. Robert Stange, eds. <u>Victorian Poetry and Poetics</u>. 2nd ed. Boston: Houghton, 1968.

Jacobus, Mary. ''Tess's Purity.'' <u>Eassays in Criticism</u> 26 (1976): 318–38.

Jonson, Ben. The Complete Masques. Ed. Stephen Orgel. Vol. 4 of The Yale Ben Jonson. New Haven: Yale UP, 1969.

Lang, Andrew. ''Ballads.'' Encyclopaedia Britannica, 1910 ed.

MacCaffrey, Isabel Gamble. Introduction. Samson Agonistes and the Shorter Poems. By John Milton. New York: New American Library, 1966. vii—xxvi.

McCabe, Bernard. ''Taking Dickens Seriously.'' Commonweal 14 May 1965: 245—46.

Mack, Maynard. ''The World of Hamlet.'' Yale Review 41 (1952): 502—23. Rpt. in Hamlet. By William Shakespeare. Ed. Edward Hubler. New York: New American Library, 1963. 234—56.

''Metaphor.'' Encylopeadia Britannica: Micropaedia. 1974 ed.

Pope, Alexander. The Correspondence of Alexander Pope. 5 vols. Ed. George Sherburn. Oxford: Clarendon Press, 1956.

Rosetti, Christina. ''Goblin Market.'' Victorian Poetry and Poetics. 2nd ed. Ed. Walter E. Houghton and G. Robert Stange. Boston: Houghton, 1968. 602—08.

Rourke, Constance. American Humor. 1931. Garden City, New York: Doubleday, 1953.

Sewell, Arthur. ''The Moral Dilemma in Tragedy: Brutus.'' Character and Society in Shakespeare. Oxford: Clarendon, 1951. 53—56. Rpt. in Twentieth Century Interpretations of Julius Caesar. Ed. Leonard F. Dean. Englewood Cliffs, N.J.: 1968. 36—38.

Sontag, Susan. ''The Aesthetics of Silence.'' In Styles of Radical Will. New York: Farrar, 1969. 3—34.

Spillers, Hortense J. ''Martin Luther King and the Style of the Black Sermon.'' The Black Scholar 3.1 (1971): 14—27.

Takayanagi, Tina. ''Publishers Expect Good Year.'' New York Times 11 Dec. 1982, Sec. 2:1+.

Vendler, Helen, Rev. of <u>Essays on Style</u>, Ed. Roger
    Fowler. <u>Essays in Criticism</u> 16 (1966):457–63.

Wimsatt, William K., Jr., and Cleanth Brooks. <u>Literary
    Criticism: A Short History</u>. New York: Knopf, 1957.

This list includes the kinds of publications you are likely to have
in your own list. Here is a guide to the list, explaining the form
of the entries. (In addition to checking this guide, check "Related
Points" [page 85] for information about giving subtitles and about
a book whose title page does not specify the publisher or the date.)

> **For an anonymous work,** check the guide below for the
> type of work — for example a book by one author, or a book
> in several volumes, or an article in an encyclopedia — and
> follow the principle set forth, except of course you cannot
> give the name of the author.
>
> **A book by one author:** see above, Douglas's *Feminization,*
> or Frye's *Fables.* Note that the author's last name is given first,
> but otherwise the name is given as on the title page. Do not
> substitute initials for names written out on the title page. But
> the publisher's name may be shortened, as in the example of
> Frye, where Harcourt stands for a company whose full name
> is Harcourt, Brace and World.
>
> Take the title from the title page, not from the cover
> or spine, but disregard unusual typography — for instance,
> the use of only capital letters, or the use of & for *and.*
> Underline title and subtitle with one continuous underline,
> but do not underline the period. The place of publication is
> indicated by the name of the city, but if the city is not well
> known, or if several cities have the same name, the name of
> the state is added, as in the entry for Rourke's *American Hu-
> mor.* If the title page lists several cities, give only the first.
>
> **A book by more than one author:** see Wimsatt and Brooks.
> Notice that the book is listed under the first author's last name
> (Wimsatt) and that the second author's name is then given
> with first name (here, Cleanth) first. If the book has more
> than two authors, give the name of only the first author (last
> name first) and follow it with et al. (Latin for "and others.")
>
> **A book in several volumes:** see Abrams, or Pope. Notice

that the total number of volumes is given after the title, regardless of the number that you have used.

If you have used more than one volume, within your essay you will indicate a reference to, for instance, page 30 of volume 3 thus: (3: 30). But if you used only one volume of a multivolume work — let's say you used only volume 2 of Abrams's anthology — in your entry in Works Cited write, after the period following the date, Vol. 2. If, instead of using the volumes as a whole, you used only an independent work within one volume — say a poem in volume 2, omit the abbreviation "Vol." and instead give an arabic 2 followed by a colon, a space, and the page numbers that encompass the selection you used. See the entry for Coleridge, which specifies that the book consists of two volumes, but that only one selection ("Kubla Khan") that occupies pages 353–55 in one volume (volume 2) was used. In the body of your essay, then, a documentary reference will be only to the page; the volume number will *not* be included.

One book with a separate title in a set of volumes: see Churchill or Jonson.

A revised edition of a book: see Chaucer.

A reprint, for instance a paper back version of an older clothbound book: see Rourke, which indicates that the Doubleday reprint of 1953 is being used.

An edited book: see Chaucer; for a reference to an editor's introduction rather than to the author's book, see Mac-Caffrey; for an anthology see Abrams, Houghton, and *Victorian Poetry and Poetics*. (You can list an anthology either under the editor's name or under the title.) If the book has one editor, the abbreviation is "ed."; if two or more, "eds." For an edited book in several volumes, see Jonson and Pope. Note that if the book is listed under the editor's name (as is the anthology by Houghton), the last name is given first, but if the book is listed under the author's last name (see Pope), the editor's name is given later in the entry, first name first.

A work in a volume of works by one author: see Sontag. This entry indicates that a short work — an essay called "The Aesthetics of Science" — appears in a book entitled

Style. Notice that the page numbers of the short work are cited — not page numbers that you may to refer to, but the page numbers of the entire piece.

A work in an anthology, that is, in a collection of works by several authors: begin with the author and the title of the work you are citing, not with the name of the anthologist or the title of the anthology. See the entry under Coleridge and, for a reprinted scholarly article, the entries under Mack and Sewell. Because the entry for Coleridge specifies that only one volume (of a two-volume work) was used, your parenthetic documentary citation within your essay will give only the page number, not the volume number.

Normally you will give the title of the work you are citing (probably an essay, short story, or poem) in quotation marks, but if it is a book-length work (for instance, a novel) underline it, to indicate italics. If the work is translated, after the period that follows the title write "Trans." and give the name of the translator, followed by a period and the name of the anthology.

If the collection is a multivolume work and you are using only one volume (see Coleridge, which indicates that only volume 2 was used), your parenthetic documentary reference within your essay need not specify the volume. Thus, although the example citing Coleridge is to a poem reprinted in a two-volume work, the entry in Works Cited indicates that the poem appears on pages 353–55 in the second volume, and so a documentary reference in your text will refer, for instance, to 354, without an indication of the volume.

The pages cited in the entry in your list of Works Cited are to the *entire selection,* not simply to pages you may happen to refer to within your paper.

If you are referring to a *reprint of a scholarly article,* give details of the original publication, as in the sample references to Mack and to Sewell.

Two or more works in an anthology: If you are referring to more than one work in an anthology, in order to avoid repeating all the information about the anthology in each entry in your list, under each author's name (in the appropriate alphabetic place) you can give the author and title of the work, then a period, two spaces, and the name of the anthologist followed by the page numbers that the selection spans. Thus, a reference to Coleridge's "Kubla Khan" would be followed only by: Abrams 353–55, rather than by a full citation of Abrams's anthology. This form, of course, requires that Abrams's anthology itself be listed, under Abrams.

Two or more works by the same author: see Frye. Notice that the works are given in alphabetical order (*Fables* precedes *Fools*) and that the author's name is not repeated but is represented by three hyphens followed by a period and two spaces. If the author is the translator or editor of a volume, the three hyphens are followed not by a period but by a comma, then a space, then the appropriate abbreviation (trans. or ed.), then — two spaces after the period — the title.

A translated book: see Gogol. But if you are discussing the translation itself, as opposed to the book, list the work under the translator's name, then put a comma, a space, and "trans." After the period following "trans." skip two spaces, then give the title of the book, a period, two spaces, and then "By" and the author's name, first name first. Continue with information about the place of publication, publisher, and date, as in any entry for a book.

An introduction, foreword, or afterword: see Mac-Caffrey. Usually a book with an introduction or some such comparable material is listed under the name of the author of the book rather than the name of the author of the editorial material (see Pope), but if you are referring to the editor's apparatus rather than to the work itself, use the form in the sample illustrated by MacCaffrey.

Words such as preface, introduction, afterword, and conclusion are capitalized in the entry but are neither enclosed within quotation marks nor underlined.

A book review: see Vendler. If Vendler's review had a title, the title would be given between the period following her name and before the abbreviation "Rev." If a review is unsigned, list it under the first word of the title, or the second word if the first word is *A, An,* or *The.* If an unsigned review has no title, begin the entry with "Rev. of" and alphabetize it under the title of the work being reviewed.

An encyclopedia: for a signed article, see Lang; for an unsigned article, see "Metaphor." A citation of a reference book that is arranged alphabetically does not have to include the publisher, place of publication, volume number, or page number. But give the edition number (if available) and the date.

An article in a scholarly journal: see the items by Jacobus and by Spillers. Notice that the title of the essay is in quotation marks, and the title of the journal (*Essays in Criticism* for Jacobus's article, *The Black Scholar* for Spillers's article) is underlined to indicate italics. Notice also that only arabic numerals — not roman numerals — are used.

Some journals are paginated consecutively; that is, the pagination of the second issue begins where the first issue leaves off, but other journals begin each issue with page one. The forms of a citation differ slightly. Jacobus's article appeared in volume 26, which was published in 1976. (Note that the volume number is followed by a space, and then by the year, in parentheses, and then by a colon, a space, and the page numbers of the entire article.) This journal, which is issued four times a year, is paginated consecutively, and so you need *not* specify the issue number. But for a journal that begins each issue with page 1 (there will be four page ones each year if such a journal is a quarterly), you must give the issue number directly after the volume number and a period, with no spaces before or after the period. See Spillers for a citation of a journal that paginates each issue separately.

An article in a weekly, biweekly, or monthly publication: See McCabe. Notice that the volume number and the issue number are omitted for publications such as *The Atlantic, Commonweal,* and *Time.*

An article in a newspaper: See Takayanagi. Because newspapers usually consist of several sections, a section number may precede the page number. The example indicates that an article begins on page 1 of section 2 and is continued on a later page.

REFERRING TO THE LIST IN THE ESSAY

In writing your paper you will refer to pages in the works listed at the end, giving credit for quotations and even for borrowed ideas that you put entirely into your own words. Thus, in your paper you may write:

```
Wimsatt and Brooks say that ''each age tends to find
in some one of the literary genres the norm of all
literary art'' (556), and they go on to suggest that
for the nineteenth century the norm was tragedy.
```

The reader understands that your quotation comes from page 556 in a book that is listed under Wimsatt and Brooks.

If you set off a long quotation, put the parenthetical citation two spaces after (not below, but *after*) the punctuation that ends the quotation.

Notice in the printed example that the citation is *not* included within the quotation marks. If your sentence ends with a quotation (for instance, if the example had ended with "literary art"), the quotation is closed after the last word of the quotation, the parenthetic citation is then given, and the sentence is concluded with a period.

Of course a sentence may include a citation of a source even if it does not include a quotation from the source:

```
Wimsatt and Brooks suggest that for the nineteenth
century the norm was tragedy (556).
```

Or perhaps for stylistic reasons you will prefer:

```
Wimsatt and Brooks (556) suggest that for the nine-
teenth century the norm was tragedy.
```

If you are using a secondhand source — say you have derived a quotation from Aristotle not directly from Aristotle but from Wimsatt and Brooks — the parenthetic citation must explain that the material is quoted secondhand:

> According to Aristotle, tragedy is ''an imitation of an action that is serious, complete, and of a certain magnitude'' (qtd. in Wimsatt and Brooks 36).

If you have listed more than one work by an author, a reference to the author and to a page number will not be adequate; you will have to amplify the parenthetic reference so that your reader will know to which one of the two or more books by the author you are referring when you cite (for instance) page 220. Notice that the sample list includes two books by Northrop Frye. A reference to Frye might run thus:

> In his discussion of Yeats's symbolism, Frye (<u>Fables</u> 220) makes a connection between Yeats's <u>Vision</u> and Poe's <u>Eureka</u>.

Of course you might also say something like this:

> In <u>Fables of Identity</u> (220) Frye makes a connection between Yeats's <u>Vision</u> and Poe's <u>Eureka</u>.

If you don't mention the source in your sentence, add it in parentheses, thus:

> Poe's <u>Eureka</u> is something like Yeats's <u>Vision</u> (Frye <u>Fables</u> 220).

It was from page 220 in Frye's book, the previous sentence indicates, that you got the idea of a connection between Yeats's work and Poe's.

For an anonymous work, use a shortened form of the title, beginning with the word under which the title is listed in Works Cited.

For a reference to one volume of a multivolume work, if you used several volumes you must specify the volume as well as the page number, thus:

```
In another letter Pope (2: 160) sets forth a very

different view.
```

The reader understands that you include in your list a multivolume work by Pope, and that you are here referring to page 160 in the second volume. *But* if in your list you indicate that you used only one volume (let's say volume 2), the parenthetic reference would cite only the page number, not the volume number.

In short, the new style of documentation requires you to provide in the text of the essay — not in a footnote — a brief reference that is made intelligible by a glance at the list of Works Cited given at the end of your essay.

RELATED POINTS

1. If a book has a subtitle (see Frye, *Fables*), add a colon immediately after the main title, skip one space, and then give the subtitle. Underline the whole, with continuous underlining, but do not underline the period at the end of the subtitle.

2. If a title includes the title that ordinarily would be underlined — let's say that a book on *The Catcher in the Rye* includes the title of Salinger's novels — the work named in the title is *not* underlined. Thus your citation would look like this:

<u>A New Interpretation of</u> The Catcher in the Rye.

Notice in the list on page 77 the form of the citation of Isabel MacCaffrey's collection of Milton's writings — a collection that includes Milton's play *Samson Agonistes* and names it in the title of the book. The title of the play is *not* italicized (underlined) when you give MacCaffrey's title, but of course you do underline *Samson Agonistes* when you mention it in other contexts. See Mac-Caffrey, and for a book which includes *Julius Caesar* in its title, see Sewell.

3. If a book does not give a publisher's name, write "n.p." (but not enclosed within quotation marks) for "no publisher." The same abbreviation, "n.p.," is used to indicate "no place" if a place of publication is not given.

4. In your essay use arabic numerals, not roman numerals, in all references to writings, thus:

Luke 14.5

<u>Macbeth</u> 2.1.5–10 (a reference to lines 5–10 in the first scene of the second act. Some instructors still prefer a capital roman numeral for the act, a lower case roman numeral for the scene, and an arabic numeral for the lines or lines, thus: II.i.5–10)

5. In citing poetry, use "line" or "lines" (rather than "1." or "11.") for the first quotation, but after that, if matters will be clear, simply use the numbers.

A reminder: for two hundred pages of explanation of these matters, covering all sorts of troublesome cases, see Joseph Gibaldi and Walter S. Achtert, *MLA Handbook for Writers of Research Papers,* 2nd ed. (New York: Modern Language Association of America, 1984).

3
Practical Applications

WRITING A REVIEW

Since a **review** is usually about a newly published work, the reviewer normally assumes that readers will be unfamiliar with it. The reviewer must acquaint the readers with the book, its contents, and its value, and help the readers decide whether or not they wish to read it. Most reviews are brief (500–1500 words), appearing as they do in newspapers and magazines; unlike explications, they cannot comment on everything. And unlike analyses, which focus on one aspect of the writing, reviews attempt in some sense to cover the work. Reviews, then, will probably contain both more summary and more evaluation than will explications or analyses.

Because the work under discussion is new, a review commonly describes it briefly in an introductory paragraph. Example:

> Although Eugène Ionesco's new play *Macbett* often stays fairly close to Shakespeare's *Macbeth,* it is not a translation or even a free adaptation. It takes the gist of Shakespeare's tragedy and for much of its duration seems to transform it into a farce. Yet ultimately *Macbett* turns into a tragedy so much darker than *Macbeth* that the end, no less than the farcical passages, is pure Ionesco.

After giving the readers some idea of the scope of the work, the reviewer normally sets out to persuade them to accept the reviewer's opinions of its strengths and weaknesses. This job of persuasion, of course, can be convincing only if evidence is adduced. Assertions that the jokes are unfunny or that some of the characterization is brilliant must be supported by some quotation or paraphrase. If the readers are to think and feel the way the reviewer thinks and feels, they must experience in some degree what the reviewer experienced. Quotations, paraphrases, summaries — but not interminable synopses that cannot be followed — can give the readers something of the flavor or feel of the book.

Organization

A review usually has something pretty close to the following structure:

1. The opening paragraph gives the reader some idea of the nature and scope of the work.

2. A paragraph or two of plot summary follows if the book is a novel. If it is a collection of stories, poems, or plays, the reviewer usually mentions approximately how many works the book contains, whether all are new or some are old pieces reprinted, and so forth. The aim is to give a rough idea of the contents.

3. Next, a paragraph discusses the theme — that is, the point or idea or vision embodied in the book.

4. A paragraph or two examines the strengths, if any.

5. Then a paragraph or two examines the weaknesses, if any.

6. Finally, the reviewer, having set forth evaluations in some detail in the earlier paragraphs, in a concluding paragraph drives the chief point home and takes leave of the work and of the reader.

Suppose you are reviewing Philip Roth's quaintly titled novel, *The Great American Novel*. The skeleton of your review might look like this:

1. An opening paragraph asserting that *The Great American Novel* isn't great, but it is about a big subject, America in the 1940s, and it is often amusing.

2. A paragraph or two explains that the novel is about a third major league in baseball, the Patriot League, which was dissolved

in 1944 because of alleged Communist infiltration; all traces of the Patriot League have been expunged from history, which is why we never heard of it. This might be the gist of the first paragraph on the plot; the second might go into a bit more detail, explaining that the team chiefly written about is the Ruppert Mundys, who in 1943 included a one-legged catcher, a one-armed outfielder, a dwarf, and so on. The Mundys lost 120 of their 154 games, and it was largely their consistent losing (losing is un-American) that aroused the suspicion of Communist infiltration.

3. There is a point, or theme, to all this fooling. The book in many passages records the author's love affair with baseball, but it is, finally, not about baseball but about America. The novel is a criticism of American social and political values. It is also something of a spoof on earlier American authors, but the literary parody is less pervasive than the social and political themes.

4. The chief strengths are that it is often funny, as, for example, in the episode when . . . , and, more important, that Roth has indeed understood the national mood of the forties, which was characterized by. . . .

5. But these strengths fight against considerable weaknesses, for the book is, in a sense, too funny. Roth cannot resist a joke, and the abundance of gags (here an example) gets in the way; Roth is too self-indulgent. Moreover, though in many ways baseball is a suitable image of America (democratic, competitive, and so forth), Roth pushes the comparison too far, manufacturing unconvincing equations, such as. . . .

6. The conclusion suggests that whether or not the reader likes baseball, the book will entertain and will interest — but it would have been a lot better if it were less insistently funny and less insistent on pushing the sports–politics analogy.

With appropriate details — including quotations to support your points and to give the reader a taste of the writing — this outline could be turned into a coherent review. But, of course, the pattern suggested here is not invariable; you may feel that the book you are reviewing has no weaknesses, or that the plot can be disposed of in a sentence in your opening paragraph. The pattern suggested is often useful, but if it doesn't seem right to you, make yourself another one.

Tone

No less important than the organization of a review, and perhaps harder to master, is the **tone** — the writer's attitude toward the reader and toward the book under review. A review in *Harper's* will have a different tone from one in *Playgirl.* Since you have not been commissioned to write your review and are essentially playing a game, you must invent your audience. It's reasonable to assume that your classmates are your audience. Write for them, not for your teacher; in effect, write something that you would be interested in reading yourself. Keep in mind, too, that a review of a comic novel will probably have a tone different from a review of a tragic novel.

This matter of tone is important. Sometimes reviewers condescend to the reader ("You will do well to ponder this important book"); sometimes they condescend to the author ("Tennessee Williams is to be congratulated for his keen understanding of genteel poverty"). On the whole, treat the reader and the subject with respect; if the subject seems unsatisfactory, there is probably more cause for regret than for scorn — and scorn will backfire because it will turn your reader against you rather than against your subject. In the following paragraph, which is the beginning of a review of the film *Nicholas and Alexandra,* the tone is about as snippy as one can get without offending the reader. Probably the reviewer holds on to our sympathy because (1) she makes clear the grounds of her dislike, and (2) she is on the side of humanity. If she is fed up with Nicholas and Alexandra, it is, we infer, not because she is a crab who is easily exasperated by people but because she is aware of how much suffering these two inadequate leaders brought to others.

> *Nicholas and Alexandra* is as obsequiously respectful as if it had been made about living monarchs who might graciously consent to attend the first performance. The seven other movie versions of the fall of the Romanovs that have played in this country have all concentrated on that mystic voluptuary Rasputin, for the good reason that he was the most dramatic character in the story. The new Sam Spiegel production, directed by Franklin J. Schaffner, sticks to those two royally dull people. Can one make a film about a stolid, well-intentioned couple whose self-preoccupation and need to prove

themselves the leaders they weren't precipitated the butchery of millions of people in a war and a revolution — can one make such a film *without irony* and expect the audience to become involved in the fate of the unfortunate couple? The picture moves in a stately progression from one fond smile they exchange to the next. Ah, yes, they care for each other — we can certainly see that. But, far from developing sympathy for them, we get so fed up with their mediocrity that we wait for their execution to liberate us from the theatre. We quickly perceive the film's point of view — that they are a decent, neurotic pair who might have been mildly happy (in a domineering-wife-and-henpecked-husband way) if only Nicholas hadn't been the head of state. But that seems to be the film's one point of view. The lack of judgment and imagination is treated not as a horrible black joke of history — two dunces sitting on a volcano — or as a key to the eruptions but merely factually, without interpretations.

Pauline Kael, *Deeper into Movies* (Boston, 1973), pp. 366–367

This paragraph has been quoted to illustrate a breezy tone, but the reader may want to know how the review proceeds. The second paragraph compares the present film with a 1932 version of the same story; the third paragraph suggests that the history with which these films deal is interesting but that the present film foolishly subordinates the Russian Revolution to the doings of the royal couple; the fourth paragraph expresses disappointment with the director of the film; the fifth comments on some of the actors' performances; and the concluding paragraph, after asserting that "the script is the heart of the trouble," clinches the point by quoting some disastrous lines. In short, one paragraph leads to the next, and each is rich in details.

Note: For a student's review of a production of a play, see page 182.

RESEARCH PAPERS

What Research Is

Because a research paper requires its writer to collect and interpret evidence — usually including the opinions of earlier investigators — one sometimes hears that a research paper, unlike a critical essay, is not the expression of personal opinion. But such a view is unjust both to criticism and to research. A critical essay is not a mere expression of personal opinion; if it is any good it offers evidence that supports the opinions and thus persuades the reader of their objective rightness. And a research paper in the final analysis is largely personal, because the author continuously uses his or her own judgment to evaluate the evidence, deciding what is relevant and convincing. A research paper is not the mere presentation of what a dozen scholars have already said about a topic; it is a thoughtful evaluation of the available evidence, and so it is, finally, an expression of what the author thinks the evidence adds up to.

Research can be a tedious and frustrating business; there are hours spent reading books and articles that prove to be irrelevant, there are contradictory pieces of evidence, and there is never enough time. Research, in short, is not a procedure that is attractive to everyone. The poet William Butler Yeats, though an indefatigable worker on projects that interested him, engagingly expressed an indifference to the obligation that confronts every researcher: to look carefully at all the available evidence. Reviewing the possible reasons why Jonathan Swift did not marry (for example, he had syphilis, or he feared he would transmit hereditary madness), Yeats says, "Mr. Shane Leslie thinks that Swift's relation to Vanessa was not platonic, and that whenever his letters speak of a cup of coffee they mean the sexual act; whether the letters seem to bear him out I do not know, for those letters bore me."★

Though research sometimes requires one to read boring works, those who engage in it feel, at least sometimes, an exhilaration, a sense of triumph at having studied a problem thoroughly and at having arrived at conclusions that, for the moment anyway, seem objective and irrefutable. Later perhaps new evidence will turn up that will require a new conclusion, but until that time one has built something that will endure wind and weather.

★ *The Variorum Edition of the Plays of Yeats,* ed. Russell K. Alspach (New York, 1966), p. 966.

Primary and Secondary Materials

The materials of literary research can be conveniently divided into two sorts, primary and secondary. The primary materials or sources are the real subject of study; the secondary materials are critical and historical accounts already written about these primary materials. If you want to know whether Shakespeare's attitude toward Julius Caesar was highly traditional or highly original (or a little of each), you read the primary materials (*Julius Caesar,* and other Elizabethan writings about Caesar), and you also read the secondary materials (post-Elizabethan essays and books on Shakespeare and on Elizabethan attitudes toward Caesar, or, more generally, on Elizabethan attitudes toward Rome and toward monarchs).

The line between these two kinds of sources, of course, is not always clear. For example, if you are concerned with the degree to which Joyce's *Portrait of the Artist as a Young Man* is autobiographical, primary materials include not only *Portrait* and Joyce's letters but perhaps also his brother Stanislaus's diary and autobiography. Although the diary and autobiography might be considered secondary sources (certainly a scholarly biography about Joyce or about his brother would be a secondary source), because Stanislaus's books are more or less contemporary with your subject and are more or less Joycean, they can reasonably be called primary sources.

Some Kinds of Research Papers

Your instructor may assign a topic, but if not, you may want to begin by thinking along one of these lines:

1. a paper on a single work, for instance on whether Caesar or Brutus is the tragic hero in *Julius Caesar* (taking account of the views of other writers on the topic), or on Ibsen's view of marriage in *A Doll's House* (taking account of Ibsen's own comments, in letters, about this topic), or the early critical response to *Catcher in the Rye* (a study on the first reviews of the novel).

2. a paper on an author's treatment of a topic in several works, such as Zen in the writings of J.D. Salinger, or suicide in Shakespeare's tragedies, or Faulkner's depiction of blacks in his late works.

3. a comparison of two works, for instance of *Julius Caesar* with its source, or of Shakespeare's *The Merchant of Venice* with Marlowe's *The Jew of Malta,* or of two lines of critical interpretation (for instance, critics who see Shylock as a tragic hero, versus those who see him as a comic villain).

From Topic to Thesis

We will assume that you have read George Orwell's *1984* and that in browsing through *The Collected Essays, Journalism and Letters* you came across a letter (17 February 1944) in which Orwell says that he has been reading Evgenii Zamyatin's *We* and that he himself had been keeping notes for "that kind of book." And in *The Collected Essays, Journalism and Letters* you also came across a review (4 January 1946) Orwell wrote of *We,* and it is apparent that *We* resembles *1984.* Or perhaps you learned in a preface to an edition of *1984* that Orwell was influenced by *We,* and you decided to look into the matter. You borrowed *We* from the library, read it, and perceived resemblances in plot, character, and theme. But it's not simply a question of listing resemblances between the two books. Your topic is: What do the resemblances add up to? After all, Orwell in the letter said he had already been working in Zamyatin's direction without even knowing Zamyatin's book, and so your investigation may find, for example, that the closest resemblances are in relatively trivial details and that there is really nothing important in *1984* that was not already implicit in Orwell's earlier books; or your investigation may find that Zamyatin gave a new depth to Orwell's thought; or it may find that though Orwell borrowed heavily from Zamyatin, he missed the depth of *We.* In the earliest stage of your research, then, you don't know what you will find, but you know that there is a topic, and it interests you, and you are ready to begin the necessary legwork.

Locating Material: First Steps

First, prepare a working bibliography; that is, a list of books and articles that must be looked at. The catalog of your library is an excellent place to begin. If your topic is Orwell and Zamyatin, you'll want at least to glance at whatever books by and about these two authors are available. When you have looked over the most promising portions of this material (in secondary sources, chapter headings and indexes often will guide you), you will have found some interesting things. But you want to get a good idea of the state of current scholarship on your topic, and you realize that you must go beyond the card catalog's listings under "Orwell," "Zamyatin," and such an obviously related topic as "utopian literature." Doubtless there are pertinent articles in journals, but you cannot start thumbing through them at random.

Bibliographic Index, a journal issued three times a year and cumulated annually, lists bibliographies — that is, it cites not only books that are wholly bibliographies, but also articles that themselves are lists of writings about a topic (for instance, a journal called *Modern Fiction Studies* occasionally publishes an article that consists of a list of writings on a modern writer); *Bibliographic Index* even cites books that happen to include bibliographies of fifty or more citations.

But perhaps *Bibliographic Index* cites no bibliography that sounds relevant to you — and yet you know that there *must* be some publications on your topic. The easiest way to locate articles and books is by consulting the *MLA International Bibliography,* which until 1969 was published as part of *PMLA (Publications of the Modern Language Association)* and since 1969 has been published separately. This bibliography annually lists scholarly studies published in a given year; you look, therefore, in the most recent issue under "Orwell" (in the section on "English Literature," the subsection on "Twentieth Century") to see if anything is listed that sounds relevant. A look at "Zamyatin" may also turn up material. (Notice that in the past few years the number of entries in the *MLA International Bibliography* has so increased that for each year from 1969 the annual bibliography consists of more than one volume. Writings on literature in English are in one volume, writings on

European literature in another; and so the volume that gives you information about Orwell will not be the one that gives you information about Zamyatin.)

Because your time is severely limited you probably cannot read everything published on your two authors. At least for the moment, therefore, you use only the last ten years of this bibliography. Presumably any important earlier material will have been incorporated into some of the recent studies listed, and if when you come to read these recent studies you find references to an article of, say, 1958, that sounds essential, of course you will read that article too.

Other Bibliographic Aids

The *MLA International Bibliography* is not the only valuable guide to scholarship. The *Year's Work in English Studies,* though concerned only with English authors (hence it will have nothing on Zamyatin, unless an article links Zamyatin with an English author), and though not nearly so comprehensive even on English authors as the *MLA International Bibliography,* is useful partly because it is selective — presumably listing only the more significant items — and partly because it includes some evaluative comments on the books and articles it lists.

For topics in American literature, there is a similar annual publication, *American Literary Scholarship,* ed. J. Albert Robbins (earlier volumes are edited by James Woodress), valuable for its broad coverage of articles and books on major and minor writers and for its evaluative comments. There are two useful guides to scholarly and critical studies of the chief American figures: James Woodress et al., eds., *Eight American Authors: A Review of Research and Criticism,* revised edition (New York, 1972), covering Poe, Emerson, Hawthorne, Thoreau, Melville, Whitman, Mark Twain, and Henry James; and Jackson R. Bryer, ed., *Sixteen Modern American Authors* (Durham, 1974), covering such figures as Sherwood Anderson, Eugene O'Neill, William Carlos Williams, and Ezra Pound (living authors are excluded). For broader (but less deep) coverage of American literature, see Clarence Gohdes, *Bibliographic Guide to the Study of the Literature of the U.S.A.,* 4th ed. (Durham, 1976). Also useful is the bibliography accompanying

Robert Spiller et al., *Literary History of the United States,* 4th ed. revised (New York, 1974).

None of the bibliographic aids mentioned thus far covers ancient writers; there is no point, then, in looking at those aids if you are writing about the Book of Job or Greek conceptions of the tragic hero or Roman conceptions of comedy. For articles on ancient literature as well as on literature in modern languages, consult the annual volumes of *Humanities Index,* issued since 1974; for the period 1965–74 it was entitled *Social Sciences and Humanities Index,* and before that (1907–64) it was *International Index.* In *Humanities Index* (to use the current title) you can find listings of articles in periodicals on a wide range of topics. This breadth is bought at the cost of depth, for *Humanities Index,* though it includes the chief scholarly journals, does not include either the less well-known scholarly journals or the more popular magazines, and it does not include books. For the more popular magazines, consult the *Readers' Guide to Periodical Literature.* If, for example, you want to do a research paper on the reception given to Laurence Olivier's films of Shakespeare, the *Readers' Guide* can quickly lead you to reviews in such publications as *Time, Newsweek,* and *The Atlantic.*

Bibliographies of the sort mentioned are guides, and there are so many of them that there are guides to these guides. Useful guides to reference works (that is, to bibliographies and also to such helpful compilations as handbooks of mythology, quotations, dates, place names, and critical terms) are Richard D. Altick and Andrew Wright, *Selective Bibliography for the Study of English and American Literature,* 5th ed. (New York, 1974); Donald F. Bond, *A Reference Guide to English Studies,* 2nd ed. (Chicago, 1971); Arthur G. Kennedy and Donald B. Sands, *A Concise Bibliography for Students of English,* 5th ed. (Stanford, 1974); and Margaret C. Patterson, *Literary Research Guide* (New York: 1976). One additional guide, not limited to works relevant to literature, is: *Guide to Reference Books,* 9th ed., compiled by Eugene P. Sheehy et al. (Chicago, 1976), and *Supplement* (1980).

And there are guides to these guides to guides: reference librarians. If you don't know where to turn to find something, turn to the librarian.

Taking Notes

Let's assume now that you have checked some bibliographies and have a fair number of references to things that you feel you must read to have a substantial knowledge of the evidence and the common interpretations of the evidence. Most researchers find it convenient, when examining bibliographies and the card catalog, to write down each reference on a three- by five-inch index card — one title per card. On the card put the author's full name (last name first), exact title of the book or of the article and the journal (with dates and pages). Titles of books and periodicals (publications issued periodically, for instance four times a year) are underlined, titles of articles and of essays in books are put within quotation marks. It's also a good idea to put the library catalog number on the card to save time if you need to get the item for a second look.

Next, you have to start reading or scanning the materials whose titles you have collected. Some of these items will prove irrelevant or silly; others will prove valuable in themselves and also in the leads they give you to further references, which you duly record on cards. Notes — aside from these bibliographic notes — are best taken on four- by six-inch cards because smaller cards do not provide enough space for your summaries of useful materials. And, on the other hand, four- by six-inch cards rather than larger cards will serve to remind you that you should not take notes on everything; be selective in taking notes.

1. In taking notes, write brief *summaries* rather than paraphrases because there is rarely any point to paraphrasing; generally speaking, either quote exactly (and put the passage in quotation marks, with a notation of the source, including the page numbers), or summarize, reducing a page or even an entire article or chapter of a book to one four- by six-inch card. Again, be sure to include the page numbers of your source. Even when you summarize, indicate your source on the card, so that you can give appropriate credit in your paper. (On plagiarism see pp. 73–75.)

2. Of course, in your summary you will sometimes quote a phrase or a sentence — putting it in quotation marks — but quote sparingly. You are not doing stenography, but rather you are

thinking and assimilating knowledge; for the most part, then, your source should be digested rather than engorged whole. Probably most of your direct quotations will be effectively stated passages or especially crucial passages or both. In your finished paper some of these quotations will provide authority and emphasis.

3. If you quote but omit some irrelevant material within the quotation, be sure to indicate the omission by three spaced periods, as explained on pp. 68–69.

4. *Never* copy a passage changing an occasional word under the impression that you are thereby putting it into your own words. Notes of this sort will find their way into your paper, your reader will sense a style other than your own, and suspicions of plagiarism may follow.

5. If possible, add your own comment to the summary or quotation — for instance: "But this overlooks Orwell's 1939 review," or "Check to see what is omitted from quote." Be sure to mark these annotations in some distinctive way — for instance by putting them within double parentheses, like this: ((. . .))

6. In the upper corner of each note card, write a brief key — for example, "Orwell's first reading of *We,*" or "Characterization," or "Thought control"— so that later you can tell at a glance what is on the card.

As you work, you'll of course find yourself returning again and again to your primary materials — and you'll probably find to your surprise that a good deal of the secondary material is unconvincing or even wrong, despite the fact that it is printed in a handsome book. One of the things we learn from research is that not everything in print is true; one of the pleasures we get from research results from this discovery.

Writing the Paper

There remains the difficult job of writing up your findings, usually in 2,000–3,000 words (eight to twelve double-spaced typed pages). Here is some advice.

1. Begin by rereading your note cards, sorting them into packets by topic. Put together what belongs together. Don't hes-

itate to reject material that — however interesting — now seems redundant or irrelevant. In doing your research you quite properly took lots of notes (as William Blake said, "You never know what is enough unless you know what is more than enough"), but now, in looking over your material, you see that some of it is unnecessary and so you reject it. Your finished paper should not sandbag the reader; keep in mind the Yiddish proverb, "Where there is too much, something is missing." After sorting and resorting, you will have a kind of first draft without writing a draft. This business of settling on the structure of your work — the composition of your work, one might say — is often frustrating. Where to begin? Should this go before that? But remember that great writers have gone through greater struggles. If you look at a page of a manuscript by almost any writer, say William Faulkner or Marianne Moore, you will see that it is so heavily revised that it is almost illegible. You can hardly expect, at the outset, to have a better grasp of your material than Faulkner or Moore had of theirs.

2. From your packets of cards you can make a first outline. (In arranging the packets into a sequence, and then in sketching an outline, you will be guided by your *thesis,* your point. Without a thesis you will have only a lot of note cards, not an essay.) This outline will indicate not only the major parts of the essay but also the subdivisions within these parts. Do not confuse this outline with a paragraph outline (i.e., with an outline made by jotting down the topic idea of each paragraph); when you come to write your essay, a single heading may require two or three or more paragraphs.

3. When you write your first draft, leave lots of space at the top and bottom of each page so that you can add material, which will be circled and connected by arrows to the proper place. For example, as you are drafting page 6, from perhaps your tenth packet, you may find a note card that now seems more appropriate to a point you made back on page 2. Write it on page 2, and put the card in the appropriate earlier packet, so that if for some reason you later have to double-check your notes, you can find it easily. And of course your opening paragraph — in which usually you define the problem and indicate your approach — may well be the last thing that you write, for you may not be able to

enunciate your thesis clearly until you have learned from drafting the rest of the essay. (On opening paragraphs, see page 59.)

4. Write or type your quotations, even in the first draft, exactly as you want them to appear in the final version. Short quotations (fewer than five lines of prose) are enclosed within quotation marks but are not otherwise set off; longer quotations, however, are set off (triple-space before them and after them), slightly indented, and are *not* enclosed in quotation marks. For more on quotations, see pages 68-72.

5. Include, right in the body of the draft, all of the relevant citations (later these will become footnotes), so that when you come to revise, you don't have to start hunting through your notes to find who said what, and where. You can, for the moment, enclose these citations within diagonal lines, or within double parentheses — anything at all to remind you that they will be your footnotes.

6. Beware of the compulsion to include every note card in your essay. You have taken all these notes, and there is a strong temptation to use them all. But, truth to tell, in hindsight many are useless. Conversely, you will probably find as you write your draft that here and there you need to do more research, to check a quotation, or to collect additional examples. Probably it is best to continue writing your draft, if possible; but remember to insert the necessary material after you get it.

7. As you revise your draft, make sure that you do not merely tell the reader "A says . . . B says . . . C says. . . ." When you write a research paper, you are not merely setting the table with other people's dinnerware; you are cooking the meal. You must have a point, an opinion, a thesis; you are working toward a conclusion, and your readers should always feel they are moving toward that conclusion (by means of your thoughtful evaluation of the evidence) rather than reading an anthology of commentary on the topic.

Thus, because you have a focus, you should say such things as "There are three common views on. . . . The first two are represented by A and B; the third, and by far the most reasonable, is C's view that . . ." or "A argues . . . but . . ." or "Although the third view, C's, is not conclusive, still . . ." or "Moreover,

C's point can be strengthened when we consider a piece of evidence that he does not make use of." You cannot merely say, "A says . . . , B says . . . , C says . . . ," because your job is not to report what everyone says but to establish the truth of a thesis. When you introduce a quotation, then, try to let the reader see the use to which you are putting it. "A says" is of little help; giving the quotation and then following it with "thus says A" is even worse. You need a lead-in such as "A concisely states the common view," "B shrewdly calls attention to a fatal weakness," "Without offering any proof, C claims that," "D admits," "E rejects the idea that. . . ." In short, it is usually advisable to let the reader know why you are quoting or, to put it a little differently, how the quotation fits into your argument.

8. Make sure that in your final version you state your thesis early, perhaps even in the title (not "Shakespeare's Juliet" but "Juliet's Swift Maturity), but if not in the title, almost certainly in your first paragraph.

While you were doing your research you may have noticed that the more interesting writers persuade the reader of the validity of their opinions by (1) letting the reader see that they know what of significance has been written on the topic; (2) letting the reader hear the best representatives of the chief current opinions, whom they correct or confirm; and (3) advancing their opinions, by offering generalizations supported by concrete details. Adopt these techniques in your own writing.

Your overall argument, then, is fleshed out with careful summaries and with effective quotations and with judicious analyses of your own, so that by the end of the paper the readers not only have read a neatly typed paper, but they also are persuaded that under your guidance they have seen the evidence, heard the arguments justly summarized, and reached a sound conclusion. They may not become better persons but they are better informed.

When you have finished your paper prepare a final copy that will by easy to read. Type the paper in accordance with the principles given on pages 68–86.

A bibliography or list of works consulted (see pp. 76–83) is usually appended to the research paper, so that readers may easily look further into the primary and secondary material if they wish; but if you have done your job well, readers will be content to leave the subject where you left it, grateful that you have set matters straight.

ESSAY EXAMINATIONS

What Examinations Are

Chapters 4, 5, 6, and 7, on writing essays about fiction, drama, poetry, and film, discuss not only the job of writing essays but also the nature of the artistic forms themselves, on the assumption that writing an essay requires knowledge of the subject as well as skill with language. Here a few words will be spent in discussing the nature of examinations; perhaps one can write better essay answers when one knows what examinations are.

An examination not only measures learning and thinking but stimulates them. Even so humble an examination as a short-answer quiz — chiefly a device to coerce students to do the assigned reading — is a sort of push designed to move students forward. Of course internal motivation is far superior to external, but even such crude external motivation as a quiz can have a beneficial effect. Students know this; indeed they often seek external compulsion, choosing a particular course "because I want to know something about . . . and I know that I won't do the reading on my own." (Teachers often teach a new course for the same reason; we want to become knowledgeable about, say, the Theater of the Absurd, and we know that despite our lofty intentions we may not seriously confront the subject unless we are under the pressure of facing a class.)

In short, however ignoble it sounds, examinations force students to acquire learning and then to convert learning into thinking. Sometimes it is not until preparing for the final examination that students — rereading the chief texts and classroom notes — see what the course was really about; until this late stage, the trees obscure the forest, but now, reviewing and sorting things out, a pattern emerges. The experience of reviewing and then of writing an examination, though fretful, can be highly exciting, as connections are made and ideas take on life. Such discoveries about the whole subject matter of a course can almost never be made by writing critical essays on topics of one's own construction, for such topics rarely require a view of the whole. Further, we are more likely to make imaginative leaps when trying to answer questions that other people pose to us, rather than questions we pose to ourselves. (Again, every teacher knows that in the classroom questions are asked that stimulate the teacher to see things and to think thoughts that would otherwise have been neglected.) And although questions posed by others cause anxiety, when they have been confronted and responded to on an examination, the student often makes yet another discovery — a self-discovery, a sudden and satisfying awareness of powers one didn't know one had.

Writing Essay Answers

Let's assume that before the examination you have read the assigned material, marked the margins of your books, made summaries of the longer readings and of the classroom comments, reviewed all this material, and had a decent night's sleep. Now you are facing the examination sheet.

Here are seven obvious but important practical suggestions.

1. Take a moment to jot down, as a sort of outline or source of further inspiration, a few ideas that strike you after you have thought a little about the question. You may at the outset realize that there are, say, three points you want to make, and unless you jot these down — three key words will do — you may spend all the allotted time on one point.

2. Answer the question: if you are asked to compare two characters, compare them; don't just write two character sketches. Take seriously such words as "compare," "summarize," and especially "evaluate."

3. You can often get a good start merely by turning the question into an affirmation, for example, by turning "In what ways is the poetry of Ginsberg influenced by Whitman?" into "The poetry of Ginsberg is influenced by Whitman in at least . . . ways."

4. Don't waste time summarizing at length what you have read unless asked to do so — but of course you may have to give

a brief summary in order to support a point. The instructor wants to see that you can *use* your reading, not merely that you have done the reading.

5. Budget your time. Do not spend more than the allotted time on a question.

6. Be concrete. Illustrate your arguments with facts — the names of authors, titles, dates, characters, details of plot, and quotations if possible.

7. Leave space for last-minute additions. Either skip a page between essays, or write only on the right-hand pages so that on rereading you can add material at the appropriate place on the left-hand pages.

Beyond these general suggestions we can best talk about essay examinations by looking at the five commonest sorts of questions·

1. A passage to explicate

2. A historical question (for example, "Trace T. S. Eliot's religious development"; "Trace the development of Shakespeare's conception of the tragic hero"; "How is Frost's nature poetry indebted to Emerson's thinking?")

3. A critical quotation to be evaluated

4. A wild question (such as "What would Virginia Woolf think of Vonnegut's *Cat's Cradle*?"; "What would Macbeth do if he were in Hamlet's place?")

5. A comparison (for example, "Compare the dramatic monologues of Browning with those of T. S. Eliot")

A few remarks on each of these types may be helpful.

1. On explication, see pp. 11–12 and pp. 204–206. As a short rule, look carefully at the tone (speaker's attitude toward self, subject, and audience) and at the implications of the words (their connotations and associations), and see if there is a pattern of imagery. For example, religious language ("adore," "saint") in a secular love poem may precisely define the nature of the lover and of the beloved. Remember, *an explication is not a paraphrase* (a putting into other words) but an attempt to show the relations of the

parts by calling attention to implications. Organization of such an essay is rarely a problem, since most explications begin with the first line and go on to the last.

2. A good essay on a historical question will offer a nice combination of argument and evidence; that is, the thesis will be supported by concrete details (names, dates, perhaps, even brief quotations). A discussion of Eliot's movement toward the Church of England cannot be convincing if it does not specify certain works as representative of Eliot in certain years. If you are asked to relate a writer or a body of work to an earlier writer or period, list the chief characteristics of the earlier writer or period, and then show *specifically* how the material you are discussing is related to these characteristics. And if you quote some relevant lines from the works, your reader will feel that you know not only titles and stock phrases but also the works themselves.

3. If you are asked to evaluate a critical quotation, read it carefully, and in your answer take account of *all* the quotation. If, for example, the quoted critic has said, "Alice Walker in her fiction always . . . but in her nonfiction rarely . . . ," you will have to write about fiction and nonfiction; it will not be enough to talk only about Alice Walker's novels or only about her essays (unless, of course, the instructions on the examination ask you to take only as much of the quotation as you wish). Watch especially for words like "always," "for the most part," "never"; that is, although the passage may on the whole approach the truth, you may feel that some important qualifications are needed. This is not being picky; true thinking involves making subtle distinctions, yielding assent only so far and no further. And (again) be sure to give concrete details, supporting your argument with evidence.

4. Curiously, a wild question, such as "What would Woolf think of *Cat's Cradle?*" or "What would Macbeth do in Hamlet's place?" usually produces rather tame answers: a half-dozen ideas about Woolf or Macbeth are neatly applied to Vonnegut or Hamlet, and the gross incompatibilities are thus revealed. But, as the previous paragraph suggests, it may be necessary to do more than set up bold and obvious oppositions. The interest in such a question and in the answer to it may be largely in the degree to which superficially different figures resemble each other in some impor-

tant ways. And remember that the wildness of the question does not mean that all answers are equally acceptable; as usual, any good answer will be supported by concrete detail.

5. On comparisons, see pp. 36–40. Because comparisons are especially difficult to write, be sure to take a few moments to jot down a sort of outline so that you know where you will be going. A comparison of Browning's and Eliot's monologues might treat three poems by each, devoting alternate paragraphs to one author; or it might first treat one author's poems and then turn to the other's, but if it adopts this second strategy, the essay may break into two parts. You can guard against this weakness by announcing at the outset that you can treat one author first, then the other; by reminding your reader during your treatment of the first author that certain points will be picked up when you get to the second author; and by briefly reminding your reader during the treatment of the second author of certain points already made in the treatment of the first.

Part Two

4

Writing about Fiction

THE WORLD OF THE STORY

Plot and Character

It is usual to say that a narrative — a story, whether a short story or a novel — has an **introduction, a complication,** and a **resolution;** that is, it gets under way, some difficulty or problem or complexity arises (usually a **conflict** of opposed wills or forces), and there is some sort of untying or settling-up — or, better, settling-down.★ These terms can be illustrated most simply in a familiar piece, O. Henry's "The Gift of the Magi." We are introduced to a young wife who has only (in addition to a husband) $1.87 and long hair; her husband has only (in addition to a wife) a treasured gold watch. It is the day before Christmas, and gifts must be bought. What to do? As everyone knows, she sells her hair to a wig-maker to buy a watch-fob, only to find that her husband has bought her a set of combs by selling his watch. And so

★A short story, of course, is not a novel synopsized. Most often a *short story* reveals only a single character at a moment of crisis, whereas a *novel* usually traces the development of an individual or a group through cumulative experiences. If the short story is very short, an essayist has a fairly good chance of elucidating the whole, or writing about all the aspects that seem important. But an essayist who writes about a longer story or a novel will have to be content with treating either a few pages or one thread that runs through the work. The last paragraph of this chapter sketches two critical approaches to long fiction.

(here is the resolution), these "two foolish children in a flat who most unwisely sacrificed for each other the greatest treasures of their house," smile and set abouit making dinner. Lest we mistake the author's tone — though his **verbal irony** is unmistakable, for his words clearly mean approximately the opposite of what they say — he adds that "these two were the wisest."

It is usual to say that "The Gift of the Magi" has a clever **plot.** And it does, if by a plot one means something like "a curious happening." It sets forth a cute idea, and no one who reads it ever forgets the idea — the surprising ending. But in one usage of the word *plot,* "The Gift of the Magi" has scarcely a plot at all. In E. M. Forster's terms, it is only a story (something alleged to have happened), not a plot (happenings that are causally connected). Forster illustrates his distinction thus:

> A plot is also a narrative of events, the emphasis falling on causality. "The king died and then the queen died," is a story. "The king died, and then the queen died of grief" is a plot. The time-sequence is preserved, but the sense of causality overshadows it.
>
> *Aspects of the Novel* (New York, 1927), p. 86

In O. Henry's tale, the impact comes from the coincidence of two trains of events (she sells her hair to buy a fob, he sells his watch to buy combs) rather than from the working out of the implications of a deed.

Some fiction has a good deal of physical action — wanderings, strange encounters, births, and deaths. But there is also fiction in which little seems to happen. These apparently plotless stories, however, usually involve a mental action — a significant perception, a decision, a failure of the will — and the process of this mental action is the plot.

The sense of causality, valued so highly by Forster, is in part rooted in **character.** Things happen, in most good fiction, at least partly because the people have certain personalities or characters (moral, intellectual, and emotional qualities) and, given their natures, because they respond plausibly to other personalities. What their names are and what they look like may help you to understand them, but probably the best guide to characters is what they do. As we get to know more about their drives and goals — especially the choices they make — we enjoy seeing the writer complete the portraits, finally presenting us with a coherent and credible picture of people in action. In this view, plot and character are inseparable. Plot is not simply a series of happenings, but happenings that come out of character, that reveal character, and that influence character. Henry James puts it thus: "What is character but the determination of incident? What is incident but the illustration of character?" But, of course, characters are not defined only by what they do. The narrator often describes them, and the characters' words and dress reveal aspects of them. David Lodge's analysis (pp. 145–149) of a page from Dickens's *Hard Times* astutely points out the devices Dickens uses to help us understand what Gradgrind is like.

You may want to set forth a character sketch, describing some person in the story or novel. You will probably plan to reveal three things: appearance, personality, and character —"character" here meaning not a figure in a literary work but the figure's moral or ethical values. Of course "character" in this sense may not be utterly distinct from "personality," but personality is more a matter of psychology than of ethics. For example, wit, irritability, and fastidiousness can be regarded as parts of personality, but generosity, cowardice, and temperance can be regarded as parts of character or of morality. The distinction is not always clear, but it is evident enough when we speak of someone as "a diamond in the rough." We probably mean that the person is morally solid (a matter of character) though given to odd or even rude expressions of personality. In preparing such a sketch take these points into consideration:

1. What the person says (but remember that what he or she says need not be taken at face value; the person may be hypocritical, or self-deceived, or biased).

2. What the person does.

3. What others (including the narrator of the story) say about the person.

4. What others *do* (their actions may help to indicate what the person could do but does not do).

5. What the person looks like — face, body, clothes. These may help to convey the personality, or they may in some measure help to disguise it.

A character sketch (remember — we have made a distinction between character and personality, but when one speaks of a "character sketch" one means all aspects of a figure in a work of literature, *not* simply the moral sense), such as "Holden Caulfield: Adolescent Snob or Suffering Saint?" can be complex and demanding, especially if the character (the figure) is complex. Notice that in the example just referred to, the writer sees that Holden might (at least at first glance) be interpreted in two very different ways, a snob or a saint. In fact, the student who wrote the essay argued that Holden has touches of the adolescent snob but is chiefly a suffering saint. An essay on a character, you will recall, is necessarily in some degree an interpretation, and thus even such an essay has a thesis or argument holding it together. Usually, however, you will want to do more than set forth your view of a character. Probably you will discuss the character's function, or contrast him or her with other characters, or trace the development of personality. (One of the most difficult topics, the character of the narrator, will be discussed later in this chapter, under the heading "Point of View.") You probably will still want to keep in mind the five suggestions for getting at a character (as well as others on page 112), but you will also want to go further, relating your findings to additional matters of the sort we will now examine.

Foreshadowing

The writer of fiction provides a coherent world in which the details work together. The **foreshadowing** that would eliminate surprise, or at least greatly reduce it, and thus destroy a story that has nothing else to offer, is a powerful tool in the hands of the writer of serious fiction. Even in such a story as Faulkner's "A Rose for Emily," where we are surprised to learn near the end that Miss Emily has slept beside the decaying corpse of her dead lover, from the outset we expect something strange; that is, we are not surprised by the surprise, only by its precise nature. The first sentence of the story tells us that after Miss Emily's funeral (the narrator begins at the end) the townspeople cross her threshold "out of curiosity to see the inside of her house, which no one save an old manservant . . . had seen in at least ten years." As the story

progresses, we see Miss Emily prohibiting people from entering
the house, we hear that after a certain point no one ever sees Homer Barron again, that "the front door remained closed," and (a
few paragraphs before the end of the story) that the townspeople
"knew that there was one room in that region above the stairs which
no one had seen in forty years." The paragraph preceding the revelation that "the man himself lay in bed" is devoted to a description of Homer's dust-covered clothing and toilet articles. In short,
however much we are unprepared for the precise revelation, we
are prepared for some strange thing in the house; and, given Miss
Emily's purchase of poison and Homer's disappearance, we have
some idea of what will be revealed. (The story is printed on pp.
294–302.)

Joyce's "Araby" is another example of a story in which the
beginning is a preparation for all that follows. Consider the first
two paragraphs.

> North Richmond Street, being blind, was a quiet street except
> at the hour when the Christian Brothers' school set the boys free.
> An uninhabited house of two storeys stood at the blind end, de-
> tached from its neighbours in a square ground. The other houses of
> the street, conscious of decent lives within them, gazed at one an-
> other with brown imperturbable faces.
>
> The former tenant of our house, a priest, had died in the back
> drawing-room. Air, musty from having been long enclosed, hung
> in all the rooms, and the waste room behind the kitchen was lit-
> tered with old useless papers. Among these I found a few paper-
> covered books, the pages of which were curled and damp: *The Ab-
> bot,* by Walter Scott, *The Devout Communicant* and *The Memoirs of
> Vidocq.* I liked the last best because its leaves were yellow. The wild
> garden behind the house contained a central apple-tree and a few
> straggling bushes under one of which I found the late tenant's rusty
> bicycle pump. He had been a very charitable priest; in his will he
> had left all his money to institutions and the furniture of his house
> to his sister.

A dead-end ("blind") street contains "imperturbable" houses, including an uninhabited one. The former tenant of the house that
the narrator lived in was a priest who died in the back drawing-
room, leaving, among other things, musty air, yellowing books,
and a rusty bicycle pump. If we have read with care and sympa-

thy, we find that Joyce gives us in these paragraphs a vision of the paralysis of Ireland that he elsewhere speaks of.

As we read further in the story, we are not surprised to learn that the boy for a while manufactured quasi-religious experiences (religion being dead — remember the dead priest and his rusty bicycle pump). In his ears, shop-boys sing "litanies," his girl friend's name springs to his lips "in strange prayers," and his vision of her is a "chalice" which he carries "safely through a throng of foes." He plans to visit a bazaar, and he promises to bring her a gift; but after he has with some difficulty arrived at the bazaar, he is vastly disappointed by the trivial conversation of the attendants, by the counting of the day's receipts (money-changers in the temple), and by the darkness ("the upper part of the hall was now completely dark"). The last line of the story runs thus: "Gazing up into the darkness I saw myself as a creature driven and derided by vanity; and my eyes burned with anguish and anger." Everything in the story coheres; the dead-end street, the dead priest, the rusty pump — all are perfect preludes to this story about a boy's recognition of the nothingness that surrounds him. The "vanity" that drives and derides him is not only the egotism that moved him to think he could bring the girl a fitting gift but also the nothingness that is spoken of in the biblical "Vanity of vanities, all is vanity."

In an essay on foreshadowing you will almost surely work through the evidence chronologically, though of course your initial paragraph may discuss the end and indicate that the remainder of the essay will be concerned with tracing the way in which the author prepares the reader for this end and simultaneously maintains the right amount of suspense. If the suspense is too slight, we stop reading, not caring what comes next. If it is too great, we are perhaps reading a story in which the interest depends entirely on some strange happening rather than a story with sufficiently universal application to make it worthy of a second reading. Your essay may study the ways in which details gain in meaning as the reader gets further into the story. Or it may study the author's failure to keep details relevant and coherent, the tendency to introduce material for its momentary value at the expense of the larger design. An essay on an uneven story may do both: it may show that although there are unfortunate irrelevancies, there is also considerable skill in arousing and interestingly fulfilling the reader's expectations. If you feel that the story is fundamentally successful, the organization of your thoughts may reflect your feelings. After an initial paragraph stating the overall position, you may discuss the failures and then go on, at greater length, to discuss the strengths, thus ending strongly on your main point. If you feel that the story is essentially a failure, perhaps first discuss its merits briefly, and then go on to your main point — the unsatisfactory nature of the story. To reverse this procedure would be to leave the reader with an impression contrary to your thesis.

Setting and Atmosphere

Foreshadowing normally makes use of **setting.** The setting or environment in the first two paragraphs of Joyce's "Araby" is not mere geography, not mere locale: it provides an **atmosphere,** an air that the characters breathe, a world in which they move. Narrowly speaking, the setting is the physical surroundings — the furniture, the architecture, the landscape, the climate — and these often are highly appropriate to the characters who are associated with them. Thus, in Emily Brontë's *Wuthering Heights* the passionate Earnshaw family is associated with Wuthering Heights, the storm-exposed moorland, whereas the mild Linton family is associated with Thrushcross Grange in the sheltered valley below.

Broadly speaking, setting includes not only the physical surroundings but a point or several points in time. The background against which we see the characters and the happenings may be specified as morning or evening, spring or fall, and this temporal setting in a good story will probably be highly relevant; it will probably be part of the story's meaning, perhaps providing an ironic contrast (think of the festive, carnival setting in Poe's "The Cask of Amontillado," a story of a murder) or perhaps exerting an influence on the characters.

Some comments on familiar examples from Thomas Hardy's novels may clarify the significance of setting. In *Tess of the D'Urbervilles* we are told of a place called Flintcomb Ash, where "the whole field was in color a desolate drab; it was a complexion without features, as if a face, from chin to brow, should be only an expanse of skin. The sky wore, in another color, the same likeness; a white vacuity of expression with the lineaments gone." Or, near the end of the novel, when, just before her arrest, Tess lies upon a great stone slab at Stonehenge, she is associated with all the victims of history and prehistory. Dorothy Van Ghent calls attention to the role that the earth plays in *Tess.* There are

> the long stretches of earth that have to be trudged in order that a person may get from one place to another, the slowness of the business, the irreducible reality of it (for one has only one's feet), its grimness of soul-wearing fatigue and shelterlessness and doubtful issue at the other end of the journey where nobody may be at home.
>
>

The English Novel (New York, 1953), p. 201

Van Ghent goes on to say, in discussing *The Mayor of Casterbridge:*

> The Roman ruins round about the town of Casterbridge are a rather . . . complicated metaphor, for they are works of man that have fallen into earth; they speak mutely of the anonymity of human effort in historical as well as in geological times; their presence suggests also the classic pattern of the Mayor's tragedy, the ancient repetitiveness of self-destruction; and they provide thus a kind of guarantee or confirming signature of the heroism of the doomed human enterprise.
>
>

The English Novel, p. 202

David Lodge, on pages 145–149, points out that Dickens's "plain, bare, monotonous vault of a schoolroom," the domain of the schoolmaster Gradgrind, is a kind of extension of Gradgrind himself, who has a "square wall of a forehead," an "inflexible" voice, and a "square coat." In short, in a good piece of fiction the setting is not merely "colorful" but relevant.

It is not enough, of course, to weave a pattern of references, a chain of images. The writer's story must be about something; and language is the net that catches it, the device whereby the author makes something we value, something which illuminates human experience. This intangible that the writer gives us has been called "felt life" and "felt reality." Here is a paragraph by another critic, Martin Green, sharply criticizing Hawthorne for naming experiences rather than catching them. Green begins by quoting from Hawthorne's "Young Goodman Brown."

> "On he flew among the black pines, brandishing his staff with frenzied gestures, now giving vent to an inspiration of horrid blas-

phemy, and now shouting forth such laughter as set all the echoes of the forest laughing like demons around him." Nothing there evokes the experience of blasphemy. Everything evokes memories of fanciful fiction. "Another verse of the hymn arose, a low and mournful strain, such as the pious love, but joined to words which expressed all that our natures can conceive of sin, and darkly hinted at far more." This is the language of empty exaggeration; after all that our natures can conceive comes "far more." "Young Goodman Brown" is not an allegory because it allegorizes nothing. There is no experience embodied in its language, and consequently no reason to construct elaborate meanings for its oddities.

Re-appraisals (New York, 1965), pp. 73–74

Green may be wrong, but notice how he makes his point: he begins with a quotation from the story, offers his criticism, and then offers another quotation that allows him to restate his criticism. He concludes the paragraph with yet another and broader restatement.

Note: although your instructor may ask you to write a paragraph describing the setting, more often he or she will want something more complicated, an essay on the *function* of the setting. For such an essay, you may find it useful to begin with a paragraph or two describing the setting or settings, but be sure to go on to analyze the significance of this material.

Symbolism

An "experience," of course, is not a happening through which the author necessarily passed; rather, it is a thought, an emotion, a vision that is meaningful and is embodied in the piece of fiction for all to read. Inevitably the writer uses **symbols.** Symbols are neither puzzles nor colorful details but are among the concrete embodiments that give the story whatever accuracy it has. Joyce's dead-end street, dead priest, apple tree (suggestive of the Garden of Eden, now fallen?), and rusty bicycle pump all help to define very precisely the condition of a thoroughly believable Dublin. In Hemingway's *Farewell to Arms* the river in which Frederic Henry swims when he deserts the army is not only symbolic of his cleansing himself from war, but it is a river, as material as the guns he flees from. Mary McCarthy, in an essay on symbolism, points out that symbols are not odd things stuck into a story but are things that properly belong in the world of the story. She effectively illustrates her point with an example from Tolstoy's *Anna Karenina*.

> . . . Toward the beginning of the novel, Anna meets the man who will be her lover, Vronsky, on the Moscow-St. Petersburg express; as they meet, there has been an accident; a workman has been killed by the train. This is the beginning of Anna's doom, which is completed when she throws herself under a train and is killed; and the last we see of Vronsky is in a train, with a toothache; he is off to the wars. The train is necessary to the plot of the novel, and I believe it is also symbolic, both of the iron forces of material progress that Tolstoy hated so and that played a part in Anna's moral destruction, and also of those iron laws of necessity and consequence that govern human action when it remains on the sensual level.
>
> One can read the whole novel, however, without being conscious that the train is a symbol; we do not have to "interpret" to feel the impact of doom and loneliness in the train's whistle — the same import we ourselves can feel when we hear a train whistle blow in the country, even today.
>
> *On the Contrary* (New York, 1962), p. 236

The symbols, to repeat, are a part of the world of the story, contributing to its sense of immediacy or reality as well as radiating suggestions or (to use Henry James's figure) casting long shadows. In Hardy's *Jude the Obscure,* for example, the pigeons that Jude and Sue are forced to sell are symbols of Jude's and Sue's caged existence, but they are also pigeons that Jude and Sue are forced to sell. Furthermore, other references to birds in the novel function similarly, as do the passages dealing with the trapped rabbit. Birds and rabbits are a part of Jude's world, meaningful on the realistic level but resonant too. An essayist who discusses symbolism in a piece of fiction will probably want to examine the degree to which the symbols are integral and interrelated.

Sample Essay: Atmosphere as Symbol

The next example, a fine essay by a student, points out that the repeated references to darkness in Joyce's *Dubliners* are an important part of the meaning of the book. The title and the first paragraph of the essay give the reader an idea of what will follow.

The next paragraph discusses the first story in the book, and the third paragraph discusses the last story. The essayist wisely avoids plodding through fifteen stories; by choosing the first and the last stories she implies that all the stories share the motif. The fourth paragraph sets forth the general implications of darkness, and it is followed by a fairly detailed paragraph analyzing the motif in one story. In the concluding paragraph the essayist concedes that the references to darkness are literal as well as symbolic, but she quietly insists that the symbolic implications are there, too.

Although this title doesn't announce the thesis, it at least announces the topic.

Thesis is stated early.

Darkness in <u>Dubliners</u>

The fifteen short stories in Joyce's collection called <u>Dubliners</u> are not simply fifteen separate stories, or even fifteen stories united only by being about people in the city for which the book is named. The unity is greater than physical locale; there is a unity of theme, which Joyce himself said was ''paralysis,''[1] and this sense of paralysis is conveyed not only by what the characters do — or, more often, what they do <u>not</u> do — but also by Joyce's insistence on the dark sky, or the darkness inside a room, in most of the stories. Darkness, especially of night, seems to surround the characters, hindering them from any advance and representing their mental condition.

The essay is not a research paper, but the student has done some digging, and gives credit to the source. (For another way of indicating a source, see pages 75–85.)

---

[1]Letter to the publisher, quoted in Harry Levin, <u>James Joyce</u> (London: Faber and Faber, 1944), p. 29.

Overall view; then narrows to reasonable choice of "the very first story."

Most of the stories are set in a dark street or a dark room. For example, the very first story, ''The Sisters,'' begins as follows:

Quotation provides evidence, and lets us hear Joyce for a moment.

There was no hope for him this time; it was the third stroke. Night after night I had passed the house (it was vacation time) and studied the lighted square of the window: and night after night I had found it lighted in the same way, faintly and evenly.

Useful brief quotations; longer ones are not needed.

As the story continues, we find that a priest has at last died. The narrator visits the house ''after sunset'' (a time of day that itself suggests the death of the day) and he learns that the dead priest ''was quite resigned'' and ''was a disappointed man.'' Near the end of the story we learn that the priest was mentally sick, and was once found ''sitting up by himself in the dark in his confession-box.'' In short, the priest's mind was darkened, and this is revealed in the episode of the confession-box and in the several references to night, a time when men do not usually work or make progress. Death and darkness are associated, and Dublin seems to be a dying city.

Reasonable choice of a second example.

If we jump, for a moment, across the entire book, to some sentences in the last paragraph of the last story, ''The Dead,'' we find remarkable connections with the first story.

Again it is night, and again we get references to a dim light surrounded by darkness. This time a man is in his bedroom, looking out of a window on a snowy night. The final paragraph includes such expressions as ''He watched sleepily the flakes, silver and dark, falling obliquely against the lamplight,'' ''journey westward,'' ''the dark central plain,'' ''their last end,'' ''falling,'' ''buried,'' and ''the living and the dead.'' In this story the whole of Dublin is wrapped in night and in a cover of snow, and the chief character falls asleep. Here as in the first story about the dead priest, the literal time of day — night — contributes to the sense of death or paralysis. The people in Dublin seem to live in darkness — that is, in frustration and spiritual emptiness.

In almost all the stories, the darkness is made the more ominous by feeble lights that seem to try to overcome it but of course fail to do so. In the first story, for example, the window was lighted ''night after night,'' but at last the time came when the priest died and the blinds were drawn. The only light inside is from candles burning at the dead man's head; this light is not seen from the street, where the window is lit only by ''tawny gold'' light reflected from the clouds. Inside, the

Brief quotations offered as evidence.

Skillful pulling together of the material so far.

Generalization has been amply supported.

We are inclined to take the writer's word about "all the stories" because we have been convinced by the previous discussion of two stories.

narrator ''groped'' his way to a chair, and
then learns of the episode in the confession-
box. Darkness takes over. Sometimes the images
of light against the dark are not literal, as
in the previous instances, but are figurative.
In ''The Dead,'' for instance, we get this
figurative description of Gabriel: ''The dull
fires of his lust began to glow angrily in his
veins.'' Here again life or vitality is asso-

Judicious references to
evidence in other sto-
ries.

ciated with light (''fire''). As in the other
stories, the light does not last, for Gabriel's lust soon disappears and he falls
asleep in the night. In another story, ''Ivy
Day in the Committee Room,'' the fire is literal; some minor politicians are discussing an
election in a room with a dying fire, and it
is clear that they are the corrupt or dying
left-overs of what was once a genuinely pa-
triotic movement. We are told that the weather
is unpleasant and that ''the short day had
grown dark.'' Several times we are told that
the room is dark, the fire being inadequate.
We learn from the dialogue that there is brib-
ery, suspicion, selfishness, a total lack of
idealism. In short, the physical locale—a
darkening room, fitfully illuminated by a
dying fire—is a way of representing the people who live in it.

Because it would be tedious to go through

Essayist offers a reasonable justification for the procedure.

each story, describing the special sorts of darkness that appear in almost all, this paper will study a single story, ''Araby,'' in a bit

Plot summary is brief and useful, not mere padding.

more detail. The gist of the plot is that a young boy, in love with a girl, promises to bring her something from a fair called Araby, but when he gets to the fair, just before closing time, he finds that his romantic visions of himself as a heroic lover, and of the fair as a sort of enchanted place, are demolished by the tawdriness of the fair. This short summary gives only one hint, in the reference to closing time, of the role that darkness plays in creating the atmosphere that helps to shape the characters, but in fact the story is filled with references to darkness.

Evidence from the text.

The narrator played in ''dark muddy lanes,'' ''dark dripping gardens,'' and ''dark odorous stables,'' and he admires the girl from inside of his room, where he has pulled the shade ''down to within an inch of the sash so that I could not be seen.'' On the day he is to go to the fair to bring back his trophy, his uncle does not get home until nine o'clock, and therefore the boy does not get to the fair until ten to ten, when ''the greater part of the hall was in darkness.'' This is the way the story ends:

Fairly long quotation is not padding; it is evidence.

I heard a voice call from one of the gallery that the light was out. The upper part of the hall was now completely dark.

Gazing up into the darkness I saw myself as a creature driven and derided by vanity; and my eyes burned with anguish and anger.

The narrator's sense of disillusionment is perfectly represented by the statement of the voice that ''the light was out.'' The voice is stating a simple fact about the light in the hall, but the reader understands its relation to the narrator's state of mind. In the last sentence of the story, the narrator looks into the dark and sees nothing; his rich illusions, or delusions, have vanished, and he is surrounded by nothing, for he now has nothing within him.

Dublin probably is often dark; certainly night comes to Dublin as it comes to every

Essayist raises a possible objection, and refutes it.

other city, and one might try to argue that Joyce is merely being accurate in his depiction of dark days, and of nights. But when one rereads the stories, and notices how few are set in the daylight, and how often the darkness is stressed, and how appropriate it is to the spiritually impoverished characters in the book, one realizes that Joyce is doing more than giving realistic pictures of Dublin at a

Quiet reaffirmation of thesis.

certain time of day. His descriptions of dark streets, dark rooms, and of fitful bits of il-

lumination, are also descriptions of a state
of mind that dominates the Dubliners in <u>Dub-
liners</u>.

POINT OF VIEW

The Dublin in *Dubliners* and the England in *Jude* are the Dublin
and England that Joyce and Hardy thought existed, but it must be
remembered that although an author *writes* a story, someone else
tells it. The story is seen from a particular **point of view,** and this
point of view in large measure determines our response to the story.
A wide variety of terms has been established to name differing
points of view, but the following labels are among the commonest. We can begin with two categories: third-person points of view
(in which the narrator is, in the crudest sense, not a participant in
the story) and first-person points of view (in which the "I" who
narrates the story plays a part in it).

Third-Person Narrators

The **third-person point of view** itself has several subdivisions. At one extreme is the **omniscient narrator,** who knows
everything that is going on, and can tell us the inner thoughts of
all the characters. The omniscient narrator may editorialize, pass
judgments, reassure the reader, and so forth, in which case he or
she may sound like the author. Here is Hardy's editorially omniscient narrator in *Tess of the D'Urbervilles,* telling the reader that
Tess was mistaken in imagining that the countryside proclaimed
her guilt: "But this encompassment of her own characterization,
based upon shreds of convention, peopled by phantoms and voices
antipathetic to her, was a sorry and mistaken creation of Tess's
fancy — a cloud of moral hobgoblins by which she was terrified
without reason." Still, even this narrator is not quite Hardy; he
does not allude to his other books, his private life, or his hope that
the book will sell. If he is Hardy, he is only one aspect of Hardy,
quite possibly a fictional Hardy, a disembodied voice with particular characteristics.

Another sort of third-person narrator, **selective omniscient,** takes up what Henry James called a "center of consciousness," revealing the thoughts of one of the characters but (for the most part) seeing the rest of the characters from the outside only. Wayne Booth, in a thoughtful study of Jane Austen's *Emma,* explains the effectiveness of selective omniscience in this novel. He points out that Emma is intelligent, witty, beautiful, and rich. But she is flawed by pride, and, until she discovers and corrects her fault, she almost destroys herself and her friends. How can such a character be made sympathetic, so that we will hope for the happy conclusion to the comedy? "The solution to the problem of maintaining sympathy despite almost crippling faults," Booth says,

> was primarily to use the heroine herself as a kind of narrator, though in third person, reporting on her own experience. . . . By showing most of the story through Emma's eyes, the author insures that we shall travel with Emma rather than stand against her. It is not simply that Emma provides, in the unimpeachable evidence of her own conscience, proof that she has many redeeming qualities that do not appear on the surface; such evidence could be given with authorial commentary, though perhaps not with such force and conviction. Much more important, the sustained inside view leads the reader to hope for good fortune for the character with whom he travels, quite independently of the qualities revealed.

> *The Rhetoric of Fiction* (Chicago, 1961), pp. 245–246

Booth goes on to point out, in a long and careful analysis, that "sympathy for Emma can be heightened by withholding inside views of others as well as by granting them of her."

In writing about point of view, one of course tries to suggest what the author's choice of a particular point of view contributes to the story. Wayne Booth shows how Jane Austen's third-person point of view helps to keep sympathetic a character who otherwise might be less than sympathetic. Booth states the problem — how to draw an intelligent but proud woman so that the reader will wish for a happy ending — and he presents his answer convincingly, moving from "It is not simply . . ." to "Much more important. . . ." (To reverse the order would cause a drop in interest.) He then moves from a discussion of the inside treatment of Emma to the outside treatment of the other characters, thus substantiating and enlarging his argument. Possibly one could reverse this procedure, beginning with a discussion of the treatment of the characters other than Emma and then closing in on Emma, but such an essay may seem slow in getting under way. The early part may appear unfocused. The reader will for a while be left wondering why in an essay on point of view in *Emma* the essayist does not turn to the chief matter, the presentation of the central character.

The third-person narrator, then, although not in the ordinary sense a character in the story, is an important voice in the story, who helps to give shape to it. Another type of third-person narrator is the so-called **effaced narrator.** This narrator does not seem to exist, for (unlike the editorially omniscient narrator) he or she does not comment in his or her own voice, and (unlike the omniscient and selective omniscient narrators) does not enter any minds. It is almost improper to speak of an effaced narrator as "he" or "he or she," for no evident figure is speaking. The reader hears dialogue and sees only what a camera or a fly on the wall would see. The following example is from Hemingway's "The Killers":

> The door of Henry's lunchroom opened and two men came in. They sat down at the counter.
> "What's yours?" George asked them.
> "I don't know," one of the men said. "What do you want to eat, Al?"
> "I don't know," said Al. "I don't know what I want to eat."

But even an effaced narrator has, if we think a moment, a kind of personality. The story the narrator records may seem "cold" or "scientific" or "reportorial" or "objective," and such a **tone** or voice (attitude of the narrator, as it is detected) may be an important part of the story. Rémy de Gourmont's remark, quoted in Ezra Pound's *Literary Essays,* is relevant: "To be impersonal is to be personal in a special kind of way. . . . The objective is one of the forms of the subjective."

In writing about a third-person narrator, speak of "the narrator," or "the speaker," not of "the author."

First-Person Narrators

To turn to **first-person,** or **participant, points of view:**
The "I" who narrates the story (recall that at the end of "Araby"
the narrator says, "I saw myself as a creature driven and derided
by vanity") may be a major character in it (as he is in "Araby,"
in *The Catcher in the Rye,* and in Dickens's *Great Expectations*), or
he may be a minor character, a mere witness (Dr. Watson narrates
tales about Sherlock Holmes, Nick Carraway narrates the story of
Gatsby in *The Great Gatsby*). Of course the narrator, even when a
relatively minor character, is still a character, and therefore in some
degree the story is about him or her. Although *The Great Gatsby*
is primarily about Gatsby, it is also about Nick's changing perception of Gatsby.

First-person narrators may not fully understand their own
report. Take Huck Finn in *The Adventures of Huckleberry Finn.* In
one passage Huck describes the "astonishing things" performed at
a circus he witnessed, including a drunk who badgered the ringmaster until he was permitted to try to ride a horse. Of course the
drunk turns out to be an expert performer and is part of the circus
act, but Huck thinks the ringmaster was genuinely deceived by a
performer who "had got up that joke all out of his own head." In
using Huck as the narrator, Mark Twain uses an **innocent eye,** a
device in which a good part of the effect consists in the discrepancy between the narrator's imperfect awareness and the reader's
superior awareness. Mark Twain makes much more important use
of the device in another passage in *Huckleberry Finn,* when Huck
is listening to Jim, an escaped slave:

> Jim talked out loud all the time while I was talking to myself.
> He was saying how the first thing he would do when he got to a
> free state he would go to saving up money and never spend a single
> cent, and when he got enough he would buy his wife, which was
> owned on a farm close to where Miss Watson lived; and then they
> would both work to buy the two children, and if their master
> wouldn't sell them, they'd get an Ab'litionist to go and steal them.
>
> It most froze me to hear such talk. He wouldn't ever dared to
> talk such talk in his life before. Just see what a difference it made
> in him the minute he judged he was about free. It was according to
> the old saying, "Give a nigger an inch and he'll take an ell." Thinks

I, this is what comes of my not thinking. Here was this nigger, which I had as good as helped to run away, coming right out flat-footed and saying he would steal his children — children that be-longed to a man I didn't even know; a man that hadn't ever done me no harm.

I was sorry to hear Jim say that, it was such a lowering of him.

Of course we hear unconscious irony in Huck's words, especially in his indignation that Jim "would steal his children — children that belonged to a man I didn't even know."

Although we sometimes feel that a first-person narrator (Conrad's Marlow in several novels is an example) is a very thinly veiled substitute for the author, the words of a first-person narrator require the same kind of scrutiny that we give to the words of the other characters in a story or play. The reader must deduce the personality from what is said. For instance, the narrator of "Araby" never tells us that he was a good student, but, from such a passage as the following, we can deduce that he was a bookish boy until he fell in love: "I watched my master's face pass from amiability to sternness; he hoped I was not beginning to idle."

A first-person narrator is not likely to give us the help that an editorially omniscient narrator gives. We must deduce that the narrator's uncle drinks too much from this passage from "Araby": "At nine o'clock I heard my uncle's latchkey in the hall-door. I heard him talking to himself and heard the hall-stand rocking when it had received the weight of his overcoat. I could interpret these signs." In a first-person narrative it is sometimes difficult for the reader to interpret the signs. In a sense the author has given the reader two stories: the story the narrator tells and the story of a narrator telling a story. Henry James's tale, *The Turn of the Screw,* is told in the first person, beginning thus:

> The story had held us, round the fire, sufficiently breathless, but except the obvious remark that it was gruesome, as, on Christmas eve in an old house, a strange tale should essentially be, I remember no comment uttered till somebody happened to say that it was the only case he had met in which such a visitation had fallen on a child.

The unnamed narrator — we can call him Henry James, but only if we remember that he exists here only as narrator, not as the

American expatriate, the brother of William James, and so on —
is one of a group which has heard a ghost story. He goes on to
introduce another member of the group, someone named Douglas:

> It was this observation that drew from Douglas — not immedi-
> ately, but later in the evening — a reply that had the interesting
> consequence to which I call attention.

The narrator proceeds to say that two nights later Douglas told
a ghost story concerning a governess and her two charges, a boy
and a girl, who had been harried by the ghosts of two former servants. Douglas did not exactly tell the story, rather he read it from
a manuscript written long ago by the governess. There are, then,
three narrators: the "I" who addresses the reader; Douglas, who
narrates the ghost story; and the governess, whose words Douglas
reads aloud to the group. The heart of *The Turn of the Screw* is,
therefore, the governess's long first-person narrative, which is read
to a group by Douglas and which is recounted to the reader by
one of the group, "I." If you are writing about point of view in
James's story, you will want to comment on this narrator within
a narrator within a narrator. You will want to ask yourself at least
two questions: What broad effects does this framework have on
the reader, and how reliable are Douglas and the governess as narrators?

Because the first question is simpler and less important, it is
probably best to treat it first and get on to the larger matter. Your
essay might, then, at the outset, touch on the suitability of having
a ghost story told by someone who has heard it from someone
who saw the ghosts. Ghost stories are like that; we usually get them
not at first hand but second or third hand, and we listen with
wonder and at the same time with a sense of doubt. The stories,
like ghosts, are not within our grasp; we wish we could question
the eyewitness, but we cannot. Having said this much, you might
add that because ghost stories belong primarily to the world of
oral literature, where stories are told to a group rather than read
by an individual, it is appropriate for this story, too, to be told to
a group. James's first line, "The story had held us, round the fire,"
in some measure takes us into the world of oral literature, a world

less intellectual than the world of books. Even this outermost narrator is simply one of "us," a nameless part of the community, a member of Douglas's audience two nights later.

Your essay on point of view in *The Turn of the Screw* will next alert the reader that the discussion of broad effects created by the framework is finished, and the essay will now turn to the second, and more important, point: the degree to which the narrators' personalities color the events. Douglas explains that he met the governess when he was a university student; she was ten years older than he, and she seemed "worthy" and "clever"; he "liked her extremely." He means to assure his audience of her reliability, but the reader senses that Douglas was infatuated with her; the reader learns, too, that Douglas did not meet her until ten years after her ordeal with the ghosts, when she was no longer an "anxious girl out of a Hampshire vicarage," "young, untried, nervous." You may decide that her personality indeed colors the happenings. If you do, then collect the details about her provincial background and her inexperience, which made awesome the responsibility of bringing up two children. You will probably devote a paragraph to what you understand her intellectual and emotional state to have been at the time she accepted the job. If you see her as unprepared and unstable, you will want to explain that Douglas's positive remarks about her must be taken only provisionally and as only Douglas's view; the real governess is not simply the "worthy" girl Douglas thinks he is describing, but she is the governess whom the reader perceives through Douglas's words and through her own. Give the evidence that supports your own view that she was unstable: various bits that emphasize her naiveté and her nervousness provide the background. Then go on to examine her less direct revelations. At one point, for example, she compares herself and the little boy in her charge to "some young couple on their wedding-journey." Maybe you notice that she sometimes says "I felt" and later reports as a fact the things she had only "felt," and that she is given to learning things in a "flash of knowledge" rather than in a more acceptable way. Maybe you notice, too, the lack of corroboration. The governess insists that the little girl saw the ghost, and she explains that the girl would lie and deny it if asked; there is, then, in her opinion, no need to check with the girl. You might well conclude that the story is not so much a ghost story as a story about a neurotic governess whose fantasies drive the children to destruction.

In this sketch of an essay on point of view in *The Turn of the Screw,* one important matter may have been omitted: Is there any evidence, other than Douglas's testimony of the governess's good character, that conflicts with the thesis that she is neurotic? If there is, it must, of course, be accounted for. *Where* it will be accounted for depends upon what it is. As we have seen, Douglas's testimony can effectively be given immediately after the discussion of Douglas as a narrator and before the detailed discussion of the governess. About the only advice one can give is to put it at the appropriate place, the place where the reader *ought* to be told. Usually, as with the comment on Douglas's comments, it should precede your detailed refutation; if it follows, your essay may seem to run downhill. But in initially setting forth a position that will be refuted, you should give your readers a clear hint of what is to come; there is no point in setting forth an argument that at first seems convincing only to inform the readers that they have accepted an insubstantial argument. A clue such as "It may seem," or "Although at first glance one may believe," will often be enough, though sometimes one may want to be even more forthright: "The argument that the governess is reliable is based on two pieces of evidence, but neither is substantial. The first. . . ." Usually the most satisfactory formula is to state your view at some length, take account of the objections at the points where they might reasonably be offered, and move steadily toward developing your thesis.

In writing about point of view in a first-person narrative, such as *Huckleberry Finn,* after an introductory remark to the effect that Huckleberry Finn narrates the story, use the character's name, or a pronoun ("Huck fails to see . . .") in speaking of the narrator.

Caution: Essays on narrative point of view have a way of slipping into essays on what the story is about. Of course point of view *is* relevant to the theme of the story, but if you are writing about point of view keep this focus in sight, explaining (for instance) how it shapes the theme.

THEME

Vision or Discourse?

Because modern fiction makes subtle use of it, point of view can scarcely be neglected in a discussion of **theme** — what a story is about. Perhaps unfairly, modern criticism is usually unhappy with suggestions of the author's voice in older fiction. We would rather see than be lectured at. We are less impressed by "It was the stillness of an implacable force brooding over an inscrutable intention" (from Conrad's *Heart of Darkness*) than by this passage from the same book:

> Black shapes crouched, lay, sat between the trees, leaning against the trunks, clinging to the earth, half coming out, half effaced within the dim light, in all the attitudes of pain, abandonment, and despair. Another mine on the cliff went off, followed by a slight shudder of the soil under my feet. The work was going on. The work! And this was the place where some of the helpers had withdrawn to die.

The second quotation, but not the first, gives us the sense of reality that we have come to expect from fiction. (Still, this is a critical assumption that can be questioned.) Hardy's novels in particular have been censured on this account; the modern sensibility is uneasy when it hears Hardy's own voice commenting on the cosmic significance of the happenings, as when in *Tess of the D'Urbervilles* the narrator says: "In the ill-judged execution of the well-judged plan of things, the call seldom produces the comer, the man to love rarely coincides with the hour for loving." The passage goes on in this vein at some length. Even in passages of dialogue we sometimes feel that we are getting not a vision of life but a discourse on it, as in this famous exchange between Tess and her brother:

> "Did you say the stars were worlds, Tess?"
> "Yes."
> "All like ours?"
> "I don't know; but I think so. They sometimes seem to be like the apples on our stubbard-tree. Most of them splendid and sound — a few blighted."

"Which do we live on — a splendid one or a blighted one?"
"A blighted one."

We prefer the picture of the field at Flintcomb Ash, the pigeons, the rabbits, Stonehenge. Partly, we feel, overt commentary (even when put into the mouths of the characters) leaves the world of fiction and invites us to judge it separately, as philosophy. Partly, of course, the difficulty is that twentieth-century novelists and readers have come to expect the novel to do something different from what Hardy and his contemporaries expected it to do. As Virginia Woolf puts it in "Mr. Bennett and Mrs. Brown," the novelists before World War I "made tools and established conventions which do their business. But those tools are not our tools, and that business is not our business. For us those conventions are ruin, those tools are death." Van Ghent concisely gives the modern objection: when the philosophic vision

> can be loosened away from the novel to compete in the general field of abstract truth — as frequently in Hardy — it has the weakness of any abstraction that statistics and history and science may be allowed to criticize; whether true or false for one generation or another, or for one reader or another, or even for one personal mood or another, its status as truth is relative to conditions of evidence and belief existing outside the novel and existing there quite irrelevant to whatever body of particularized life the novel itself might contain.
>
> *The English Novel,* p. 197

Van Ghent goes on to explain that the philosophic vision has its proper place in the novel when it is "local and inherent there through a maximum of organic dependencies." She illustrates her point by quoting this passage from *Tess,* which describes the coming of morning after Tess's horse has been accidentally stabbed to death by the shaft of a mail cart.

> The atmosphere turned pale, the birds shook themselves in the hedges, arose, and twittered, the lane showed all its white features, and Tess showed hers, still whiter. The huge pool of blood in front of her was already assuming the iridescence of coagulation; and when the sun rose, a million prismatic hues were reflected from it. Prince lay alongside still and stark, his eyes half open, the hole in his chest looking scarcely large enough to have let out all that had animated him.

Part of Van Ghent's comment runs thus:

> With the arousal and twittering of the birds we are aware of the oblivious manifold of nature stretching infinite and detached beyond the isolated human figure; the iridescence of the coagulating blood is, in its incongruity with the dark human trouble, a note of the same indifferent cosmic chemistry that has brought about the accident; and the smallness of the hole in Prince's chest, that looked "scarcely large enough to have let out all that had animated him," is the minor remark of that irony by which Tess's great cruel trial appears as a vanishing incidental in the blind waste of time and space and biological repetition. Nevertheless, there is nothing in this event that has not the natural "grain" of concrete fact; and what it signifies — of the complicity of doom with the most random occurrence, of the cross-purposing of purpose in a multiple world, of cosmic indifference and of moral desolation — is a local truth of a particular experience and irrefutable as the experience itself.
>
> *The English Novel,* pp. 198–99

Determining and Discussing the Theme

First, we can distinguish between *story* and *theme* in fiction. Story is concerned with "How does it turn out? What happens?" But theme is concerned with "What does it add up to? What motif holds the happenings together? What does it make out of life, and, perhaps, what wisdom does it offer?" ★ In a good work of fiction, the details add up, or, to use Flannery O'Connor's words, they are "controlled by some overall purpose." In F. Scott Fitzgerald's *The Great Gatsby,* for example, there are many references to popular music, especially to Negro jazz. These references of course contribute to our sense of the reality in Fitzgerald's depiction of America in the twenties, but they do more: they help to comment on the shallowness of the white middle-class characters and they

---

★A theme in a literary work is sometimes distinguished from a thesis, an arguable message such as "People ought not to struggle against Fate." The theme, it might be said, is something like "The struggle against Fate" or "The Process of Maturing" or "The Quest for Knowledge." In any case, the formulation of a theme normally includes an abstract noun or a phrase, but of course it must be remembered that such formulations as those in the previous sentence are, finally, only shorthand expressions for highly complex statements. For some further comments on theme, see pp. 161–164 and 261–263.

sometimes (very gently) remind us of an alternative culture. One might study Fitzgerald's references to music with an eye toward getting a deeper understanding of what the novel is about.

Perhaps a discussion of James Joyce's "The Dead" will clarify what is meant by theme. The story tells of Gabriel's arrival at a party, the events at the party, his subsequent departure, and his realization that his wife is taken up with the thought of a boy, unknown to Gabriel, who had loved her. As David Daiches points out in an essay (in *The Novel and the Modern World*), about three-fourths of the story is devoted to episodes at the party. Daiches suggests that these episodes modify each other and embody the theme. That theme, he says, is the liberation of Gabriel from his own egotism. Here is the skeleton of Daiches's essay:

The theme of "The Dead" is the liberation of Gabriel from his own egotism; this theme determines the episodes:

The first attack on his egotism: The caretaker's daughter is not impressed by him.

Gabriel's response: He is a little distressed.

The second attack: Miss Ivors attacks his individualism and questions his patriotism.

Gabriel's response: He is distressed, but he calms himself by denigrating her, and he regains his composure when he sits at the head of the table.

The third attack: D'Arcy's favorable reference to Caruso reveals the provincialism of the rest of the group, whose members have hardly heard of him.

Gabriel continues in his role as the center of attention.

The fourth attack: D'Arcy's singing and playing take the limelight from Gabriel.

The fifth attack: Confident and desirous of his wife, Gabriel learns that her thoughts are of a boy he does not even know.

Gabriel's response: Humbled, he dozes off and becomes a part of all the blank, snow-covered world around him.

Gabriel's new attitude resembles Joyce's ideal aesthetic attitude.

Daiches's method, clearly, is to move through the story, episode by episode.

Another method of talking about the theme is to focus on a single speech. A work, especially if it is told from an editorially omniscient point of view, may include an explicit statement of the theme, but it need not; think twice before you detach any passage and say that it states the theme. Be especially wary of assuming that the words of any character state the theme, though of course this is not to say that no character in any work of fiction ever says anything that can serve as a statement of the theme. The difficulty is that a character has a personality, and what he or she says is usually colored by this personality and the momentary situation. The statement, apt in the immediate context, may not adequately cover the entire work.

Take Phoebe's comment to her brother Holden Caulfield in *The Catcher in the Rye:* "You don't like *any*thing that's happening." Many readers believe that Phoebe has put her finger on the matter: Holden doesn't like anything. But with a little work one can find a number of things Holden likes. He likes the kettle drummer at Radio City, he likes *The Return of the Native,* he likes the music of carousels, he likes his brother Allie, and he likes talking to Phoebe. She mentions that Allie is dead and so he "really" doesn't count, but Holden replies:

> I know he's dead! Don't you think I know that? I can still like him, though, can't I?

And when Phoebe says that talking to her "isn't anything *really*," he insists it is:

> It is something *really*! Certainly it is! Why the hell isn't it? People never think anything is anything *really*. I'm getting goddam sick of it.

Phoebe may have touched on an important point. An essay suggesting that *The Catcher* is about a boy whose perception of corruption is so keen that it overwhelms him and in turn corrupts his vision will make use of Phoebe's statement, but it will also establish the limitations of that statement. The essay may, for instance, go on to argue that Holden's perception of "phoniness" — for example, Ossenburger's speech in the chapel at Pencey Prep — is thoroughly warranted. One might, in fact, write an interesting essay on exactly what sorts of things Holden finds "phony."

One other statement has fairly often been thought of as summarizing the theme of *The Catcher*. It is Mr. Antolini's diagnosis:

> This fall I think you're riding for — it's a special kind of fall, a horrible kind. The man falling isn't permitted to feel or hear himself hit bottom. He just keeps falling and falling. The whole arrangement's designed for men who, at some time or other in their lives, were looking for something their own environment couldn't supply them with. So they gave up looking. They gave it up before they ever really even got started. . . . I can very clearly see you dying nobly, one way or another, for some highly unworthy cause.

Is this what *The Catcher* is about? Perhaps, but Mr. Antolini's words must be tested carefully against one's own perception of Holden. If your essay on the theme of *The Catcher* argues that Mr. Antolini states the theme with precision, you must go on to give evidence supporting this idea. Probably in its early stages you will want to indicate why Antolini can be taken as a reliable spokesman. You will, for example, have to face the objection that Salinger apparently alienates us from Mr. Antolini by making him a homosexual whose adjustment to his environment has in part taken the form of marriage to a woman whose close presence he avoids. Even before Mr. Antolini touches Holden, Holden has noticed that the Antolinis "were never in the same room at the same time. It was sort of funny." If you believe that Mr. Antolini is a judicious spokesman, your reply may be threefold: Mr. Antolini must have some sort of distinguishing trait if he is to be believable; the fact that he is a homosexual does not in itself mean that he cannot state the theme of the book; and possibly his own alienation from the normal world may even help to give him awareness of Holden's alienation. The thesis of the overall argument, then, is not simply "The theme of *The Catcher in the Rye*" but something with more shape, "Mr. Antolini's diagnosis is apt."

Some such angle as this is necessary when trying to write about the theme of a novel; such a work is much too long to proceed through, episode by episode, as Daiches does (pp. 138–139) with Joyce's story, "The Dead." The essayist must, of course, be thoroughly familiar with the entire novel, but because he does not have at his disposal the space to guide his reader through some fifty or sixty episodes, he must take hold of the theme in another way. Here is the skeleton of an essay arguing that Mr. Antolini's speech brings us to the theme of the book:

> *Topic idea of introductory paragraph:* At the end of the novel, Holden has had a collapse and is undergoing psychoanalytic treatment. Mr. Antolini had predicted a fall.
>
> *Topic idea of next paragraph:* Although Mr. Antolini himself is an embodiment of the corrupt sexuality and phoniness that obsess Holden, his own alienation from the normal world may even help to give him an awareness of Holden's alienation.
>
> *Topic idea of next paragraph:* Holden fits Mr. Antolini's diagnosis in the following details. . . . (Whether or not the presentation of this evidence will take more than one paragraph depends upon the nature of the evidence. One paragraph might be devoted to evidence that Holden is looking for something that his environment cannot provide, another paragraph to evidence that Holden is likely to settle "for some highly unworthy cause.")
>
> *Topic idea of concluding paragraph:* Although Mr. Antolini's words do not seem to make any impression on Holden, they impress the reader by their accuracy.

With detailed evidence fleshing these bare bones, we might get an essay that convinces and illuminates.

CONCLUDING REMARKS

Here are some questions that may trigger ideas for essays on fiction:

Plot: What is the conflict, or what are the conflicts? Does the plot grow out of the characters, or does it depend on chance or coincidence? Are some episodes irrelevant, or do episodes that at first seem irrelevant have a function? If the development is not strictly chronological, what is gained by the arrangement? Does surprise play an important role, or does foreshadowing? Is the title a good one?

Character: Is a particular character highly individual, or, rather, highly typical (for example, representative of a social class or age)? Are we chiefly interested in the character's psychology, or does he or she seem to be an allegorical representation? Are there characters who by their similarities and differences define each other? How else is a particular character defined? (Words, actions — including thoughts and emotions — dress, setting, narrative, point of view?) To what extent does a character change, and what causes the change? What are the functions of minor characters?

Remember, unless you are simply writing a character sketch, your essay should advance a thesis. Suppose, for example, you feel that by the end of the story or novel a character has changed. You may want to propose one of several theses: the character is inconsistent and therefore unsatisfying; or the character is inconsistent but acceptable because (for example) the change is for the better and we approve of it even though we don't believe it; or (again for example) it is acceptable because the overall structure of the work requires this inconsistency; or the change is well motivated and psychologically plausible.

Point of view: Who is the narrator? Does the point of view change? If so, what is the effect? How does the point of view help to shape the theme? After all, the basic story of "Little Red Riding Hood" remains unchanged whether told from the wolf's point of view or from the girl's, but (to simplify grossly) if we hear the story from the wolf's point of view we may feel that the story is about terrifying yet pathetic compulsive neurotic behavior; if from the girl's point of view, about terrified innocence.

Setting: What is the relation of the setting to the plot and the characters? To what degree does the work illustrate Henry James's assertion that in fiction "landscape is character"? What would be lost if the setting were changed? Where does the author describe the setting? Only at the beginning, or at various points in the story? Is there some significance to this disposition of material?

Style: What role is played by the author's style? Is the style (not only the words but also the sentence structure) simple, understated, figurative, or what, and why?

Theme: Does the story imply a meaning (or meanings), a relation to the outside world? The title may be especially significant, and so too may certain passages that explicitly offer ideas. But remember that these passages may be offered by an unreliable narrator or by particular characters whose views are probably shaped by their personalities and by the circumstances in which they speak. Or the author may be imposing a theme that the rest of the work does not really support.

The least fruitful way to study a novel is to seek to extract whatever overt philosophizing it seems to contain and to discuss it as philosophy; the most fruitful way is to pay close attention to all the words. In writing an essay on a very short piece of fiction — for example, a short short story — one can perhaps study in some detail all aspects of it — or all that one sees. But most fiction is too big for such analysis. Normally one decides either to examine a particular passage (sometimes a bit pretentiously called the **textural approach**) or to examine some significant thread (sometimes called the **structural approach**).

In this book, David Lodge's essay (pp. 145–149) on the first chapter of Dickens's *Hard Times* is an example of the textural approach; John Daremo's essay (pp. 149–153) on point of view in Faulkner's "A Rose for Emily" is an example of the structural approach. Notice, by the way, that Lodge wisely chooses the *first* chapter of *Hard Times*. Because the meaning of a later chapter is in part determined by what has preceded it, discussion of a later chapter is more cumbersome. (On the other hand, one must realize that an early passage derives part of its meaning from what happens later; the description of the blind street and the stuffy house in "Araby" achieves its fullest meaning at the end of the story, when the boy's imaginative world is dispersed and he finds himself in darkness.) A second difficulty with the textural approach is that the chosen passage may not be typical of the work as a whole. To choose the right passage one must have a good understanding of all the passages.

The structural approach comes closer to dealing with the whole, but it too has a danger: in following a thread, say, the point of view in a novel, the role of landscape in a story, or a particular theme, it inevitably neglects other threads that, if followed, might lead to a rather different reading of the work. This means that even though the topic must be narrowed, one must have a grasp of the whole work and must follow a thread that is significant.

SAMPLE ESSAYS

The two essays printed next reveal different approaches. David Lodge, using the textural approach, examines a page from Dickens's *Hard Times,* giving it the sort of close reading that is commonly reserved for poetry. He shows how Dickens makes every word contribute to his portrait of Gradgrind and how the portrait contributes to the novel's central concern. John Daremo, using a structural approach, stands a little further back from his subject, surveying Faulkner's "A Rose for Emily" by examining the narrative point of view which controls our understanding of all that happens in the story. Where Lodge looks hard at words, Daremo looks hard at the narrator's interpretation of action in the light of character. (Lodge of course has ideas about the actions and the characters of the novel as a whole, and Daremo has ideas about the individual words, but on the whole the treatments are different.)

Because Lodge's essay is part of a chapter in a book, it does not have the neat opening and closing paragraphs that a good independent essay usually has. But it is carefully organized. The first paragraph is chiefly devoted to quoting the passage he will study. The next paragraph explains that in the quoted passage Dickens introduces "a judgment of a concept of education," and the following paragraph tells us that "fact" is a key word in this concept. Lodge supports his assertion by telling us exactly how often the word occurs, and by quoting an illustrative sentence. Next he says that the "concept of education" can be broken down into three categories, which he lists and goes on to discuss in the listed order. When he has finished with the third category he links it to the first. There is no need in this headnote to discuss further the organization; if you read the essay you will find that you move easily from paragraph to paragraph — the sign of a well-organized essay.

Daremo's essay too is well organized. The title accurately conveys its contents, and the opening paragraph moves from the large matter of Faulkner's alleged sensationalism to a study of it in one story whose plot is briefly summarized, thereby letting the readers get their bearings. The body of the essay studies the problem, first by rejecting the idea that the narrator is an innocent eye and then by offering proof of the narrator's perceptive sympathy in recounting what superficially is a sensational tale. There are a fair number of supporting quotations, but most of them are brief and are therefore welcome. The final paragraph nicely turns back to the very beginning of the story, commenting on the relevance of the title to the story as Daremo interprets it.

The Rhetoric of a Page of Hard Times ★

David Lodge

The very first chapter of *Hard Times* ["The One Thing Needful"] affords an excellent illustration of Dickens's rhetoric, and it is short enough to be quoted and analyzed in its entirety.

"Now, what I want is, Facts. Teach these boys and girls nothing but Facts. Facts alone are wanted in life. Plant nothing else, and root out everything else. You can only form the minds of reasoning animals upon Facts: nothing else will ever be of any service to them. This is the principle on which I bring up my own children, and this is the principle on which I bring up these children. Stick to Facts, Sir!"

The scene was a plain, bare, monotonous vault, of a school-room, and the speaker's square forefinger emphasised his observations by underscoring every sentence with a line on the school-master's sleeve. The emphasis was helped by the speaker's square wall of a forehead, which had his eyebrows for its base, while his eyes found commodious cellarage in two dark caves, over-shadowed by the wall. The emphasis was helped by the speaker's mouth, which was wide, thin, and hard set. The emphasis was helped by the speaker's voice, which was inflexible, dry, and dictatorial. The emphasis was helped by the speaker's hair, which bristled on the skirts of his bald head, a plantation of firs to keep the wind from its shining surface, all covered with knobs, like the crust of a plum pie, as if the head had scarcely warehouseroom for the hard facts stored inside. The speaker's obstinate carriage, square coat, square legs, square shoulders — nay, his very neckcloth, trained to take him by the throat with an unaccommodating grasp, like a stubborn fact, as it was — all helped the emphasis.

★ Mr. Lodge's essay is here retitled.

"In this life, we want nothing but Facts, Sir; nothing but Facts!"

The speaker, and the schoolmaster, and the third grown person present, all backed a little, and swept with their eyes the inclined plane of little vessels then and there arranged in order, ready to have imperial gallons of facts poured into them until they were full to the brim.

This chapter communicates, in a remarkably compact way, both a description and a judgment of a concept of education. This concept is defined in a speech, and then evaluated — not in its own terms, but in terms of the speaker's appearance and the setting. Dickens, of course, always relies heavily on the popular, perhaps primitive, assumption that there is a correspondence between a person's appearance and his character; and as Gradgrind is a governor of the school, its design may legitimately function as a metaphor for his character. Dickens also had a fondness for fancifully appropriate names, but — perhaps in order to stress the representativeness of Gradgrind's views — he does not reveal the name in this first chapter.[1]

Because of the brevity of the chapter, we are all the more susceptible to the effect of its highly rhetorical patterning, particularly the manipulation of certain repeated words, notably *fact, square,* and *emphasis.* The kind of education depicted here is chiefly characterized by an obsession with facts. The word occurs five times in the opening speech of the first paragraph, and it is twice repeated towards the end of the second, descriptive paragraph to prepare for the reintroduction of Gradgrind speaking — " 'we want nothing but Facts, Sir; nothing but Facts' "; and it occurs for the tenth and last time towards the end of the last paragraph. In Gradgrind's speeches the word is capitalized, to signify his almost religious devotion to Facts.

Gradgrind's concept of education is further characterized in ways we can group into three categories, though of course they are closely connected:

1. It is authoritarian, fanatical and bullying in its application.
2. It is rigid, abstract and barren in quality.
3. It is materialistic and commercial in its orientation.

[1] Mary McCarthy has suggested that an anonymous "he" at the beginning of a novel usually will move the reader to sympathetic identification. That the effect is quite the reverse in this example indicates that the effect of any narrative strategy is determined finally by the narrator's language.

The first category is conveyed by the structure of the second paragraph, which is dominated by "emphasis." This paragraph comprises six sentences. In the first sentence we are told how the "speaker's square forefinger emphasised his observations." The next four, central sentences are each introduced, with cumulative force, by the clause "The emphasis was helped," and this formula, translated from the passive to the active voice, makes a fittingly "emphatic" conclusion to the paragraph in the sixth sentence: "all helped the emphasis." This rhetorical pattern has a dual function. In one way it reflects or imitates Gradgrind's own bullying, over-emphatic rhetoric, of which we have an example in the first paragraph; but in another way it helps to *condemn* Gradgrind, since it "emphasizes" the narrator's own pejorative catalogue of details of the speaker's person and immediate environment. The narrator's rhetoric is, as it must be, far more skilful and persuasive than Gradgrind's.

The qualities in category 2 are conveyed in a number of geometrical or quasi-geometrical terms, *wide, line, thin, base, surface, inclined plane* and, particularly, *square* which recurs five times; and in words suggestive of barren regularity, *plain, bare, monotonous, arranged in order, inflexible.* Such words are particularly forceful when applied to human beings — whether Gradgrind or the children. The metamorphosis of the human into the nonhuman is, as we shall find confirmed later, one of Dickens's main devices for conveying his alarm at the way Victorian society was moving.

Category 3, the orientation towards the world of commerce, is perhaps less obvious than the other categories, but it is unmistakably present in some of the boldest tropes of the chapter: *commodious cellarage, warehouseroom, plantation, vessels, imperial gallons.*

The authoritarian ring of *"imperial"* leads us back from category 3 to category 1, just as *"underscoring* every sentence with a *line"* leads us from 1 to 2. There is a web of connecting strands between the qualities I have tried to categorize: it is part of the rhetorical strategy of the chapter that all the qualities it evokes are equally applicable to Gradgrind's character, person, ideas, his school and the children (in so far as he has shaped them in his own image).

Metaphors of growth and cultivation are of course commonplace in discussion of education, and we should not overlook the ironic invocation of such metaphors, with a deliberately religious, prophetic implication (reinforced by the Biblical echo of the chapter heading, "The One Thing Needful"[2]) in the title of the Book,

---

[2] Chapter 2 of Book I is called "Murdering the Innocents."

"SOWING," later to be followed by Book the Second, "REAP-ING," and Book the Third, "GARNERING." These metaphors are given a further twist in Gradgrind's recommendation to "Plant nothing else and root out everything else" (except facts).

If there is a flaw in this chapter it is the simile of the plum pie, which has pleasant, genial associations alien to the character of Gradgrind, to whose head it is, quite superfluously, applied. Taken as a whole, however, this is a remarkably effective and densely woven beginning of the novel.

The technique of the first chapter of *Hard Times* could not be described as "subtle." But subtle effects are often lost in a first chapter, where the reader is coping with the problem of "learning the author's language." Perhaps with some awareness of this fact, sharpened by his sense of addressing a vast, popular audience, Dickens begins many of his novels by nailing the reader's attention with a display of sheer rhetorical power, relying particularly on elaborate repetition. One thinks, for instance, of the fog at the be-ginning of *Bleak House* or the sun and shadow in the first chapter of *Little Dorrit*. In these novels the rhetoric works to establish a symbolic atmosphere; in *Hard Times,* to establish a thematic Idea — the despotism of Fact. But this abstraction — Fact — is invested with a remarkable solidity through the figurative dimension of the lan-guage.

The gross effect of the chapter is simply stated, but analysis reveals that it is achieved by means of a complex verbal activity that is far from simple. Whether it represents fairly any actual educa-tional theory or practice in mid-nineteenth-century England is really beside the point. It aims to convince us of the *possibility* of children being taught in such a way, and to make us recoil from the imag-ined possibility. The chapter succeeds or fails as rhetoric; and I think it succeeds.

Dickens begins as he means to continue. Later in the novel we find Gradgrind's house, which, like the school-room, is a function of himself, described in precisely the same terms of fact and rigid measurement, partly geometrical and partly commercial.

> A very regular feature on the face of the country, Stone Lodge was. Not the least disguise toned down or shaded off that uncompromising fact in the landscape. A great square house, with a heavy portico darkening the principal windows, as its master's heavy brows over-shadowed his eyes. A calculated, cast up, balanced and proved house. Six windows on this side of the door, six on that side; a total of twelve in

this wing, a total of twelve in the other wing; four and twenty carried over to the back wings. A lawn and garden and an infant avenue, all ruled straight like a botanical account-book.

(I, iii)

It has been observed that Dickens individualizes his characters by making them use peculiar locutions and constructions in their speech, a technique which was particularly appropriate to serial publication in which the reader's memory required to be frequently jogged. This technique extends beyond the idiosyncratic speech of characters, to the language in which they are described. A key-word, or group of key-words, is insistently used when the character is first introduced, not only to identify him but also to evaluate him, and is invoked at various strategic points in the subsequent action. Dickens's remarkable metaphorical inventiveness ensures that continuity and rhetorical emphasis are not obtained at the expense of monotony. The application of the key-words of the first chapter to Mr. Gradgrind's house gives the same delight as the development of a metaphysical conceit. The observation that Mrs. Gradgrind, "whenever she showed a symptom of coming to life, was invariably stunned by some weighty piece of fact tumbling on her" (I, iv), affords a kind of verbal equivalent of knock-about comedy, based on a combination of expectancy (we know the word will recur) and surprise (we are not prepared for the particular formulation).

Insight into Horror: The Narrator in
Faulkner's "A Rose for Emily" ★

John Daremo

Having admitted, in the preface to the Modern Library edition of *Sanctuary* (1932), that after some failures he set out to make money by writing about the horrible and the obscene, Faulkner was regularly accused of turning out meaningless narratives which had only their sensationalism to recommend them. (In fact, however, the in-

★Faulkner's story is reprinted in Appendix B to this book, pp. 294–302.

famous preface to *Sanctuary* made the point that although he began the book with the crudest of motives, he rewrote it at the cost of time and money to make it into something worthy.) His most popular short story, "A Rose for Emily," written at about the same time as *Sanctuary,* on the surface at least shares a concern with the horrible and the obscene: Miss Emily Grierson, it turns out, has poisoned a lover who was about to desert her, has kept the rotting corpse in an upstairs bedroom, and on at least one occasion has lain next to it. Murder and a hint of necrophilia are pretty strong stuff, and yet, when one first reads this rather drily narrated story of a southern lady who retreated into a world of her own, one scarcely is aware of any sensationalism at all until the very end, when the corpse is discovered in bed, and a strand of Miss Emily's hair is found upon the adjacent pillow. This is shocking, no doubt. But on re-reading the story one sees that one's first reading was right: the story is not simply a horror story, designed to thrill, but a story in which horror plays a meaningful part. Despite the decaying mansion, the silent servant, and the corpse, all the usual properties in rather old-fashioned thrillers, "A Rose for Emily" — whether on the first reading or on the tenth — seems closely related to experience. Not that we know anyone who in fact has behaved precisely in this mad way; but, as Miss Emily's behavior is narrated, it seems plausible, fully in accord not merely with some arbitrary fictional world but with our understanding of human behavior.

In large measure this sense of plausibility is conveyed to us by the unnamed narrator, who unobtrusively gives us a sense of the world in which Miss Emily lives, and whose responses — sometimes commonplace and sometimes deeply sympathetic — help to assure us that the story we hear is one that speaks to mankind. This narrator is never very precisely identified, and there are moments when he almost seems to be an Innocent Eye, a simple-minded recorder of a story whose implications escape him but reach us. Sometimes he seems to be a good deal less than deeply sensitive: he speaks of Miss Emily's aunt as "old Lady Wyatt, the crazy woman"; he talks easily of "niggers"; he confesses that because he and the other townspeople felt that Miss Emily's family "held themselves a little too high for what they really were," when at thirty Miss Emily was still unmarried "we were not pleased exactly, but vindicated." When her father died and Miss Emily was left in poverty, the narrator, like the other townspeople, could take some pleasure in seeing her reduced to the common level: "Now she too would know the old thrill and the old despair of a penny more or less."

But of course, as even this last brief quotation suggests, the narrator is no simpleton. If his feelings are those of common humanity, he not only shares our feelings, but, more important, he *knows* what these feelings are, he can describe them and thus he helps us to understand the character and also ourselves. We recognize this ability, and we therefore have confidence in his narrative: we heed the story not only because it is curious but because, guided by the narrator, we feel that it deserves our respectful attention. These are both motifs introduced in the first sentence: "When Miss Emily Grierson died, our whole town went to her funeral: the men through a sort of respectful affection for a fallen monument, the women mostly out of curiosity to see the inside of her house, which no one save an old manservant — combined gardener and cook — had seen in at least ten years." The narrator shares the women's curiosity and the men's respect, and by reading the story we too become implicated. There is, of course, a certain snoopiness involved in telling a story about someone else, or in reading one, but there can also be respect for the subject, and this the narrator of "A Rose for Emily" unobtrusively but abundantly conveys.

For example, the narrator sees old Miss Emily's ugliness ("She looked bloated. . . . Her eyes, lost in the fatty ridges of her face, looked like two small pieces of coal pressed into a lump of dough"), but he also remembers her when, many years earlier, her father drove with a horsewhip a suitor from the door, and Miss Emily was "a slender figure in white in the background." After the death of her tyrannical father, and before she became bloated, she bore "a vague resemblance to those angels in colored church windows — sort of tragic and serene." On the whole, the narrator is compassionate. He helps us to understand why Miss Emily for three days after the death of her father insisted that he was not dead: We did not say she was crazy then. "We believed she had to do that. We remembered all the young men her father had driven away, and we knew that with nothing left, she would have to cling to that which had robbed her, as people will."

The insight is presented simply, almost as an afterthought: Miss Emily acted "as people will," and it is easy for us to give no thought to the narrator even while we accept his explanation that a woman whose father has robbed her of a husband will cling to the only man who had played an important role in her life, even when he is dead. (And of course later she will cling to her lover, Homer Barron, by murdering him and keeping his corpse in the bedroom. The narrator does not go on to put it this way, but, given his comments

on Miss Emily's relationship to her father, we easily make the connection. We do so not because we are superior to a simple-minded
Innocent Eye narrator, but because the narrator has astutely shown
us the way, and then in a gentlemanly fashion has not gone on to
labor the point.)

I have been saying that if we regard Miss Emily with some
respect — as well as with some curiosity and with some horror —
it is largely because the narrator treats her, on the whole, with respect. We can, of course, say that Miss Emily earns respect by her
aloofness and her strength of purpose when, for example, she scorns
the town's opinions and drives in the buggy with Homer Barron,
a Yankee laborer, or when she cows the druggist into selling arsenic, or when she cows the aldermen who come to collect taxes.
But we learn all such things through the narrator, and if we speak
of her aloofness or strength of purpose rather than of, say, her ar-
rogance or madness, it is because he has helped us to think this way
of her, to see her not as a monster but as a human being with feelings like our own. The narrator's imaginative sympathy is evident
throughout, even in its wry tolerance of "a member of the rising
generation" who is unable to tolerate the stench on Miss Emily's
property, but the sympathy is perhaps most evident in the won-
derful description of the memories of the very old men who come
to Miss Emily's funeral. For old men, the narrator tells us, "the
past is not a diminishing road, but, instead, a huge meadow which
no winter ever quite touches, divided from them now by the narrow bottleneck of the most recent decade of years." The two metaphors, meadow and bottleneck, give us a sense of what the minds
of old people may be like, conveying both rich expansiveness and
narrowness. And just as the narrator had not been so presumptuous
as to tell us that Miss Emily's mad (but understandable) insistence
that her father was not dead is related to her later murder of Homer
Barron in her mad effort to preserve their relation as lovers, so now
he does not presume to tell us that Miss Emily, like these old men
at her funeral, had shut off "the most recent decade" and had been
living, with Homer's corpse, in a meadow of memory.

But of course the horror is not revealed until the last two paragraphs, when we learn that Miss Emily had murdered Homer and
had kept the rotting corpse in bed. The horror is not minimized. In
the penultimate paragraph we are told of the "fleshless grin" and
the "rotted" body. But here too we sense a compassionate voice.
The talk of "niggers" and of "the crazy woman," which earlier had

at most been sporadic, now is totally banished and the language and the vision evoke the Bible:

> The body had apparently once lain in the attitude of an embrace, but now the long sleep that outlasts love, that conquers even the grimace of love, had cuckolded him. What was left of him, rotted beneath what was left of the nightshirt, had become inextricable from the bed in which he lay; and upon him and upon the pillow beside him lay that even coating of the patient and biding dust.

The final paragraph, commenting on the strand of hair on the pillow beside Homer, makes it clear that Emily had lain next to the corpse, and the effect is shocking but the revelation is not inconsistent with what has come before.

Nor is the final paragraph, I think, the last word in the story. I suppose that at the end almost every reader calls back to mind the title of the story, and briefly wonders why it is "A Rose for Emily." Almost immediately, I suppose, the question answers itself, even in the mind of the reader who has not thought much about the unobtrusive narrator of the story. The telling of this tale about a woman who, deprived of a husband, murdered her lover before he could desert her, is itself the rose, the community's tribute (for the narrator insistently speaks of himself as "we") to the intelligible humanity in a woman whose unhappy life might seem monstrous to less sympathetic observers.

5

Writing about Drama

TYPES OF PLAYS

Most of the world's great plays written before the twentieth century may be regarded as one of two kinds: **tragedy** or **comedy.** Roughly speaking, tragedy dramatizes the conflict between the vitality of the single life and the laws or limits of life (the tragic hero reaches his heights, going beyond the experiences of other men, at the cost of his life), and comedy dramatizes the vitality of the laws of social life (the good life is seen to reside in the shedding of an individualism that isolates, in favor of a union with a genial and enlightened society). A third kind of drama, somewhat desperately called **tragicomedy,** is harder to epitomize, but most of the tragicomedies of our century use extravagant comic scenes to depict an absurd, senseless world. These points must be amplified a bit before we go on to the further point that, of course, any important play does much more than can be put into such crude formulas.

Tragedy

Most tragic heroes are males. There are a few splendid exceptions, such as Antigone, Medea, Juliet, Cleopatra, and Phèdre, but for the most part women in tragic plays are pathetic rather than tragic, that is, they are relatively passive, chiefly being images of vulnerability rather than of exceptional strength at its breaking point. The following remarks, then, will speak of the tragic "hero" and of "his" actions, partly because repetition of "hero or heroine" and "his or her" is tiresome, but chiefly because tragic heroines are relatively few.

The tragic hero usually goes beyond the standards to which reasonable people adhere; he does some fearful deed which ultimately destroys him. This deed is often said to be an act of *hubris*, a Greek word meaning something like "overweening pride." It may involve, for instance, violating a taboo, such as that against taking life. But if the hubristic act ultimately destroys the person who performs it, it also shows him (paradoxically) to be in some way more fully a living being — a person who has experienced life more fully, whether by heroic action or by capacity for enduring suffering — than the people around him. Othello kills Desdemona, Lear gives away his crown and banishes his one loving daughter, Antony loses his share of the Roman Empire; but all of these men seem to live more fully than the other characters in the plays — for one thing, they experience a kind of anguish unknown to those who surround them and who outlive them. (If the hero does not die, he usually is left in some deathlike state, as is the blind Oedipus in *King Oedipus*.) In tragedy, we see humanity pushed to an extreme; in his agony and grief the hero enters a world unknown to most and reveals magnificence. After his departure from the stage, we are left in a world of littler people. The closing lines of almost any of Shakespeare's tragedies can be used to illustrate the point. *King Lear,* for example, ends thus:

> The oldest hath borne most: we that are young
> Shall never see so much, nor live so long.

Tragedy commonly involves **irony** of two sorts: unconsciously ironic deeds and unconsciously ironic speeches. **Ironic deeds** have some consequence more or less the reverse of what the doer intends. Macbeth thinks that by killing Duncan he will gain happiness, but he finds that his deed brings him sleepless nights. Brutus thinks that by killing Caesar he will bring liberty to Rome, but he brings tyranny. In an unconsciously **ironic speech,** the speaker's words mean one thing to him but something more sig-

nificant to the audience, as when King Duncan, baffled by Caw-
dor's treason, says:

> There's no art
> To find the mind's construction in the face:
> He was a gentleman on whom I built
> An absolute trust.

At this moment Macbeth, whom we have already heard meditating the murder of Duncan, enters. Duncan's words are true, but
he does not apply them to Macbeth, as the audience does. A few
moments later Duncan praises Macbeth as "a peerless kinsman."
Soon Macbeth will indeed become peerless, when he kills Duncan
and ascends to the throne.★ Sophocles' use of ironic deeds and
speeches is so pervasive, especially in *King Oedipus,* that **Sopho-
clean irony** has become a critical term. Here is a critic summarizing the ironies of *King Oedipus:*

> As the images unfold, the enquirer turns into the object of enquiry,
> the hunter into the prey, the doctor into the patient, the investiga-
> tor into the criminal, the revealer into the thing revealed, the finder
> into the thing found, the savior into the thing saved ("I was saved,
> for some dreadful destiny"), the liberator into the thing released ("I
> released your feet from the bonds which pierced your ankles" says
> the Corinthian messenger), the accuser becomes the defendant, the
> ruler the subject, the teacher not only the pupil but also the object
> lesson, the example.
>
> Bernard Knox, "Sophocles' Oedipus," in *Tragic Themes in
> Western Literature,* ed. Cleanth Brooks (New Haven, 1955),
> pp. 10–11

Notice, by the way, the neatness of this sentence; it is unusually
long, but it does not ramble, it does not baffle, and it does not
suggest a stuffy writer. The verb "turns" governs the first two-
thirds; and after the second long parenthesis, when there is danger

---

★ *Dramatic irony* (ironic deeds, or happenings, and unconsciously ironic
speeches) must be distinguished from *verbal irony,* which is produced when the
speaker is conscious that his words mean something different from what they say.
In *Macbeth* Lennox says: "The gracious Duncan / Was pitied of Macbeth. Marry,
he was dead! / And the right valiant Banquo walked too late. /. . ./ Men must
not walk too late." He says nothing about Macbeth having killed Duncan and Banquo, but he *means* that Macbeth has killed them.

that the messenger's speech will cause the reader to forget the verb, the writer provides another verb, "becomes."

When the deed backfires, or has a reverse effect such as Macbeth's effort to gain happiness has, we have what Aristotle called a **peripeteia,** or a **reversal.** When a character comes to perceive what has happened (Macbeth's "I have lived long enough: my way of life / Is fall'n into the sere, the yellow leaf"), he experiences (in Aristotle's language) an **anagnorisis, or recognition.** Strictly speaking, for Aristotle the recognition was a matter of literal identification, for example, that Oedipus was the son of a man he killed. In *Macbeth,* the recognition in this sense is that Macduff, "from his mother's womb / Untimely ripped," is the man who fits the prophecy that Macbeth can be conquered only by someone not "of woman born." In his analysis of drama Aristotle says that the tragic hero comes to grief through his **hamartia,** a term sometimes translated as **tragic flaw** but perhaps better translated as **tragic error.** Thus, it is a great error for Othello to trust Iago and to strangle Desdemona, for Lear to give away his kingdom, and for Macbeth to decide to help fulfill the prophecies. If we hold to the translation "flaw," we begin to hunt for a fault in their characters; and we say, for instance, that Othello is gullible, Lear self-indulgent, Macbeth ambitious, or some such thing. In doing this, we may overlook their grandeur. To take a single example: Iago boasts he can dupe Othello because

> The Moor is of a free and open nature
> That thinks men honest that but seem to be so.

We ought to hesitate before we say that a man who trusts men because they seem to be honest has a flaw.

When writing about tragedy, probably the commonest essay topic is on the tragic hero. Too often the hero is judged mechanically: he must be noble, he must have a flaw, he must do a fearful deed, he must recognize his flaw, he must die. The previous paragraph suggests that Shakespeare's practice makes doubtful one of these matters, the flaw. Be similarly cautious about accepting the rest of the package unexamined. (This book has several times urged you to trust your feelings; don't assume that what you have been taught about tragedy must be true, and that you should therefore trust such assertions even if they go against your own responses to a given play.) On the other hand, if "tragedy" is to have any meaning — any use as a term — it must have some agreed-upon attributes. An essay that seeks to determine whether or not a character is a tragic character ought at its outset to make clear its conception of tragedy and the degree of rigidity, or flexibility, with which it will interpret some or all of its categories. For example, it may indicate that although nobility is a *sine qua non,* nobility is not equivalent to high rank. A middle-class figure with certain mental or spiritual characteristics may, in such a view, be an acceptable tragic hero.

An essay closely related to the sort we have been talking about measures a character by some well-known theory of tragedy. For example, one can measure Willy Loman, in *Death of a Salesman,* against Miller's essays on tragedy or against Aristotle's remarks on tragedy. The organization of such an essay is usually not a problem: isolate the relevant aspects of the theoretical statement, and then examine the character to see if, point by point, he illustrates them. But remember that even if Willy Loman fulfills Arthur Miller's idea of a tragic figure, you need not accept him as tragic; conversely, if he does not fulfill Aristotle's idea, you need not deny him tragic status. Aristotle may be wrong.

Comedy

In comedy, the fullest life is seen to reside within enlightened social norms: at the beginning of a comedy we find banished dukes, unhappy lovers, crabby parents, jealous husbands, and harsh laws; but at the end we usually have a unified and genial society, often symbolized by a marriage feast to which everyone, or almost everyone, is invited. Early in *A Midsummer Night's Dream,* for instance, we meet quarreling young lovers and a father who demands that his daughter either marry a man she does not love or enter a convent. Such is the Athenian law. At the end of the play the lovers are properly matched, to everyone's satisfaction.

Speaking broadly, most comedies fall into one of two classes: **satiric comedy** and **romantic comedy.** In the former, the emphasis is on the obstructionists — the irate fathers, hardheaded businessmen, and other members of the Establishment who at the beginning of the play seem to hold all the cards, preventing joy from reigning. They are held up to ridicule because they are repressive monomaniacs enslaved to themselves, acting mechanistically (always irate, always hardheaded) instead of responding genially to the ups and downs of life. The outwitting of these obstructionists, usually by the younger generation, often provides the resolution of the plot. Jonson, Molière, and Shaw are in this tradition; their comedy, according to an ancient Roman formula, "chastens morals with ridicule" — that is, it reforms folly or vice by laughing at it. On the other hand, in romantic comedy (one thinks of Shakespeare's *Midsummer Night's Dream, As You Like It,* and *Twelfth Night*) the emphasis is on a pair or pairs of delightful people who engage our sympathies as they run their obstacle race to the altar. There are obstructionists here too, but the emphasis is elsewhere.

Essays on comedy often examine the nature of the humor. Why is an irate father, in this context, funny? Or why is a young lover, again in this context, funny? Commonly one will find that at least some of the humor is in the disproportionate nature of their activities (they get terribly excited) and in their inflexibility. In both of these qualities they are rather like the cat in animated cartoons, who repeatedly chases the mouse to his hole and who repeatedly bangs his head against the wall. The following is a skeleton of a possible essay on why Jaques in *As You Like It* is amusing:

> Jaques is insistently melancholy. In the Eden-like Forest of Arden, he sees only the dark side of things.
>
> His monomania, however, is harmless to himself and to others; because it causes us no pain, it may entertain us.
>
> Indeed, we begin to look forward to his melancholy speeches. We delight in hearing him fulfill our expectations by wittily finding gloom where others find mirth.
>
> We are delighted, too, to learn that this chastiser of others has in fact been guilty of the sort of behavior he chastises.
>
> At the end of the play, when four couples are wed, the inflexible Jaques insists on standing apart from the general rejoicing.

Such might be the gist of an essay. It needs to be supported with details, and it can be enriched, for example, by a comparison between Jaques's sort of jesting and Touchstone's; but it is at least a promising draft of an outline.

Tragicomedy

The word *tragicomedy* has been used to denote (1) plays that seem tragic until the happy ending, (2) plays that combine tragic and comic scenes, and (3) plays that combine the anguish of tragedy with the improbable situations and unheroic characters and funny dialogue of comedy. It is this last sort of tragicomedy (also called "black comedy") that will occupy us here, because it has attracted most of the best dramatists of our time, for example, Beckett, Genet, and Ionesco. They are the dramatists of the Absurd in two senses: the irrational and the ridiculous. These writers differ from one another, of course, and they differ from play to play; but they are all preoccupied with the loneliness of people in a world without the certainties afforded by God or by optimistic rationalism. This loneliness is heightened by a sense of impotence derived partly from an awareness of our inability to communicate in a society that has made language meaningless, and partly from an awareness of the precariousness of our existence in an atomic age.

Landmarks on the road to people's awareness of their littleness are Darwin's *The Origin of Species* (1859), which reduced human beings to the product of "accidental variations"; Marx's writings, which attributed people's sense of alienation to economic forces and thus implied that people had no identity they could properly call their own; and Freud's writings, which by charting people's unconscious drives and anarchic impulses induced a profound distrust of the self.

The result of such developments in thought seems to be that a "tragic sense" in the twentieth century commonly means a despairing or deeply uncertain view, something very different from what it meant in Greece and in Elizabethan England. This uncertainty is not merely about the cosmos but even about character or identity. In 1888, in the Preface to *Miss Julie,* Strindberg called attention to the new sense of the instability of character:

I have made the people in my play fairly "characterless." The middle-class conception of a fixed character was transferred to the stage, where the middle class has always ruled. A character there came to mean an actor who was always one and the same, always drunk, always comic or always melancholy, and who needed to be characterized only by some physical defect such as a club foot, a wooden leg, or a red nose, or by the repetition of some such phrase such as, "That's capital," or "Barkis is willin'.". . . Since the persons in my play are modern characters, living in a transitional era more hurried and hysterical than the previous one at least, I have depicted them as more unstable, as torn and divided, a mixture of the old and the new.

Along with the sense of characterlessness, or at least of the mystery of character, there developed in the drama (and in the underground film and novel) a sense of plotlessness, or of the fundamental untruthfulness of the traditional plot that moved by cause and effect. Ionesco, for example, has said that a play should be able to stop at any point; it ends only because — as in life — the audience at last has to go home to bed. Moreover, Ionesco has allowed directors to make heavy cuts, and he has suggested that endings other than those he wrote are possibilities. After all, in a meaningless world one can hardly take a dramatic plot seriously.

Every play, of course, is different from every other play; each is a unique and detailed statement, and the foregoing paragraphs give only the broadest outlines — tragedies, comedies, and tragicomedies seen at a distance, as it were. The analyst's job is to try to study the differences as well as the similarities in an effort (in Henry James's words) "to appreciate, to appropriate, to take intellectual possession, to establish in fine a relation with the criticized thing and make it one's own."

ASPECTS OF DRAMA

Theme

The best way to make a work of art one's own is (again in Henry James's words) "to be one of the people on whom nothing is lost." If we have perceived the work properly, we ought to be

able to formulate its **theme,** its underlying idea, and perhaps we
can even go so far as to say its moral attitudes, its view of life, its
wisdom. Some critics, it is true, have argued that the concept of
theme is meaningless. They hold that *Macbeth,* for example, gives
us only an extremely detailed history of one imaginary man. In
this view, *Macbeth* says nothing to you or me; it only says what
happened to some imaginary man. Even *Julius Caesar* says nothing
about the historical Julius Caesar or about the nature of Roman
politics. Here we can agree; no one would offer Shakespeare's play
as evidence of what the historical Caesar said or did. But surely
the view that the concept of theme is meaningless, and that a work
tells us only about imaginary creatures, is a desperate one. We *can*
say that we see in *Julius Caesar* the fall of power, or (if we are
thinking of Brutus) the vulnerability of idealism, or some such
thing.

   To the reply that these are mere truisms, we can counter: Yes,
but the truisms are presented in such a way that they take on life
and become a part of us rather than remain things of which we
say "I've heard it said, and I guess it's so." And surely we are in
no danger of equating the play with the theme that we sense underlies it. If, for example, we say (as Ionesco himself said of his
play) that *Rhinoceros* is "an attack on collective hysteria and the ep-
idemics that lurk beneath the surface of reason," we do not believe that our statement of the theme is the equivalent of the play
itself. We recognize that the play presents the theme with such detail that our statement is only a wedge to help us enter into the
play so that we may more fully appropriate it. Joseph Wood Krutch
discusses at some length the themes of *Death of a Salesman* and *A
Streetcar Named Desire* (pp. 190–194), but a briefer illustration may
be helpful here. A critic examining Ibsen's achievements begins by
trying to see what some of the plays are in fact about.

> We must not waste more than a paragraph on such fiddle-faddle as
> the notion that *Ghosts* is a play about venereal disease or that *A Doll's
> House* is a play about women's rights. On these terms, *King Lear* is
> a play about housing for the elderly and *Hamlet* is a stage-debate
> over the reality of spooks. Venereal disease and its consequences are
> represented onstage in *Ghosts;* so, to all intents and purposes, is in-
> cest; but tht theme of the play is inherited guilt, and the sexual pa-
> thology of the Alving family is an engine in the hands of that theme.

A Doll's House represents a woman imbued with the idea of becoming a person, but it proposes nothing categorical about women becoming people; in fact, its real theme has nothing to do with the sexes. It is the irrepressible conflict of two different personalities which have founded themselves on two radically different estimates of reality.

> Robert M. Adams, "Ibsen on the Contrary," in *Modern Drama,* ed. Anthony Caputi (New York, 1966), p. 345

Such a formulation can be most useful; a grasp of the theme helps us to see what the plot is really all about, what the plot suggests in its universal meaning or applicability.

A few words about the preceding quotation may be appropriate here. Notice that Adams's paragraph moves from a vigorous colloquial opening through some familiar examples, including a brief comparison with plays by another dramatist, to a fairly formal close. The disparity in tone between opening and closing is not distressing because even in the opening we sense the writer's mastery of his material, and we sympathize with his impatience. Adams's next paragraph, not given here, extends his suggestion that the plays are not about nineteenth-century problems: he argues that under the bourgeois décor, under the frock coat and the bustle, we detect two kinds of people — little people and great people. His third paragraph elaborates this point by suggesting that, allowing for variations, the dichotomy consists of satyrs and saints, and he provides the details necessary to make this dichotomy convincing. Among Ibsen's little people, or satyrs, are Parson Manders, Peter Stockmann, Hjalmar Ekdal, and Torvald Helmer; among the great people, or saints, are Mrs. Alving, Thomas Stockmann, Gregers Werle, and Nora Helmer. In short, Adams's argument about Ibsen's themes advances steadily, and is convincingly illustrated with concrete references.

Some critics (influenced by Aristotle's statement that a drama is an imitation of an action) use **action** in a sense equivalent to theme. In this sense, the action is the underlying happening — the inner happening — for example, "the enlightenment of someone," or "the coming of unhappiness," or "the finding of the self by self-surrender." One might say that the theme of *Macbeth,* for example, is embodied in some words that Macbeth himself utters: "Blood will have blood." Of course this is not to say that these words and no other words embody the theme or the action. Francis Fergusson suggests that another expression in *Macbeth,* to the effect that Macbeth "outran the pauser, reason," describes the action of the play:

> To "outrun" reason suggests an impossible stunt, like lifting oneself by one's own bootstraps. It also suggests a competition or race, like those of nightmare, which cannot be won. As for the word "reason," Shakespeare associates it with nature and nature's order, in the individual soul, in society, and in the cosmos. To outrun reason is thus to violate nature itself, to lose the bearings of common sense and of custom, and to move into a spiritual realm bounded by the irrational darkness of Hell one way, and the superrational grace of faith the other way. As the play develops before us, all the modes of this absurd, or evil, or supernatural, action are attempted, the last being Malcolm's and Macduff's acts of faith.
>
> *The Human Image in Dramatic Literature* (New York, 1957), p. 118

Critics like Fergusson, who are influenced by Aristotle's *Poetics,* assume that the dramatist conceives of an action and then imitates it or sets it forth by means of, first a plot and characters, then by means of language, gesture, and perhaps spectacle and music. When the Greek comic dramatist Menander told a friend he had finished his play and now had only to write it, he must have meant that he had the action or the theme firmly in mind, and had worked out the plot and the requisite characters. All that remained was to set down the words.

Plot

Plot is variously defined, sometimes as equivalent to "story" (in this sense a synopsis of *Julius Caesar* has the same plot as *Julius Caesar*), but more often, and more usefully, as the dramatist's particular *arrangement of the story*. Thus, because Shakespeare's *Julius Caesar* begins with a scene dramatizing an encounter between plebeians and tribunes, its plot is different from that of a play on Julius Caesar in which such a scene (not necessary to the story) is omitted. Richard G. Moulton, discussing the early part of Shakespeare's plot in *Julius Caesar,* examines the relatonship between the first two scenes.

. . . The opening scene strikes appropriately the key-note of the whole action. In it we see the tribunes of the people — officers whose whole *raison d'être* is to be the mouthpiece of the commonalty — restraining their own clients from the noisy honors they are disposed to pay Caesar. To the justification in our eyes of a conspiracy against Caesar, there could not be a better starting-point than this hint that the popular worship of Caesar, which has made him what he is, is itself reaching its reaction-point. Such a suggestion moreover makes the whole play one complete *wave* of popular fickleness from crest to crest.

The second is the scene upon which the dramatist mainly relies for the *crescendo* in the justification of the conspirators. It is a long scene, elaborately contrived so as to keep the conspirators and their cause before us at their very best, and the vicitm at his very worst. . . .

Shakespeare as a Dramatic Artist (Oxford, 1893), pp. 188–189

Moulton's discussion of the plot continues at length. One can argue that he presents too favorable a view of the conspirators (when he says we see the conspirators at their best he seems to overlook their fawning), but that is not our concern here; here we have been talking about the process of examining juxtaposed scenes, a process Moulton's words illustrate well.

Handbooks on the drama often suggest that a plot (arrangement of happenings) should have a **rising action,** a **climax,** and a **falling action.** This sort of plot can be diagramed as a pyramid: the tension rises through complications or **crises** to a climax, at which point the climax is the apex, and the tension allegedly slackens as we witness the **dénouement** (unknotting). Shakespeare sometimes used a pyramidal structure, placing his climax neatly in the middle of what seems to us to be the third of five acts. Roughly the first half of *Romeo and Juliet,* for example, shows Romeo winning Juliet; but when in III.i he kills her cousin Tybalt, Romeo sets in motion (it is often said) the second half of the play, the losing of Juliet and of his own life. Similarly, in *Julius Caesar,* Brutus rises in the first half of the play, reaching his height in III.i, with the death of Caesar; but later in this scene he gives Marc Antony permission to speak at Caesar's funeral, and thus he sets in motion his own fall, which occupies the second half of the play.

In *Macbeth,* the protagonist attains his height in III.i ("Thou hast it now: King"), but he soon perceives that he is going downhill:

> I am in blood
> Stepped in so far, that, should I wade no more,
> Returning were as tedious as go o'er.

In *Hamlet,* the protagonist proves to his own satisfaction Claudius's guilt in III.ii, by the play within the play, but almost immediately he begins to worsen his position, by failing to kill Claudius when he is an easy target (III.iii) and by contaminating himself with the murder of Polonius (III.iv).

Of course, no law demands such a structure, and a hunt for the pyramid usually causes the hunter to overlook all the crises but the middle one. William Butler Yeats once suggestively diagramed a good plot not as a pyramid but as a line moving diagonally upward, punctuated by several crises. And it has been said that in Beckett's *Waiting for Godot,* "nothing happens, twice." Perhaps it is sufficient to say that a good plot has its moments of tension, but that the location of these will vary with the play. They are the product of **conflict,** but it should be noted that not all conflict produces tension; there is conflict but little tension in a ball game when the home team is ahead 10–0 and the visiting pitcher comes to bat in the ninth inning with two out and none on base.

Regardless of how a plot is diagramed, the **exposition** is that part which tells the audience what it has to know about the past, the **antecedent action.** Two gossiping servants who tell each other that after a year away in Paris the young master is coming home tomorrow with a new wife are giving the audience the exposition. The exposition in Shakespeare's *Tempest* is almost ruthlessly direct: Prospero tells his naive daughter, "I should inform thee farther," and for about one hundred and fifty lines he proceeds to tell her why she is on an almost uninhabited island. Prospero's harangue is punctuated by his daughter's professions of attention; but the Elizabethans (and the Greeks) sometimes tossed out all pretense at dialogue, and began with a **prologue,** like the one spoken by the Chorus at the opening of *Romeo and Juliet:*

> Two households, both alike in dignity
> In fair Verona, where we lay our scene,

> From ancient grudge break to new mutiny,
>   Where civil blood makes civil hands unclean.
> From forth the fatal loins of these two foes
>   A pair of star-crossed lovers take their life. . . .

But the exposition may also extend far into the play, being given in small, explosive revelations.

Exposition has been discussed as though it consists simply of informing the audience about events, but exposition can do much more. It can give us an understanding of the characters who themselves are talking about other characters, it can evoke a mood, and it can generate tension. When we summarize the opening act, and treat it as "mere exposition," we are probably losing what is in fact dramatic in it. Moulton, in his analysis of the first two scenes in *Julius Caesar,* does not make the mistake of thinking that the first scenes exist merely to tell the audience certain facts.

An analysis of plot, then, will consider the arrangement of the episodes and the effect of juxtapositions, as well as the overall story. A useful essay can be written on the function of one scene. Such an essay may point out, for example, that the long, comparatively slow scene (IV.iii) in *Macbeth,* in which the Malcolm, Macduff, an English doctor, and Ross converse near the palace of the King of England, is not so much a leisurely digression as may at first be thought. After reading it closely, you may decide that it has several functions. For example, it serves to indicate the following:

1. The forces that will eventually overthrow Macbeth are gathering.

2. Even good men must tell lies during Macbeth's reign.

3. Macbeth has the vile qualities that the virtuous Malcolm pretends to have.

4. Macbeth has failed — as the King of England has not — to be a source of health to the realm.

It probably will take an effort to come to these or other conclusions, but once you have come to some such ideas, the construction of an essay on the function of a scene is usually fairly simple: an introductory paragraph announces the general topic and thesis — an apparently unnecessary scene will be shown to be functional — and the rest of the essay demonstrates the functions, usually in climactic order if some of the functions are more important than others. If you think they are all equally important, perhaps you will organize the material from the most obvious to the least obvious, thereby keeping the reader's attention to the end. If, on the other hand, you believe that although justifications for the scene can be imagined, the scene is nevertheless unsuccessful, say so; announce your view early, consider the alleged functions one by one, and explain your reasons for finding them unconvincing as you take up each point.

Sometimes an analysis of the plot will examine the relationships between the several stories in a play: *A Midsummer Night's Dream* has supernatural lovers, mature royal lovers, young Athenian lovers, a bumpkin who briefly becomes the lover of the fairy queen, and a play (put on by the bumpkins) about legendary lovers. How these are held together and how they help to define each other and the total play are matters that concern anyone looking at the plot of *A Midsummer Night's Dream*. Richard Moulton suggests that Shakespeare's subplots "have the effect of assisting the main stories, smoothing away their difficulties and making their prominent points yet more prominent." He demonstrates his thesis at some length, but a very brief extract from his discussion of the Jessica-Lorenzo story in *The Merchant of Venice* may be enough to suggest the method. The main story concerns Shylock and his rivals, Antonio, Bassanio, and Portia. Shylock's daughter Jessica is not needed for the narrative purpose of the main story. Why then did Shakespeare include her? (Remember: When something puzzles you, you have an essay topic at hand.) Part of Moulton's answer runs thus:

> A Shylock painted without a tender side at all would be repulsive . . . and yet it appears how this tenderness has grown hard and rotten with the general debasement of his soul by avarice, until, in his ravings over his loss, his ducats and his daughter are ranked as equally dear.
>
> > I would my daughter were dead at my foot, and the jewels in her ear! Would she were hearsed at my foot, and the ducats in her coffin!

For all this we feel that he is hardly used in losing her. Paternal feeling may take a gross form, but it is paternal feeling none the less, and cannot be denied our sympathy; bereavement is a common ground upon which not only high and low, but even the pure and the outcast, are drawn together. Thus Jessica at home makes us hate Shylock; with Jessica lost we cannot help pitying him.

Shakespeare as a Dramatic Artist, p. 79

Sample Essay on Structure

The example that follows is a student's essay on the structure of Tennessee Williams's *Glass Menagerie*. It proceeds a bit mechanically, moving (after the first two paragraphs) scene by scene through the play, but the writer notices some interesting things about the shape of the plot and he makes his points clearly.

Title is focused; it announces topic and thesis.

Opening paragraph closes in on thesis.

Reasonable organization; the paragraph touches on the beginning and the end.

The Solid Structure of The Glass Menagerie

In the ''Production Notes'' Tennessee Williams calls The Glass Menagerie a ''memory play,'' a term that the narrator in the play also uses. Memories often consist of fragments of episodes which are so loosely connected that they seem chaotic, and therefore we might think that The Glass Menagerie will consist of very loosely related episodes. However, the play covers only one episode and though it gives the illusion of random talk, it really has a firm structure and moves steadily toward a foregone conclusion.

Tennessee Williams divides the play into seven scenes. The first scene begins with a sort of prologue and the last scene concludes with a sort of epilogue that is related to the prologue. In the prologue Tom addresses the audience and comments on the 1930s as a time

Brief but effective quotations.

when America was ''blind'' and was a place of ''shouting and confusion.'' Tom also mentions that our lives consist of expectations, and though he does not say that our expectations are unfulfilled, near the end of the prologue he quotes a postcard that his father wrote to the family he deserted: ''Hello—Goodbye.'' In the epilogue Tom tells us that he followed his ''father's footsteps,'' deserting the family. And just before the epilogue, near the end of Scene VII, we see what can be considered another desertion: Jim explains to Tom's sister Laura that he is engaged and therefore cannot

Useful generalization based on earlier details.

visit Laura again. Thus the end is closely related to the beginning, and the play is the steady development of the initial implications.

Chronological organization is reasonable. Opening topic sentence lets readers know where they are going.

The first three scenes show things going from bad to worse. Amanda is a nagging mother who finds her only relief in talking about the past to her crippled daughter Laura and her frustrated son Tom. When she was young she was beautiful and was eagerly courted by rich young men, but now the family is poor and this harping on the past can only bore or infuriate Tom and embarrass or depress Laura, who have no happy past to look back to, who see no happy future, and who can only be upset by Amanda's insistence that they should behave as she behaved long ago. The second scene deepens

Brief plot summary
supports thesis.

the despair: Amanda learns that the timorous
Laura has not been attending a business school
but has retreated in terror from this confrontation with the contemporary world. Laura's
helplessness is made clear to the audience,
and so is Amanda's lack of understanding. Near
the end of the second scene, however, Jim's
name is introduced; he is a boy Laura had a
crush on in high school, and so the audience
gets a glimpse of a happier Laura and a sense
that possibly Laura's world is wider than the
stifling tenement in which she and her mother
and brother live. But in the third scene
things get worse, when Tom and Amanda have so
violent an argument that they are no longer on
speaking terms. Tom is so angry with his
mother that he almost by accident destroys his
sister's treasured collection of glass animals, the fragile lifeless world which is her
refuge. The apartment is literally full of the
''shouting and confusion'' that Tom spoke of
in his prologue.

Useful summary and
transition.

    The first three scenes have revealed a
progressive worsening of relations; the next
three scenes reveal a progressive improvement
in relations. In Scene IV Tom and his mother
are reconciled, and Tom reluctantly--appar-
ently in an effort to make up with his mother-
-agrees to try to get a friend to come to dinner so that Laura will have ''a gentleman

caller.'' In Scene V Tom tells his mother that
Jim will come to dinner on the next night, and
Amanda brightens, because she sees a possibility of security for Laura at last. In Scene VI
Jim arrives, and despite Laura's initial terror, there seems, at least in Amanda's mind,
to be the possibility that things will go
well.

The seventh scene, by far the longest, at
first seems to be fulfilling Amanda's hopes.
Despite the ominous fact that the lights go
out because Tom has not paid the electric
bill, Jim is at ease. He is an insensitive
oaf, but that doesn't seem to bother Amanda,
and almost miraculously he manages to draw
Laura somewhat out of her sheltered world.
Even when Jim in his clumsiness breaks the
horn off Laura's treasured glass unicorn, she
is not upset. In fact, she is almost relieved
because the loss of the horn makes the animal
less ''freakish'' and he ''will feel more at
home with the other horses.'' In a way, of
course, the unicorn symbolizes the crippled
Laura, who at least for the moment feels less
freakish and isolated now that she is somewhat
reunited with society through Jim. But this is
a play about life in a blind and confused
world, and though in a previous age the father
escaped, there can be no escape now. Jim reveals that he is engaged, Laura relapses into

''desolation,'' Amanda relapses into rage and bitterness, and Tom relapses into dreams of escape. In a limited sense Tom does escape. He leaves the family and joins the merchant marine, but his last speech or epilogue tells us that he cannot escape the memory of his sister: ''Oh, Laura, Laura, I tried to leave you behind me, but I am more faithful than I intended to be!'' And so the end of the last scene brings us back again to the beginning of the first scene: we are still in a world of ''the blind'' and of ''confusion.'' But now at the end of the darkness is deeper, the characters are lost forever in their unhappiness as Laura ''blows the candles out,'' the darkness being literal but also symbolic of their extinguished hopes.

The essayist is thinking and commenting, not merely summarizing the plot.

Numerous devices, such as repeated references to the absent father, to Amanda's youth, to Laura's Victrola and of course to Laura's glass menagerie help to tie the scenes together into a unified play. But beneath these threads of imagery, and recurring motifs, is a fundamental pattern that involves the movement from nagging (Scenes I and II) to open hostilities (Scene III) to temporary reconciliation (Scene IV) to false hopes (Scenes V and VI) to an impossible heightening of false hopes and then, in a swift descent, to an inevitable collapse (Scene VII). Tennessee Williams has

Useful, thoughtful summary of thesis.

constructed his play carefully. G. B. Tennyson says that a ''playwright must 'build' his speeches, as the theatrical expression has it.''[1] But a playwright must do more, he must also build his play out of scenes. Like Ibsen, if Williams had been introduced to an architect he might have said, ''Architecture is my business too.''

Documentation. (For another way of indicating a source, see pages 75–85.)

---

[1]*An Introduction to Drama* (New York: Holt, Rinehart and Winston, 1967), p. 13.

The danger in writing about structure, especially if one proceeds by beginning at the beginning and moving steadily to the end, is that one will simply tell the plot. This essay on *The Glass Menagerie* manages to say things about the organization of the plot even as it tells the plot. It has a point, hinted at in the pleasantly paradoxical title, developed in the body of the essay, and wrapped up in the last line.

Conventions

Artists and their audience have some tacit — even unconscious — agreements. When we watch a motion picture and see an image dissolve and then reappear, we understand that some time has passed. Such a device, unrealistic but widely accepted, is a **convention.** In the theater, we sometimes see on the stage a room, realistic in all details except that it lacks a fourth wall; were that wall in place, we would see it and not the interior of the room. We do not regret the missing wall, and indeed we are scarcely aware that we have entered into an agreement to pretend that this strange room is an ordinary room with the usual number of walls. Sometimes the characters in a play speak verse, although outside the theater no human beings speak verse for more than a few moments. Again we accept the device because it allows the author to make a play, and we want a play. In *Hamlet* the characters are understood to be speaking Danish, in *Julius Caesar* Latin, in *A*

Midsummer Night's Dream Greek, yet they all speak English for our benefit.

Two other conventions are especially common in older drama: the **soliloquy** and the **aside.** In the former, although a solitary character speaks his thoughts aloud, we do not judge him to be a lunatic; in the latter, a character speaks in the presence of others but is understood not to be heard by them, or to be heard only by those to whom he directs his words. The soliloquy and the aside strike us as artificial — and they are. But they so strike us only because they are no longer customary. Because we are accustomed to it, we are not bothered by the artificiality of music accompanying dialogue in a motion picture. The conventions of the modern theater are equally artificial but are so customary that we do not notice them. The Elizabethans, who saw a play acted without a break, would probably find strange our assumption that, when we return to the auditorium after a ten-minute intermission, the ensuing action may be supposed to follow immediately the action before the intermission.

Gestures and Settings

The language of a play, broadly conceived, includes the **gestures** that the characters make and the **settings** in which they make them. As Ezra Pound somewhere says, "The medium of drama is not words, but persons moving about on a stage using words." When Shaw's Major Barbara, in a Salvation Army shelter, gives up the Army's insignia, pinning it on the collar of her millionaire father, who has, she says, bought the Army, the gesture is at least as important as the words that accompany it. Gesture can be interpreted even more broadly: the mere fact that a character enters, leaves, or does not enter may be highly significant. John Russell Brown comments on the actions and the absence of certain words that in *Hamlet* convey the growing separation between King Claudius and his wife, Gertrude:

> Their first appearance together with a public celebration of marriage is a large and simple visual effect, and Gertrude's close concern for her son suggests a simple, and perhaps unremarkable modification. . . . But Claudius enters without Gertrude for his "Prayer Scene" (III.iii) and, for the first time, Gertrude enters without

him for the Closet Scene (III.iv) and is left alone, again for the first time, when Polonius hides behind the arras. Thereafter earlier accord is revalued by an increasing separation, often poignantly silent, and unexpected. When Claudius calls Gertrude to leave with him after Hamlet has dragged off Polonius' body, she makes no reply; twice more he urges her and she is still silent. But he does not remonstrate or question; rather he speaks of his own immediate concerns and, far from supporting her with assurances, becomes more aware of his own fears:

> O, come away!
> My soul is full of discord and dismay.
>
> (IV.i.44–45)

Emotion has been so heightened that it is remarkable that they leave together without further words. The audience has been aware of a new distance between Gertrude and Claudius, of her immobility and silence, and of his self-concern, haste and insistence.

> *Shakespeare's Plays in Performance* (New York, 1967), p. 139

Sometimes the dramatist helps us to interpret the gestures; Shaw and O'Neill give notably full stage directions, but detailed stage directions before the middle of the nineteenth century are rare.

Drama of the nineteenth and early twentieth centuries (for example, the plays of Ibsen, Chekhov, and Odets) is often thought to be "realistic," but of course even a realistic playwright or stage designer selects his materials. A realistic **setting** (indication of the locale), then, can say a great deal, can serve as a symbol. Here is Ibsen on nonverbal devices:

> I can do quite a lot by manipulating the prosaic details of my plays so that they become theatrical metaphors and come to mean more than what they are; I have used costume in this way, lighting, scenery, landscape, weather; I have used trivial everyday things like inky fingers and candles; and I have used living figures as symbols of spiritual forces that act upon the hero. Perhaps these things could be brought into the context of a modern realistic play to help me to portray the modern hero and the tragic conflict which I now understand so well.
>
> Quoted by John Northam, "Ibsen's Search for the Hero," in *Ibsen*, ed. Rolf Fjelde (Englewood Cliffs, N.J., 1965), p. 99

In the setting of *Hedda Gabler,* for example, Ibsen uses two suggestive details as more than mere background: early in the play Hedda is distressed by the sunlight that shines through the opened French doors, a detail that we later see helps to reveal her fear of the processes of nature. More evident and more pervasive is her tendency, when she cannot cope with her present situation, to move to the inner room, at the rear of the stage, in which hangs a picture of her late father. And over and over again in Ibsen we find the realistic setting of a nineteenth-century drawing room, with its heavy draperies and its bulky furniture, helping to convey his vision of a bourgeois world that oppresses the individual who struggles to affirm other values.

Twentieth-century dramatists are often explicit about the symbolic qualities of the setting. Here is an example from O'Neill's *Desire under the Elms.* Only a part of the initial stage direction is given.

> The house is in good condition but in need of paint. Its walls are a sickly grayish, the green of the shutters faded. Two enormous elms are on each side of the house. They bend their trailing branches down over the roof. They appear to protect and at the same time subdue. There is a sinister maternity in their aspect, a crushing, jealous absorption. . . . They are like exhausted women resting their sagging breasts and hands and hair on its roof. . . .

A second example is part of Miller's description of the set in *Death of a Salesman:*

> Before us is the Salesman's house. We are aware of towering, angular shapes behind it, surrounding it on all sides. Only the blue light of the sky falls upon the house and forestage; the surrounding area shows an angry glow of orange. As more light appears, we see a solid vault of apartment houses around the small, fragile-seeming home.

These directions and the settings they describe are symbols that help to give the plays their meaning. Not surprisingly, O'Neill's play has Freudian overtones, Miller's (in a broad sense) Marxist overtones. O'Neill is concerned about passion, Miller (notice the "solid vault of apartment houses" that menaces the salesman's house) about social forces that warp the individual. An essay might examine in detail the degree to which the setting contributes to the theme of the play. Take, for example, O'Neill's setting. The maternal elms are the most important aspect, but an essayist might first point out that the "good condition" of the house suggests it was well built, presumably some years ago. The need of paint, however, suggests both present neglect and indifference to decoration, and indeed the play is partly concerned with a strong, miserly father who regards his sons as decadent. The house, "a sickly grayish," helps to embody the suggestion of old strength but present decadence. One might continue through the stage directions, explaining the relevance of the details. Contrasts between successive settings can be especially important.

Because Shakespeare's plays were performed in broad daylight on a stage that (compared with Ibsen's, O'Neill's, and Miller's) made little use of scenery, he had to use language to manufacture his settings. But the attentive ear, or the mind's eye, responds to these settings too. Early in *King Lear,* when Lear reigns, we hear that we are in a country "With plenteous rivers, and wide-skirted meads"; later, when Lear is stripped of his power, we are in a place where "For many miles about / There's scarce a bush." (Incidentally, the vogue for the relatively bare stage which has been with us for a couple of decades is not merely an attempt to clear the stage of unnecessary furniture; in many plays it functions as a symbol of humanity's barren existence or existential plight. In Samuel Beckett's *Waiting for Godot* — that is, in today's theater — the very sparseness of the décor or the black backdrop says something about the people who move on the stage.)

In any case, a director staging Shakespeare must provide some sort of setting — even if only a bare stage — and this setting will be part of the play. A recent production of *Julius Caesar* used great cubes, piled on top of each other, as the background for the first half of the play, suggesting the pretensions, and the littleness, of the figures who strutted on the stage. In the second half of the play, when Rome is in the throes of a civil war, the cubes were gone: a shaggy black carpet, darkness at the rear of the stage, and a great net hanging above the actors suggested that they were wretched little creatures groping in blindness. In a review of a production you will almost surely want to pay some attention to the function of the setting.

Characterization and Motivation

Characterization, or personality, is defined, as in fiction (see p. 113), by what the characters do (a stage direction tells us that "Hedda paces up and down, clenching her fists"), by what they say (she asks her husband to draw the curtains), by what others say about them, and by the setting in which they move. The characters are also defined in part by other characters whom they in some degree resemble. Hamlet, Laertes, and Fortinbras have each lost their fathers, but Hamlet spares the praying King Claudius, whereas Laertes, seeking vengeance on Hamlet for murdering Laertes's father, says he would cut Hamlet's throat in church; Hamlet meditates about the nature of action, but Fortinbras leads the Norwegians in a military campaign and ultimately acquires Denmark. Here is Kenneth Muir commenting briefly on the way in which Laertes helps us to see Hamlet more precisely. (Notice how Muir first offers a generalization, then supports it with details, and finally, drawing a conclusion from the details he has just presented, offers an even more important generalization that effectively closes his paragraph.)

> In spite of Hamlet's description of him as "a very noble youth," there is a coarseness of fibre in Laertes which is revealed throughout the play. He has the stock responses of a man of his time and position. He gives his sister copy-book advice; he goes to Paris (we are bound to suspect) to tread the primrose path; and after his father's death and again at his sister's grave he shows by the ostentation and "bravery of his grief" that he pretends more than he really feels. He has no difficulty in raising a successful rebellion against Claudius, which suggests that the more popular prince could have done the same. Laertes, indeed, acts more or less in the way that many critics profess to think Hamlet ought to act; and his function in the play is to show precisely the opposite. Although Hamlet himself may envy Laertes' capacity for ruthless action we ought surely to prefer Hamlet's craven scruples.

> *Shakespeare: The Great Tragedies* (London, 1961), pp. 12–13

Muir returned to the subject two years later, treating it more fully in an essay reprinted on pp. 188–190. A comparison of the two versions reveals that the longer one is by no means simply a wordier version. The additional words convey additional perceptions.

Other plays, of course, provide examples of such **foils,** or characters who set one another off. Macbeth and Banquo both hear prophecies, but they act and react differently; Brutus is one kind of assassin, Cassius another, and Casca still another. In *Waiting for Godot,* the two tramps Didi and Gogo are contrasted with Pozzo and his slave Lucky, the former two suggesting (roughly) the contemplative life, the latter two the practical or active (and, it turns out, mistaken) life. Any analysis of a character, then, will probably have to take into account, in some degree, the other characters that help to show what he or she is, that help to set forth his or her motivation (grounds for action, inner drives, goals). In Ibsen's *Doll's House,* Dr. Rank plays a part in helping to define Nora:

> This is not Rank's play, it is Nora's. Rank is a minor character — but he plays a vital dramatic role. His function is to act as the physical embodiment, visible on the stage, of Nora's moral situation as she sees it. Nora is almost hysterical with terror at the thought of her situation — almost, but it is part of her character that with great heroism she keeps her fears secret to herself; and it is because of her reticence that Rank is dramatically necessary, to symbolize the horror she will not talk about. Nora feels, and we feel, the full awfulness of Rank's illness, and she transfers to herself the same feeling about the moral corruption which she imagines herself to carry. Nora sees herself, and we see her seeing herself (with our judgment), as suffering from a moral disease as mortal, as irremediable as Rank's disease, a disease that creeps on to a fatal climax. This is the foe that Nora is fighting so courageously.
>
> John Northam, "Ibsen's Search for the Hero," p. 103

Writing a Review of a Production

A reviewer normally assumes that the reader is unfamiliar with the production being reviewed, and unfamiliar with the play if the play is not a classic. Thus, the first paragraph usually provides a helpful introduction, along these lines:

> Marsha Norman's new play, *'night, Mother,* a tragedy with only two actors and one set, shows us a woman's preparation for suicide. Jessie has concluded that she no longer wishes to live, and so she tries to

put her affairs into order, which chiefly means preparing her rather uncomprehending mother to get along without her.

Inevitably some retelling of the plot is necessary if the play is new, and a summary of a sentence or two is acceptable even for a familiar play, but the review will chiefly be concerned with describing, analyzing, and especially with evaluating. If the play is new, much of the evaluation may center on the play itself, but if the play is a classic, the evaluation probably will chiefly be devoted to the acting, the set, and the direction.

Other points:

1. Save the playbill; it will give you the names of the actors, and perhaps a brief biography of the author, a synopsis of the plot, and a photograph of the set, all of which may be helpful.

2. Draft your review as soon as possible, while the performance is still fresh in your mind. If you can't draft it immediately after seeing the play, at least jot down some notes about the setting and the staging, the acting, and the audience's response.

3. If possible, read the play — ideally, before the performance and again after it.

4. In your first draft, don't worry about limitations of space; write as long a review as you can, putting down everything that comes to mind. Later you can cut it to the required length, retaining only the chief points and the necessary supporting details, but in your first draft try to produce a fairly full record of the performance and your response to it, so that a day or two later, when you revise, you won't have to trust a fading memory for details.

A Sample Review

If you read reviews of plays in *Time, Newsweek,* or a newspaper, you will soon develop a sense of what reviews normally do. The following example, an undergraduate's review of a production of *Macbeth,* is typical except in one respect: reviews of new plays customarily include a few sentences summarizing the plot and classifying the play (a tragedy, a farce, a rock musical, or whatever), perhaps briefly putting it into the context of the author's other works, but because *Macbeth* is so widely known the reviewer has chosen not to insult his readers by telling them that *Macbeth* is a tragedy by Shakespeare.

An Effective <u>Macbeth</u>

Opening paragraph is informative, letting the reader know the reviewer's overall attitude.

<u>Macbeth</u> at the University Theater is a thoughtful and occasionally exciting production, partly because the director, Mark Urice, has trusted Shakespeare and has not imposed a gimmick on the play. The characters do not wear cowboy costumes as they did in last year's production of <u>A Midsummer Night's Dream</u>.

Reviewer promptly turns to a major issue.

Probably the chief problem confronting a director of <u>Macbeth</u> is how to present the witches so that they are powerful supernatural forces and not silly things that look as though they came from a Halloween party. Urice gives us ugly but not absurdly grotesque witches, and he introduces them most effectively. The stage seems to be a bombed-out battlefield littered with rocks and great chunks of earth, but some of these begin to stir -- the earth seems to come alive -- and the clods move, unfold, and become the witches, dressed in brown and dark gray rags. The suggestion is that the witches are a part of nature, elemental forces that can hardly be escaped. This effect is increased by the moans and creaking noises that they make, all of which could be comic but which in this production are impressive.

The witches' power over Macbeth is further emphasized by their actions. When the witches first meet Macbeth, they encircle him, touch him, caress him, even embrace him, and he seems helpless, almost their plaything. Moreover, in the scene in which he imagines that he sees a dagger, the director has arranged for one of the witches to appear, stand near Macbeth, and guide his hand toward the invisible dagger. This is, of course, not in the text, but the interpretation is reasonable rather than intrusive. Finally, near the end of the play, just before Macduff kills Macbeth, a witch appears and laughs at Macbeth as Macduff explains that he was not ''born of woman.'' There is no doubt that throughout the tragedy Macbeth has been a puppet of the witches.

Macbeth (Stephen Beers) and Lady Macbeth (Tina Peters) are excellent. Beers is sufficiently brawny to be convincing as a battle-field hero, but he also speaks the lines sensitively, and so the audience feels that in addition to being a hero he is a man of insight and imagination, and even a man of

gentleness. One can believe Lady Macbeth when she says that she fears he is ''too full of the milk of human kindness'' to murder Duncan.

Lady Macbeth is especially effective in the scene in which she asks the spirits to ''unsex her.'' During this speech she is reclining on a bed and as she delivers the lines she becomes increasingly sexual in her bodily motions, deriving excitement from her own stimulating words. Her attachment to Macbeth is strongly sexual, and so too is his attraction to her. The scene when she persuades him to kill Duncan ends with them passionately embracing. The strong attraction of each for the other, so evident in the early part of the play, disappears after the murder, when Macbeth keeps his distance from Lady Macbeth and does not allow her to touch him. The acting of the other performers is effective, except for Duncan (John Berens), who recites the lines mechanically and seems not to take much account of their meaning.

Description, but also analysis.

The set consists of a barren plot at the rear on which stands a spidery framework of piping, of the sort used by construction companies, supporting a catwalk. This framework

Concrete details.

fits with the costumes (lots of armor, leather, heavy boots), suggesting a sort of elemental, primitive, and somewhat sadistic world. The catwalk, though effectively used when Macbeth goes off to murder Duncan (whose room is presumably upstairs and offstage) is not much used in later scenes. For the most part it is an interesting piece of scenery but it is not otherwise helpful. For instance,

Concrete details to support evaluation. there is no reason why the scene with Macduff's wife and children is staged on it. The costumes are not in any way Scottish — no plaids — but in several scenes the sound of a bagpipe is heard, adding another weird or primitive tone to the production.

Summary This <u>Macbeth</u> appeals to the eye, the ear, and the mind. The director has given us a unified production that makes sense and that is faithful to the spirit of Shakespeare's play.

CONCLUDING REMARKS

First, a word about mechanics. Although acts used to be indicated by capital roman numerals, scenes by lower-case roman numerals, and lines by arabic numerals (for instance, III.ii.78–82), it is now the fashion to use arabic numerals throughout (3.2.78–82). Similarly, one now writes "In act 3 of *Hamlet* . . . ," rather than "In Act III. . . ."

Among the questions you may ask as you sit down to write about a play are: What sort of character is So-and-so? How is he or she defined? (See especially pp. 179–180.) Your instructor may want you to go beyond the personality, and to set forth your idea of the character's appearance (face and body), voice, and mannerisms, along with a discussion of how these qualities help to shape our perception of the figure. If the character is tragic, does the tragedy proceed from a moral fault, from an intellectual error, from the malice of others, from sheer chance, or from some combination of these? If the character is comic, do we laugh *with* or *at* the character? Are the characters adequately motivated? What are their functions in the plot? Does the plot depend on chance? If there is a subplot, is it related in theme to the main plot? Are there irrelevant scenes? What is the function of a particular scene? Is the resolution satisfactory? Is the setting functional? Does the setting help to reveal character? Or to provide atmosphere? Does it have symbolic implications?

Questions about conflict, too, may stimulate topics. What kinds of conflict are there? One character against another, one group against another, one part of a personality against another part in the same character? How is the conflict resolved? By an unambiguous triumph of one side, or by a triumph that is also in some degree a loss for the triumphant side?

In writing about drama, most of us are likely to pay attention chiefly to the dialogue, the words on the page, an understandable procedure if we regard drama as literature. Probably the great majority of essays are about the characterization of So-and-so. These essays usually look at a character's words, actions, and the setting in which he moves, as well as at what others say about him and do to him. With a play of great complexity — for example, one of Shakespeare's major plays — in a short essay you may do well to take an even smaller topic, such as Iago's use of prose (Why does he sometimes speak in prose, sometimes in verse, and what does it tell us about him?) or Hamlet's bawdy talk (Why does this prince sometimes make dirty remarks?). Even here we will not be able merely to hunt through the play looking at Iago's prose or Hamlet's bawdry; we will have to pay some attention to other uses of prose in *Othello*, or to other jesting in *Hamlet*, if we are to see the exact nature of the problem we have chosen to isolate.

But words are not, it has been argued above, the only language of drama, and a student will sometimes want to explore matters of staging. What is especially difficult, for most of us confronted with only a printed page, is to catch the full dramatic quality of a play — to read the words and also to have a sense of how they will sound in the context of gestures and a setting. We tend to read drama as literature rather than as dramatic literature, or theater. When the author is Shakespeare or Shaw, we can sometimes justly examine his works as literature, although even here we may find that things that seem flat on the page come alive in the theater. (Those unfunny clowns in Shakespeare are usually performed today by minor actors on the assumption that the parts are of no value; when cast well — in Shakespeare's day some of the best-known actors were those who played the clowns — these parts of the play take on meaning.) Of the two essays on drama given next, Kenneth Muir's is the more theatrical. Muir tries to give us a sense of contrasting characters. Joseph Wood Krutch discusses the themes of *Death of a Salesman* and of *A Streetcar Named Desire,* with a glance at the tradition of tragic literature. Both methods can be fruitful.

SAMPLE ESSAYS

Kenneth Muir's essay on "Hamlet's Foil" is about Laertes, but like any good essay on a relatively minor aspect of a play it illuminates a larger matter. Muir's title itself, like most good titles, hints at the point: Laertes is seen in relation to Hamlet. Muir proceeds chronologically, giving us a sense of Laertes's doings from beginning to end, but he does not merely tell the plot. Rather, while he seems to be telling the plot he is commenting on Laertes's personality and on Hamlet's too, usually pointing out Hamlet's superiority. (He misses a chance in the first sentence of the second paragraph, when he says that Hamlet and Laertes have both returned to Denmark for Claudius's coronation; surely Hamlet returned for his father's funeral.) This *summary* of the action — really much more than a summary because it is accompanied by thoughtful commentary — is framed by an opening paragraph that makes the basic point that Laertes is Hamlet's foil, and by a closing paragraph that draws some broad conclusions.

Muir's topic is relatively narrow, a *comparison* between two characters in one play. Joseph Wood Krutch, however, ranges over Arthur Miller's *Death of a Salesman* and Tennessee Williams's *Streetcar Named Desire,* seeking to get at the broad underlying ideas and to place them in a tradition of tragic drama. Krutch's first paragraph introduces both Arthur Miller and Tennessee Williams, and the next two paragraphs talk about both playwrights, but once the frame has been established Krutch sets out to discuss Miller first, and then Williams. The procedure is sensible, in accord with the usually sound advice, "One thing at a time." *Death of a Salesman* is not, of course, forgotten in the latter part of the essay, where it is contrasted thus in a discussion of *A Streetcar Named Desire:*

"Even more conspicuously than in the case of Arthur Miller's play, an alternate reading of the situation [in *A Streetcar*] is possible." But Miller does eventually disappear from the discussion, as he almost surely would not disappear if these pages (extracted from a book on modern drama) had originally been intended to stand by themselves.

Hamlet's Foil

Kenneth Muir

Laertes, like Fortinbras and Horatio, is Hamlet's foil; and his situation in the second half of the play is very like Hamlet's own. Hamlet has a father killed and a mother stained, and he has the task of vengeance imposed upon him by the ghost of his father; Laertes has a father killed, he is afraid that his sister will be stained, and she is driven mad — and the culprit in both cases is the avenger of the main plot.

Laertes, like Hamlet, has come to Elsinore for Claudius's coronation; he wishes to return to France, as Hamlet wishes to return to Wittenberg. The two men are on the stage at the same time, but they do not speak to each other. In the next scene Laertes warns Ophelia against Hamlet, apparently believing that he will try to seduce her. Ophelia, aware of the double standard for men and women, mildly retorts that she hopes he will practise what he preaches. Laertes, in his turn, has to listen to a sermon from his father. In the very revealing scene between Polonius and Reynaldo, it is clear that they both expect Laertes to be a bit of a rake. Polonius's method of extracting information about his son reveals a lack of trust and a coarseness of fibre in the father, and it suggests that, compared with Hamlet, Laertes is less idealistic and more easy-going in his morals.

Laertes returns from Paris on receiving the news of his father's death. Although it is obvious that he is not so devoted to his father as Hamlet was to his, he immediately takes steps to avenge Polonius's death, raises a rebellion, storms the palace, and has Claudius at his mercy. We are meant to understand that the more popular Prince could have done the same.

One has the feeling that Laertes knows exactly how he should react to every situation, according to the conventional views of the time, and that he behaves accordingly. It was the natural result of being brought up in a house where "what is done" was always more important than what ought to be done. When, for example, the Queen urges him to be calm, he bursts out:

> That drop of blood that's calm proclaims me bastard;
> Cries cuckold to my father. . . .

The rhetorical over-emphasis, apparent also in the graveyard scene, shows how even his initial sincerity becomes vulgarised. The King has no difficulty in persuading Laertes that he is not to blame for Polonius's death, and he is about to tell him of the news he is expecting from England, when letters arrive from Hamlet himself, and he knows that his plot has failed. Immediately, he begins another plot, casting Laertes as the chief actor. He approaches the subject very gingerly, but when Laertes declares that he would cut Hamlet's throat in the church, the King realises that he need not have been so careful; and we are reminded of the way Hamlet would not kill the King while he was praying. The plot requires that Hamlet shall not peruse the foils, and Claudius admits that his intended victim is "Most generous, and free from all contriving." This plot has the advantage that the Queen might suppose that the unbated foil was an accident; but Laertes nullifies this advantage, even though it makes Hamlet's death more certain, by proposing to anoint his sword with poison. To buy poison in case of need exhibits a deeper depravity in Laertes than he has yet revealed; and it is this refinement which is the cause of his own death. The King, who has used poison before, decides to provide a poisoned chalice in case Hamlet escapes the "venom'd stuck"; but, as Macbeth reminds us, "even-handed justice Commends the ingredience of our poison'd chalice To our own lips." The murderous pact is sealed by the news of Ophelia's death.

The next time we see Laertes, at the grave of his sister, Hamlet calls him with unconscious irony "a very noble youth." But he regains some sympathy by his exchange with the churlish priest, and does not entirely lose it when he leaps into the grave and asks to be buried alive. But, here again, Laertes is going beyond what he really feels, as Hamlet is quick to recognise. This is the first time that Shakespeare brings the two men face to face. Hamlet has only just learnt that Ophelia is dead, that the Queen hoped they would marry, that his killing of her father had led to her madness, and to her death; and, though he rants to outface Laertes, he convinces us that he loved her more than one brother, if not more than forty thousand. The encounter by the grave of the woman they both loved confirms

Laertes in his resolution to murder Hamlet. Yet, when it comes to the point, he is ashamed of what he is doing. In answer to Hamlet's apology that he had "shot his arrow o'er the house" and hurt his brother (as Laertes would have been if Hamlet had married Ophelia), Laertes says that although he will not be officially reconciled until his case has been considered by a tribunal, he will nevertheless receive Hamlet's "offer'd love like love, And will not wrong it."

When Laertes asks for a foil, Hamlet quibbles on the word:

I'll be your foil, Laertes; in mine ignorance
Your skill shall, like a star i' th' darkest night,
Stick fiery off indeed.

But Laertes, as we have seen, is a foil to Hamlet in another sense.

We may suppose that Laertes's guilty conscience prevents him from displaying the skill of which Lamord had spoken, for Hamlet scores the first two hits. At last, almost against his conscience, Laertes attacks Hamlet before he is ready and scores the necessary hit. Hamlet, although not realising the full extent of the treachery, disarms Laertes and secures the unbated rapier. Laertes is wounded before the King can intervene, and admits that he has met his deserts. In his dying moments he reveals the King's villainy and exchanged forgiveness with Hamlet.

Laertes is the ruthless avenger that Hamlet, with half his mind, wishes to be; and he throws into relief the hesitations and craven scruples of the hero. He is almost what some of Hamlet's critics blame him for not being, and he might almost have been put into the play to show them how wrong they were. "By the image of my cause," Hamlet told Horatio earlier, "I see the portraiture of his." It is one measure of the gulf between the two avengers that Laertes could never have used these words about Hamlet.

Moral Vision in Arthur Miller and Tennessee Williams ★
Joseph Wood Krutch

Neither Miller's *Death of a Salesman* nor Tennessee Williams's *A Streetcar Named Desire* is a cheerful play. Both end with what looks less like a tragic affirmation than like a simple confession of defeat. Neither Willy Loman nor Blanche DuBois is likely to strike the

★The essay is here retitled.

spectator as a very dignified or very noble character, and both are completely destroyed — as, say, Hamlet and Othello are not completely destroyed — when the story ends. Loman is a suicide and Blanche is being led away to a madhouse.

Obviously neither Miller nor Williams plainly commits himself as do Maxwell Anderson and O'Neill to either the form or the ethical content of classic tragedy. Moreover, neither exhibits, as plainly as it seems to me O'Neill exhibits, a determination to seek persistently for something in the universe outside man to which he can appeal and "belong." It is possible to interpret *Death of a Salesman* as brutal naturalism and *A Streetcar Named Desire* as a sort of semisurrealist version of the Strindbergian submission to destructive obsessions.

If such is a proper summation, then Miller and Williams, the two most widely discussed American playwrights of the moment, follow O'Neill and Anderson only as Sean O'Casey followed Synge. They represent, that is to say, the collapse of a reaction and illustrate, as did O'Casey, an irresistible pull in the direction of nihilism and despair.

Perhaps, indeed, that is the proper interpretation to be put upon their work and their current popularity. I am unwilling, however, to leave the subject without suggesting the possibility that there may be something to be said on the other side, and at the risk of being accused of overinterpretation, I should like to say it.

So far as *Death of a Salesman* is concerned, it seems reasonable to suppose that it is intended as something a little more than merely detached "scientific" naturalism. Most spectators, I think, assume that it embodies some "social criticism," and most, I imagine, assume that the social criticsm is of a sort by now very traditional. In this view, Willy Loman is the victim of an unjust competitive society. He was first corrupted by its false ideals and then exploited by those shrewder and more ruthless than himself. Society made him what he was, and in a better society his fate would have been a happier one. In all this there is, of course, nothing incompatible with what I have been loosely calling "modernism." The doctrine and methods of the naturalists lend themselves very readily to such "social significance."

What makes it impossible to dismiss *Death of a Salesman* as merely left-wind naturalism is the curious fact that Miller himself seems to be some sort of pluralist and that his play could be interpreted, not as a demonstration of the workings of social determinism, but as a study of the effects of moral weakness and irresponsibility. Willy Loman is a victim of society, but he is also a victim of himself. He accepted an essentially vulgar and debased as well as a false system of values. He himself says, and the audience seems to be expected to believe him, that he might have led a happy life if he had followed his own bent and become, for example, a carpenter, instead of submitting to the prejudice which makes a salesman more respectable than a man who works with his hands. His tragic guilt — and it is his, not society's — was, in this view, a very old-fashioned one. He was not true to himself. Thus the moral of the play becomes a classical moral and must necessarily presume both the existence of the classical ego and the power to make a choice.

Seen in this light, Miller becomes a moralist, at least in the sense and in much the same fashion that Ibsen was still a moralist. He has found his way back along the road which leads to determinism and the disappearance of the ego at least to the point where the dramatic disciples of Ibsen first entered upon it, and *Death of Salesman* thus becomes a qualified reaffirmation of the individual's privilege of being, within certain limits, what he chooses to be.

The case of Tennessee Williams is different but equally dubious. As I have already suggested, the most obvious interpretations put him plainly among the despairing explorers of pathological states of mind just as the obvious interpretations put Arthur Miller among the sociological naturalists. In all his most striking plays, *The Glass Menagerie, Summer and Smoke,* and *A Streetcar Named Desire,* the chief character is obsessed, and in the last two the obsession takes a sexual form. Madness seems to interest the author more than anything else, and at least in the third and most successful of the plays a quasi-expressionist technique is used for the purpose of persuading the audience to see certain of the events from the standpoint of the heroine's abnormality rather than from its own presumably objective point of view.

In each of the three plays there is another recurrent theme. Each of the heroines numbers among her obsessions the fact that she is or was "a lady." In each the ideal of respectability, the sense that her parents and her remoter ancestors lived in accordance with some code to which she herself would like to be loyal but which no one with whom she comes in contact acknowledges, is so strong as to appear crucial. In *The Glass Menagerie* the mother sees her family disintegrating because it no longer finds her dream of respectability anything but annoying. In both *Summer and Smoke* and *A Streetcar Named Desire* the heroine seems to succumb to crude sexuality because she has so fanatically refused to accept a normal life among people who appear to her as hopelessly unrefined.

Tennessee Williams grew up in the South. Like so many other

Southern writers, the existence of a decayed aristocracy was one of the inescapable facts of the society with which he was most familiar. That representatives of such a decayed aristocracy should appear in his plays may mean no more than that they were part of his experience. Nevertheless it seems to me obvious that his persistent concern with them does have a greater significance. These helpless survivors from the past, feeble and pathetic clingers to a dead tradition, take on the importance of symbols. They are not accidental facts; they mean something.

Upon the answer to the question "What do they mean? Of what are they symbols?" depends the whole meaning of the plays so far as our own special theme is concerned. Let us consider it in connection with *A Streetcar Named Desire.*

Blanche DuBois, a decayed aristocrat and a fanatical lady, has already lost her position as a schoolteacher because she is also a nymphomaniac. As the curtain rises we see her arriving alone and seeking refuge in the squalid home of her sister Stella, who has married a crude and brutal young man of foreign extraction. This sister has made what the psychologists would call "a satisfactory adjustment." She has rejected and forgotten the traditions of her past. She has accepted the frank squalor of her surroundings and the ignorant brutality of her husband, chiefly because she is reveling delightedly in his abundant and animalistic sexuality. Blanche, the nymphomaniac, is horrified by what some would call her sister's "normality." She makes a feeble and ridiculous attempt to instruct both the sister and her husband in the genteel tradition, and she is violently repelled by their contented animality. But because she can neither lead their life nor the genteel life of which she dreams, her last defenses crumble and she is led away to an asylum, certifiably insane.

Everything depends upon, as the phrase goes, which side the author is on. It appears that to many members of the audience this question presents no difficulty. They are, and they assume that the author is, on the side of the sister. She is "healthy," "adjusted," "normal." She lives in the present; she accepts things as they are; and she will never be confined to a madhouse. Her husband is crude, even somewhat brutal, but he is also virile; he is the natural man and one of literature's many kinsmen of Lady Chatterley's lover. Virility, even orgiastic virility, is the proper answer to decadence. Stella, the representative of a decayed aristocracy, is rejuvenated by a union with a representative of "the people."

Even more conspicuously than in the case of Arthur Miller's play, an alternate reading of the situation is possible. In Miller one suspects a sort of pluralism. In Williams the question presents itself instead under the form of an ambiguity.

By this I mean that while one section of the audience takes the side of Stella almost as a matter of course another section understands and shares Blanche's revulsion. Her instincts are right. She is on the side of civilization and refinement. But the age has placed her in a tragic dilemma. She looks about for a tradition according to which she may live and a civilization to which she can be loyal. She finds none. Ours is a society which has lost its shape.

Behind her lies a past which, at least in retrospect, seems to have been civilized. The culture of the Old South is dead, and she has good reason to know that it is. It is, however, the only culture about which she knows anything. The world of Stella and of her husband is a barbarism, — perhaps, as its admirers would say, a vigorous barbarism — but a barbarism nonetheless. Blanche chooses the dead past and becomes the victim of that impossible choice. But she does choose it rather than the "adjustment" of her sister. At least she has not succumbed to barbarism.

As I have said, one's choice of sides will depend largely upon one's attitude toward Stella's "virile" husband. The real question is whether he is villain or hero. If we knew which he is to his creator, we should know whether Williams should be classified among that group of "moderns" who see in a return to the primitive the possible rejuvenation of mankind or whether he belongs rather with traditionalists, such as the esoteric T. S. Eliot on the one hand or the popular Maxwell Anderson on the other, who maintain that from the past itself we shall still have to learn if we are ever to learn at all what civilization means.

I cannot tell you what Williams thinks or says. I can, after due warning, report a very significant thing which he is said to have said. At third hand I have it when queried in conversation about the meaning of *A Streetcar Named Desire,* or rather about the significance of its chief male character, he replied: "It means that if you do not watch out the apes will take over."

If this report is accurate, and I repeat that I have it only at third hand, the question is answered. Williams, despite all the violence of his plays, despite what sometimes looks very much like nihilism, is really on the side of what modernists would call the Past rather than the Future — which means, of course, on the side of those who believe that the future, if there is to be any civilized future, will be less new than most modern dramatists from Ibsen on have professed to believe.

6

Writing about Poetry

First, a warning: Because this chapter assumes that the reader may already be familiar with the explication of a poem given on pp. 11–12, it is in no hurry to get down to a discussion of writing about poetry. Before it deals directly with that topic, it talks about reading and experiencing poetry, and it offers definitions of terms used in writing about poetry. Therefore, the reader who wants some quick advice at the outset may wish to begin by jumping to the "Concluding Remarks" near the end of the chapter (pp. 221–224).

HARMONY AND MIMICRY

Aristotle suggested that the arts arise out of two impulses: the impulse for harmony and the impulse to imitate. Let us take these one at a time.

We are all familiar with the desire to make a pattern. We straighten pictures on the walls (we like parallel lines), and we arrange the silverware on the table in a way that pleases. (Even chimpanzees are said to show what is called an instinct for closure. If they are given paint and a brush and a paper on which two-thirds of a circle has been painted, they will sometimes complete the circle.) We make patterns too out of sounds; if we forget a line of a song, we do not leave an unpleasant blank, but we feel compelled to fill it out by humming or by uttering nonsense syllables such as *da da da da da*. Sometimes the sounds make a sort of sense, but the sense scarcely seems important. The following lines have pleased for generations, presumably because of their catchiness rather than because of any message.

> Pease-porridge hot,
>   Pease-porridge cold,
> Pease-porridge in the pot
>   Nine days old.

Something about meter, rhythm, and rhyme will be said below, but for the moment we can say that one source of pleasure in poetry is afforded by its harmonious pattern of sounds.

The meaning affords a second source of pleasure. Poetry is sound and sense, and in this connection we may briefly consider Aristotle's statement that the second psychological impulse behind the arts is the impulse to imitate. Children mimicking their parents or playing cops and robbers provide examples of the impulse to imitate. And it is easy to see that a landscape painting is a sort of imitation (in pigment) of a landscape; a piece of sculpture is an imitation (in wood or stone) of, say, Moses; a historical novel is an imitation (in words) of some aspect of a period of time; a play is an imitation (in words and gestures) of the doings of people. Because in ordinary language, however, "imitation" has a pejorative overtone, the idea may become more acceptable if we substitute "representation" or "re-creation." Now, this representation is not an exact duplicate; as the previous chapter mentioned, no one believes that *Julius Caesar* is a mirror image of what happened in Rome two thousand years ago. Shakespeare took some hints from history (a leader assassinated), but he invented speeches and even some characters. And his *Julius Caesar* offers itself as a coherent and meaningful work; Caesar may never have said this or done that, but Shakespeare's words combine to give us an imitation that helps us to see the invisible relationships in our own world, somewhat as a mimic of X suddenly — by heightening certain features of X's gestures and intonations — makes us see and hear things we had not before noticed in X. Through the imitation, we perceive, let us say, the insecurity that underlies X's words and gestures. But this is to speak of drama and impersonation, not specifically of poetry. In what sense is nondramatic poetry an imitation? And let us make the problem more difficult by eliminating such narratives as *The Odyssey* and *Paradise Lost,* for clearly they imitate — that is, they present in words — actions that allegedly happened long ago. Let us talk at first about what is ordinarily called lyric poetry.

Varieties of Imitation

The **lyric** commonly presents a speaker expressing an emotion. The name suggests that it was once a song to be accompanied by a lyre, and although the genre now includes much that cannot possibly be sung, let us begin with the singable.

> Should auld acquaintance be forgot,
>   And never brought to mind?
> Should auld acquaintance be forgot,
>   And auld lang syne!   4
>
>   For auld land syne, my jo,
>   For auld lang syne,
>   We'll tak a cup o' kindness yet
>   For auld lang syne.   8
>
> And surely ye'll be your pint-stowp!°   *pay for your pint-cup*
>   And surely I'll be mine!
> And we'll tak a cup o' kindness yet
>   For auld lang syne.   12
>
> We twa hae run about the braes,°   *slopes*
>   And pu'd the gowans° fine;   *daisies*
> But we've wander'd mony a weary fitt
>   Sin auld lang syne.   16
>
> We twa hae paidl'd i' the burn,°   *brook*
>   From morning sun till dine;°   *dinner, noon*
> But seas between us braid hae roar'd,
>   Sin auld lang syne.   20
>
> And there's a hand, my trusty fiere!°   *friend*
>   And gie's a hand o'thine!
> And we'll tak a right guid-willie-waught,°   *hearty swig*
>   For auld lang syne.   24
>
>   Robert Burns, "Auld Lang Syne"

It is not stretching a point to say that Burns's song imitates, or re-creates, a state that we all know in some degree. There are moments of conviviality that are suffused with a sense of the irrevocable past. This last sentence is an inept summary of the poem, but it affords a prologue to a simple question that may clarify the point: Do we not — and do not innumerable people who sing

"Auld Lang Syne" on New Year's Eve — feel that Burns has perfectly caught, or imitated, a state of mind? Is not "Auld Lang Syne" an embodiment or imitation of a human experience? We value its sound (we may not even know the meanings of some of the words), and we also value its sense, the representation of a moment of human behavior. We hear a voice that is not at all literally like any voice we have ever heard (no one talks in rhymes) but that nevertheless makes us say, "Yes, I understand that experience. I see what that state of mind is."

Almost any good blues song — maybe "St. Louis Woman," or "St. James Infirmary" — can similarly illustrate the point that a lyric is a highly artificial (and artful) expression that precisely communicates to us a particular state of mind. It is valuable not only to the singer, who may gain some relief from sorrow by singing about it, but to the hearer, who at least for the moment feels that a state of mind is being revealed with a clarity almost never encountered in ordinary talk.

Now here is another voice, very far from a singing one. The speaker is addressing his friend Henry St. John (pronounced "Sin-jun").

> Awake, my St. John! leave all meaner things
> To low ambition, and the pride of kings.
> Let us (since life can little more supply
> Than just to look about us and to die)
> Expatiate free o'er all this scene of Man;   5
> A mighty maze! but not without a plan;
> A wild, where weeds and flowers promiscuous shoot,
> Or garden, tempting with forbidden fruit.
> Together let us beat this ample field,
> Try what the open, what the covert yield;   10
> The latent tracts, the giddy heights, explore
> Of all who blindly creep, or sightless soar;
> Eye nature's walks, shoot folly as it flies,
> And catch the manners living as they rise;
> Laugh where we must, be candid where we can,   15
> But vindicate the ways of God to man.

> Alexander Pope, from *An Essay on Man*

This poem proceeds for hundreds of lines, and we may not feel that Pope shows the justice of the ways of God to man, but again we catch a human voice. It begins authoritatively ("Awake") and yet playfully (low things, it says, are the concern of kings). Then, in the third and fourth lines, a touch — but a highly controlled touch — of pathos is introduced in the parenthetic reference to the brevity of man's life. Next, the speaker suggests that the world is a sort of large estate harboring all sorts of creatures. He almost seems supercilious in his reference to shooting down folly (that is, some people are compared to stupid game birds), but his good-natured "Laugh where we must, be candid [that is, generous] where we can" reminds us of the traditional and reasonable view that wrongdoing appears funny (because it is self-defeating) to the good man. We continue to listen with interest to this dramatization of the mind of a speaker who, in the last line of this verse paragraph, reaffirms his high purpose with an echo from Milton's *Paradise Lost*. (Milton said he sought to "justify the ways of God to man.") What we have is a man talking easily and intimately about something important. We read Pope's *Essay on Man,* looking out both for the "ideas" he sets forth, which may or may not prove convincing, and for the voice or mind or personality, that is, for an imitation of a man thinking.

The Speaker and the Poet

The **voice,** or **mask,** or **persona** (Latin for "mask") that speaks the poem is not identical with the poet who writes it. The author counterfeits the speech of a person in a particular situation. Robert Browning invented a Renaissance duke who speaks "My Last Duchess"; Robert Frost in "Stopping by Woods on a Snowy Evening" invented the speech of a man who, sitting in a horse-drawn sleigh, is surveying woods that are "lovely, dark and deep."

The speaker's voice, of course, often has the ring of the author's own voice, and to make a distinction between speaker and author may at times seem perverse. Much contemporary American poetry is highly autobiographical: Robert Lowell, Sylvia Plath, and Anne Sexton, for instance, have not hesitated to draw upon their own experiences, writing about matters usually considered private. Older poetry, too, is often autobiographical. Robert Burns sometimes lets us know that the poem is spoken by "Rob"; he may address his wife by name; beneath the title "To a Mouse" he writes, "On Turning Up Her Nest with the Plow, November, 1785," and beneath the title "To a Mountain Daisy" he writes, "On Turning One Down with the Plow in April, 1786." Still, even in these allegedly autobiographical poems, it may be convenient to distinguish between author and speaker; the speaker is Burns the lover, or Burns the meditative man, or Burns the compassionate man, not simply Robert Burns the poet. And even "confessional poets," such as Lowell, Plath, and Sexton choose a particular voice — though a voice apparently very near to their own when their singing robes are off.

THE LANGUAGE OF POETRY

Diction and Tone

From the whole of language, one consciously or unconsciously selects certain words and grammatical constructions; this selection constitutes one's **diction.** It is partly by the diction that we come to know the speaker of a poem. "Auld" and "twa" tell us that the speaker of "Auld Lang Syne" is a Scot. In the passage from Pope's *Essay on Man,* "expatiate," "promiscuous," and "vindicate" tell us that the speaker is an educated man. Of course, some words are used in both poems: "my," "to," "and." The fact remains, however, that although a large part of language is shared by all speakers, some parts of language are used only by certain speakers.

Like some words, some grammatical constructions are used only by certain kinds of speakers. Consider these two passages:

> In Adam's fall
> We sinnèd all.
>
> from *The New England Primer*

> Of Man's first disobedience, and the fruit
> Of that forbidden tree whose mortal taste
> Brought death into the World, and all our woe,
> With loss of Eden, till one greater Man
> Restore us, and regain the blissful seat,
> Sing, Heavenly Muse, that, on the secret top
> Of Oreb, or of Sinai, didst inspire

4

That shepherd who first taught the chosen seed   8
In the beginning how the heavens and earth
Rose out of Chaos. . . .

    Milton, from *Paradise Lost*

There is an enormous difference in the diction of these two passages. Milton, speaking as an inspired poet who regards his theme as "a great argument," appropriately uses words and grammatical constructions somewhat removed from common life. Hence, while the anonymous author of the primer speaks directly of "Adam's fall," Milton speaks allusively of the fall, calling it "Man's first disobedience." Milton's sentence is nothing that any Englishman ever said in conversation; its genitive or possessive beginning ("Of Man's"), its length (the sentence continues for six lines beyond the quoted passage), and its postponement of the main verb until the sixth line mark it as the utterance of a poet working in the tradition of Latin poetry. The primer's statement, by its choice of words as well as by its brevity, suggests a far less sophisticated speaker.

    The voice in a poem is established not only by broad strokes but by such details as **alliteration** (repetition of initial consonants), **assonance** (repetition of vowel-sounds), and rhyme. (More will be said about rhyme later.) F. W. Bateson, in *English Poetry,* aptly notes that the role that alliteration plays in reinforcing the contemptuous tone we hear in "Die and endow a college or a cat," a line from Pope's "Epistle to Bathurst." Bateson points out that "the *d*'s hint that there is a subtle identity in the dying and the endowing (the only interest that the world takes in this particular death is in the testamentary endowments), and the *c*'s point the contrast between founding colleges and financing cats' homes."

    A speaker (or voice, to use the previous terminology) has attitudes toward himself, his subject, and his audience, and (consciously or unconsciously) he chooses his words, pitch, and modulation accordingly; all these add up to his **tone.** In written literature, tone must be detected without the aid of the ear, though it's a good idea to read poetry aloud, trying to find the appropriate tone of voice. That is, the reader must understand by the selection and sequence of words the way (whether playfully, angrily, confidentially, ironically, or whatever) in which they are meant to be heard. The reader must catch what Frost calls "the speaking tone of voice somehow entangled in the words and fastened to the page for the ear of the imagination."★

Paraphrase and Explication

Our interest in the shifting tones in the voice that speaks the words should not, of course, cause us to neglect the words themselves, the gist of the idea expressed. Take the first two lines of a passage from Pope's *Essay on Man,* already quoted on p. 198:

> Awake, my St. John! leave all meaner things
> To low ambition, and the pride of kings.

If we *paraphrase* (reword) these two lines we get something like this: "Wake up, my friend St. John ["my" implies intimacy], leave low things to such lowly people as are ambitious and [equally low] to arrogant monarchs." A paraphrase at least has the virtue of making us look hard at all the words. We have just seen that in paraphrasing Pope, we become aware that "my" in the first line reveals the intimacy which Pope feels toward St. John. If you paraphrase the next six lines of Pope's *Essay,* and then closely compare your paraphrase with Pope's words, you are doing some of the homework that precedes writing an **explication** (see pp. 11–13) of the lines. To take the most obvious example: You will probably be able to see the implication that is in Pope's "garden, tempting with forbidden fruit." You may need a dictionary to see the multiple meanings in "Expatiate" (to speak at length, *and* to wander about) and "promiscuous" (consisting of unrelated individuals, *and* indiscriminate). But the point of a paraphrase is not to enlarge your vocabulary; it is an exercise designed to help you understand at least the surface meaning, and it will usually help you to understand at least some of the implicit meaning. Furthermore, a paraphrase makes you see that the poet's words — if the poem is a good one — are exactly right, better than the words you might substitute. It becomes clear that the thing said in the poem —

★This discussion concentrates on the speaker's tone. But sometimes one can also talk of the author's tone, that is, of the author's attitude toward the invented speaker. The speaker's tone might, for example, be angry, but the author's tone (as detected by the reader) might be humorous.

not only the "idea" expressed but the precise tone with which it is expressed — is a sharply defined experience.

The following is an anonymous quatrain, written in England about 1500.

> Western wind, when wilt thou blow,
>   The small rain down can rain?
> Christ, if my love were in my arms,
>   And I in my bed again!

This poem defies paraphrase, not because it is obscure or non-sensical, but because the surface statement is so lucid. The most one can do in paraphrasing the first line is to say something like "O west wind [the opening is vocative, the wind is being addressed], when will you come?" About the only distortion from ordinary language in the poem is "small rain," where we would normally speak of the "light rain" or "gentle rain." But an explication will point out that much more is going on in the poem than a word-for-word substitution can indicate. The first two lines suggest that the speaker longs for the spring — the time of light rain and the time when the west wind (warmed by the Gulf Stream) blows in England. In the next two lines he expresses his unhappiness that he is not with his beloved. What is the connection between the first two and the last two lines? Among the answers are these: spring is commonly associated with lovers; spring is a time of warmth and revitalization, and love is associated with warmth and with new birth. The first two lines implicitly tell us it is winter, and the lover in effect compares the world's wintry state with his own wintriness (sense of coldness, barrenness) caused by the absence of his beloved. "Christ" in the third line may be both an agonized expletive and an invocation: he calls on Christ, who Himself was reborn in the spring (the Resurrection), and who is the giver of new life to those who sense the emptiness of their present lives. The previous sentences are tiresomely wordy (about a hundred words in place of the poem's twenty-six), but perhaps they help to illuminate the highly complex experience that we overhear in these four lines. Again, we are overhearing or witnessing an experience, not receiving an edifying message. The poem does not offer any answers to the questions: How shall I live? How can I regain the lover I have lost? It does, however, in memorable words, so perfectly catch a human experience that we feel the experience is available for us to look at, in contrast to our own daily experiences, which are so much a welter that we can scarcely know them.

A Sample Explication

An explication of a poem was given on pp. 202–204; here is another poem (published in 1945), with a student's explication. A reminder: Explication is a study of the parts of a work and their relation to the whole. It normally ignores biographical matters and the historical context — though it may unobtrusively make use of such things, as in the reference below to World War II.

> From my mother's sleep I fell into the State,
> And I hunched in its belly till my wet fur froze.
> Six miles from earth, loosed from its dream of life,
> I woke to black flak and the nightmare fighters.
> When I died they washed me out of the turret with a hose.
>
> Randall Jarrell, "The Death of the Ball Turret Gunner"

The student's explication runs thus:

Randall Jarrell's ''The Death of the Ball

Turret Gunner''

Reading the first line aloud, one pauses slightly after ''sleep,'' dividing the line in half. The halves make a sharp contrast. The point of transition in this line is ''I fell,'' a helpless movement from the mother to the State, from sleep to the State. The mother and the State make an evident contrast, and so do ''sleep'' and ''the State,'' which resemble each other in their first sound and in their position at the end of a half-line but which have such different associations, for sleep is comforting and the State is associated with totalitarianism. (''The country'' or ''the land'' might be comforting and nourishing, but ''the State'' has no such warm suggestions.) We will soon see in the poem that life in the ''belly'' of the State is mindless and cold, a death-like life which ends with a sudden and terrible death. A mother, even in her ''sleep,'' naturally protects and nourishes the child in her warm womb; the State unnaturally cramps the man in its icy belly. He ''hunched in its belly'' until his ''wet fur froze.'' We gather from the title that ''its'' refers not only to the State but also to the airplane in whose womblike ball turret he led his confined existence and died. Given the title, the fur probably literally refers to the fur collar of the jackets that fliers wore in World War II, and it also suggests the animal-like existence he led while confined by this unfeeling foster parent, the State-airplane. His unnatural existence is further emphasized by the fact that, in the airplane, he was ''Six miles from earth.'' From such an existence, far from the ''dream of life'' that people hope for, and still hunched in the turret like a baby in the womb, he was born again, that is, he awoke to (or became aware of) not a rich fulfillment of the dream but a horrible reality that is like a nightmare. ''Woke to black flak'' imitates, in its rattling *k*'s at the ends of words, the sound of the gunfire that simultaneously awakened and killed him. His awakening or birth is to a nightmarish reality and death. It is not surprising,

but it is certainly horrifying, that in this world of
an impersonal State that numbs and destroys life, his
body is flushed out of the turret with a hose. This is
the third horrible release: the first was from the
mother into the State; the second was from the belly
of the State into the belly of the airplane; and now
in shreds from the belly of the airplane into nothing.
That this life-history is told flatly, with no note of
protest, of course increases the horror. The simplicity of the last line more effectively brings out the
horror of the experience than an anguished cry or an
angry protest could do.

A suggestion: before setting out to write an explication, type the poem with double-spacing, or write it out with ample space between the lines. Typing or writing the poem will in itself help you to get to know it, and the sheet will then be useful as a worksheet on which you can draw lines linking repeated words or sounds, and make other annotations.

Figurative Language

Robert Frost has said, "Poetry provides the one permissible way of saying one thing and meaning another." This, of course, is an exaggeration, but it shrewdly suggests the importance of **figurative language** — saying one thing in terms of something else. Words have their literal meaning, but they can also be used so that something other than the literal meaning is implied. "My love is a rose" is, literally, nonsense, for she is not a five-petaled, many-stamened plant with a spiny stem. But the suggestions of "rose" include "delicate beauty," "soft," "perfumed," and thus the word "rose" can be meaningfully applied — figuratively rather than literally — to "my love." The girl is fragrant; her skin is perhaps like a rose in texture and (in some measure) color, she will not keep her beauty long. The poet, that is, has communicated a perception very precisely. His discovery is not world-shaking; it is less important than the discovery of America or the discovery that the meek are blessed, but is *is* a discovery and it offers that "clarification" and "momentary stay against confusion" that Frost spoke of.

People who write about poetry have found it convenient to name the various kinds of figurative language. Just as the student of geology employs special terms, such as "kames" and "eskers," the student of literature employs special terms to name things as accurately as possible. The next few pages give the most common terms.

In a **simile** items from different classes are explicitly compared by a connective such as "like," "as," or "than," or by a verb such as "appears" or "seems." (If the objects compared are from the same class, for example, "New York is like London," no simile is present.)

> Float like a butterfly, sting like a bee.
>
> > Muhammad Ali
>
> It is a beauteous evening, calm and free.
> The holy time is quiet as a Nun,
> Breathless with adoration.
>
> > Wordsworth
>
> How sharper than a serpent's tooth it is
> To have a thankless child.
>
> > Shakespeare
>
> Seems he a dove? His feathers are but borrowed.
>
> > Shakespeare

A **metaphor** asserts the identity, without a connective such as "like" or a verb such as "appears," of terms that are literally incompatible.

> She is the rose, the glory of the day.
>
> > Spenser
>
> Yes! it's true all my visions
> have come home to roost at last.
>
> > Brautigan

Notice how in the last example only one of the terms ("visions") is stated; the other ("chickens") is implied in "have come home to roost." In the following poem, Keats's excitement on reading Chapman's translation of Homer is communicated first through a metaphor and then through a simile.

> Much have I traveled in the realms of gold,
> And many goodly states and kingdoms seen;
> Round many western islands have I been
> Which bards in fealty to Apollo hold.
> Oft of one wide expanse have I been told.   5
> That deep-browed Homer ruled as his demesne;
> Yet did I never breathe its pure serene
> Till I heard Chapman speak out loud and bold:
>
> Then felt I like some watcher of the skies
> When a new planet swims into his ken;   10
> Or like stout Cortez when with eagle eyes
> He stared at the Pacific — and all his men
> Looked at each other with a wild surmise —
> Silent, upon a peak in Darien.
>
>> John Keats, "On First Looking into
>> Chapman's Homer"

We might pause for a moment to take a closer look at Keats's poem. If you write an essay on the figurative language in this sonnet, you will probably discuss the figure involved in asserting that reading is a sort of traveling (it brings us to unfamiliar worlds), and especially that reading brings us to realms of gold. Presumably the experience of reading is valuable. "Realms of gold" not only continues and modifies the idea of reading as travel, but in its evocation of El Dorado (an imaginary country in South America, thought to be rich in gold and therefore the object of search by Spanish explorers of the Renaissance) it introduces a suggestion of the Renaissance appropriate to a poem about a Renaissance translation of Homer. The figure of traveling is amplified in the next few lines, which assert that the "goodly states and kingdoms" and "western islands" are ruled by poets who owe allegiance to a higher authority, Apollo. The beginning of the second sentence (line 5) enlarges this already spacious area with its reference to "one wise expanse," and the ruler of this area (unlike the other rulers) is given the dignity of being named. He is Homer, "deep-browed," "deep" suggesting not only his high, or perhaps furrowed, forehead but the profundity of the thoughts behind the forehead. The speaker continues the idea of books as remote places, but now he also seems to think of this place as more than a rich area; instead of merely saying that until he read Chapman's translation he had not "seen" it (as in line 2) or "been" there (line 3), he says he never breathed its air. That is, the preciousness is not material but ethereal, not gold but something far more exhilarating and essential. This reference to air leads easily to the next dominant image, that of the explorer of the illimitable skies (so vast is Homer's world) rather than of the land and sea. But the explorer of the skies is conceived as watching an *oceanic* sky. In hindsight we can see that the link was perhaps forged earlier in line 7, with "serene" (a vast expanse of air *or* water); in any case, there is an unforgettable rightness in the description of the suddenly discovered planet as something that seems to "swim" into one's ken. After this climactic discovery we return to the Renaissance Spanish explorers (though, in fact, Balboa, and not Cortez, was the discoverer of the Pacific) by means of a simile that compares the speaker's rapture with Cortez's as he gazed at the expanse before him. The writer of an essay on the figurative language in a poem should, in short, try to call attention to the aptness (or ineptness) of the figures and to the connecting threads that make a meaningful pattern.

Two types of metaphor deserve special mention. In **synecdoche** the whole is replaced by the part, or the part by the whole. For example, "bread," in "Give us this day our daily bread," replaces all sorts of food. In **metonymy** something is named that replaces something closely related to it. For example, James Shirley names certain objects, using them to replace social classes to which they are related:

> Scepter and crown must tumble down
> And in the dust be equal made
> With the poor crooked scythe and spade.

The attribution of human feelings or characteristics to abstractions or to inanimate objects is called **personification.**

> The fixed bells rang, their voices
> came like boats over the oil-slicks.
>
> Olson

Olson attributes voices to bells. Of all figures, personification most surely gives to airy nothings a local habitation and a name:

> There's Wrath who has learnt every trick of guerilla warfare,
> The shamming dead, the night-raid, the feinted retreat.
>
> Auden

> Hope, thou bold taster of delight.
>
> Crashaw

Crashaw's personification, "Hope, thou bold taster of delight," is also an example of the figure called **apostrophe,** an address to a person or thing not literally listening. Wordsworth begins a sonnet by apostrophizing Milton:

> Milton, thou shouldst be living at this hour,

and Ginsberg apostrophizes "gusts of wet air":

> Fall on the ground, O great Wetness.

What conclusions can we draw about figurative language? First, figurative language, with its literally incompatible terms, forces the reader to attend to the connotations (suggestions, associations) rather than to the denotations (dictionary definitions) of one of the terms. Second, although figurative language is said to differ from ordinary discourse, it is found in ordinary discourse as well as in literature. "It rained cats and dogs," "War is hell," "Don't be a pig," "Mr. Know-all," and other tired figures are part of our daily utterances. But through repeated use, these, and most of the figures we use, have lost whatever impact they once had and are only a shade removed from expressions which, though once figurative, have become literal: the *eye* of a needle, a *branch* office, the *face* of a clock. Third, good figurative language is usually concrete, condensed, and interesting. The concreteness lends precision and vividness; when Keats writes that he felt "like some watcher of the skies / When a new planet swims into his ken," he more sharply characterizes his feelings than if he had said, "I felt excited." His simile isolates for us a precise kind of excitement, and the metaphoric "swims" vividly brings up the oceanic aspect of the sky. The effect of the second of these three qualities, condensation, can be seen by attempting to paraphrase some of the figures. A paraphrase will commonly use more words than the original, and it will have less impact — as the gradual coming of night usually has less impact on us than a sudden darkening of the sky, or as a prolonged push has less impact than a sudden blow. The third quality, interest, is largely dependent on the previous two: the successful figure often makes us open our eyes wider and take notice. Keats's "deep-browed Homer" arouses our interest in Homer as "thoughtful Homer" or "meditative Homer" does not. Similarly, when W. B. Yeats says:

> An aged man is but a paltry thing,
> A tattered coat upon a stick, unless
> Soul clap its hands and sing, and louder sing
> For every tatter in its mortal dress,

the metaphoric identification of an old man with a scarecrow jolts us out of all our usual unthinking attitudes about old men as kind, happy folk who are content to have passed from youth into age.

Imagery and Symbolism

When we read "rose," we may more or less call to mind a picture of a rose, or perhaps we are reminded of the odor or texture of a rose. Whatever in a poem appeals to any of our senses (including sensations of heat as well as of sight, smell, taste, touch, sound) is an image. In short, images are the sensory content of a work, whether literal or figurative. When a poet says "My rose," and he is speaking about a rose, we have no figure of speech — though we still have an image. If, however, "My rose" is a shortened form of "My love is a rose," some would say that he is using a metaphor, but others would say that because the first term is omitted ("My love is"), the rose is a **symbol.** A poem about the transience of a rose might compel the reader to feel that the transience of female beauty is the larger theme even though it is never explicitly stated.

Some symbols are **conventional symbols** — people have agreed to accept them as standing for something other than their literal meanings: a poem about the cross would probably be about Christianity; similarly, the rose has long been a symbol for love. In Virginia Woolf's novel *Mrs. Dalloway,* the husband communicates his love by proffering this conventional symbol: "He was holding out flowers — roses, red and white roses. (But he could not bring himself to say he loved her; not in so many words.)" Objects that are not conventional symbols, however, may also give rise to rich, multiple, indefinable associations. The following poem uses the traditional symbol of the rose, but uses it in a nontraditional way:

> O rose, thou art sick!
> The invisible worm
> That flies in the night,
> In the howling storm,
>
> Has found out thy bed
> Of crimson joy,
> And his dark secret love
> Does thy life destroy.
>
> William Blake, "The Sick Rose"

One might perhaps argue that the worm is "invisible" (line 2) merely because it is hidden within the rose, but an "invisible worm / That flies in the night" is more than a long, slender, soft-bodied, creeping animal; and a rose that has, or is, a "bed / Of crimson joy" is more than a gardener's rose. Blake's worm and rose suggest things beyond themselves — a stranger, more vibrant world than the world we are usually aware of. One finds oneself half thinking, for example, that the worm is male, the rose female, and the poem is about the violation of virginity. Or that the poem is about the destruction of beauty: woman's beauty, rooted in joy, is destroyed by a power that feeds on her. But these interpretations are not fully satisfying: the poem presents a worm and a rose, and yet it is not merely about a worm and a rose. These objects resonate, stimulating our thoughts toward something else, but the something else is elusive, whereas it is not elusive in Burns's "My love is like a red, red rose."

A symbol, then, is an image so loaded with significance that it is not simply literal, and it does not simply stand for something else; it is both itself *and* something else that it richly suggests, a kind of manifestation of something too complex or too elusive to be otherwise revealed. Blake's poem is about a blighted rose and at the same time about much more. In a symbol, as Thomas Carlyle wrote, "the Infinite is made to blend with the Finite, to stand visible, and as it were, attainable there."

Sample Essay on the Speaker in a Poem

Here is a student's essay on Blake's "The Sick Rose" (p. 212), relating the symbolism to the speaker and audience.

Title announces topic.

Speaker and Audience in ''The Sick Rose''

The essayist advances by clarifying the title of the essay.

Blake's ''The Sick Rose'' seems, on first reading, to be addressed to a rose, but despite ''O rose'' of the first line, further reading reveals two other audiences: the speaker, if he is not a madman, is addressing a special kind of rose, a rose that can listen, and, second, he is addressing himself. Another way of putting these points is to say that the rose is to some extent a woman, and second, it is to some extent any person, male or female, here including the speaker.

The first point, that the rose is no ordinary rose, is evident from the fact that it is

Useful brief quotations.

attacked by an ''invisible worm / That flies in the night'' and that feels a ''dark secret love'' for the rose. Of course the worm might be invisible merely because it is concealed within the rose, and the ''bed'' of line 5 might simply be a flower bed, but other words,

Evidence supports the assertion.

such as ''joy'' (line 6) and ''love'' (line 7) serve to bring the rose and the worm close to the human world. The flower bed thus suggests

The generalization is based on evidence.

a bed of love, or rather (since the love is specifically said to be ''dark'' and ''se-

cret'' and destructive) a bed of lust. The
worm suggests the destructive male, partly because it is phallic, partly perhaps because
the biblical tradition holds that the serpent
in the garden is male, and mostly because the
worm may reasonably be conceived of as different in sex from the flower, the rose being
conventionally female.

Brief summary of point thus far.

Thus far the poem would seem, then, to be
addressed to a woman, or at least to a rose
that partakes of human female characteristics.

The transitional word "But" tel . readers there will now be a twist in the argument.

But repeated rereading suggests that the poet
is not so much addressing something or someone
in front of him, but is thinking aloud. Despite ''O rose,'' he is in good measure addressing himself, meditating upon a fact of
life. Beauty and love are destroyed in the
''night'' and ''howling storm'' by furtive
lust (''dark secret love''). The first step
beyond seeing the rose and worm as merely a
rose and a worm is to see them as also a woman
and a man; the next step is to see them as the
beauty that anyone, regardless of gender, may
have, and the destructiveness that is similarly beyond gender. Because the speaker is
clearly so sympathetic to the object he addresses that he is virtually soliloquizing, it
is reasonable to say that the speaker and his
audience and his subject are one. He may reasonably be thought of as thinking about a pro-

cess that is going on inside of himself, as well as about some external destruction of feminine beauty by male lust.

Faint apology, usually to be avoided in a concluding paragraph, but tactful here.

The previous sentences, with their abstractions, may seem far from the poem, and indeed their language and the language of the poem are utterly different. But the language of the poem sets up vibrations or emanations that may be legitimately pursued; to say that the poem starts with a rose and a worm and leads us back to the speaker and even to ourselves is scarcely an exaggeration.

This essay on symbolism is temperate, but essays on symbolism often have a way of seeming far-fetched. As a rough rule of thumb, beware of saying X equals, or symbolizes, Y, unless there are rather evident and insistent connections between X and Y. One reference to the darkness of night does not justify talking about the night as symbolic of evil; one reference to water does not justify talking about water as symbolic of life-giving forces. But a pattern of contrasting references to day and night, or to water versus an arid landscape, calls for such interpretations. Similarly, in "Stopping by Woods on a Snowy Evening," Robert Frost's *repetition* of "miles to go before I sleep" forces us to give the words more than their usual significance, transforms "miles" and "sleep" into symbols.

Remember, too, that although some things by their nature are likely to be symbolic of certain qualities (for example, railroad trains of unfeeling industrialism, stars of spiritual or intellectual illumination, water of life), we should not respond automatically to these things as we do to red and green traffic lights. The poet shapes our responses, and an automatic response may preclude a more appropriate response. In Matthew Arnold's "To Marguerite — Continued," the sea plays an important role. The poem begins "Yes! in the sea of life enisled," and it ends with a reference to "The unplumbed, salt, estranging sea." In this poem Arnold conceives of humans as islands, creatures tragically *separated* by water. The student who writes about the life-giving symbol of water in this poem ignores the fact that Arnold specifies that it estranges and is salty, that is, undrinkable. Such a reading will distort the poem more than a reading that sees the water only as water rather than emblematic of the gulfs (figurative language keeps slipping in, even in analysis) that separate us. Mary McCarthy's comments on symbolism in fiction (p. 120) are relevant here. Keep in mind the fact that in literature things *are;* they may also *represent,* but don't lose sight of what they are.

STRUCTURE

Repetitive

The arrangement of the parts, the manner of organization of the entire poem, is its **structure.** Every poem has its own structure, but if we stand back from a given poem we may see that the structure is one of three common sorts: repetitive, narrative, or logical. **Repetitive structure** is especially common in lyrics that are sung, where a single state of mind is repeated from stanza to stanza so that the stanzas are pretty much interchangeable As we read through "Auld Lang Syne," for instance, we get reaffirmation rather than progression. Here is a passage from Whitman's "By Blue Ontario's Shore" that similarly has a repetitive structure:

> I will confront these shows of the day and night,
> I will know if I am to be less than they,
> I will see if I am not as majestic as they,
> I will see if I am not as subtle and real as they,
> I will see if I am to be less generous than they.

Narrative

In a poem with a **narrative structure** (we are not talking about "narrative poems," poems that tell a story, such as *The Odyssey* or *The Rime of the Ancient Mariner,* but about a kind of lyric poem) there is a sense of advance. Blake's "The Sick Rose" (p. 212) is an example. What comes later in the poem could not come earlier. The poem seems to get somewhere, to settle down to an end. A lyric in which the speaker at first grieves and then derives some comfort from the thought that at least he was once in love similarly has a narrative structure. Here is a short but detailed examination by F. W. Bateson of a poem with narrative structure, Wordsworth's "A slumber did my spirit seal." Although "She" in line 3 is unnamed, it is customary to call her Lucy because that name is given in some other poems associated with this one in Wordsworth's *Lyrical Ballads*. The poem consists of two quatrains:

> A slumber did my spirit seal;
>   I had no human fears:
> She seemed a thing that could not feel
>   The touch of earthly years.
>
> No motion has she now, no force;
>   She neither hears nor sees;
> Rolled round in earth's diurnal course,
>   With rocks, and stones, and trees.

Bateson writes:

> The structural basis of the poem is clearly the contrast between the two verses. Verse one deals with the past (there are no less than four verbs in a past tense — *did, had, seemed, could*). Lucy had been such a vital person that the possibility of her growing old or dying had not crossed Wordsworth's mind. Verse two concerns the present (in addition to the *now* in the first line there are three main verbs in the present tense — *has, hears, sees*), Lucy is dead. The invulnerable Ariel-like creature is now as lifeless and immobile as rocks and stones. And the contrast is emphasized by the repetition of *earth*: Lucy, who had seemed immune from the passage of *earthly years,* must now submit to *earth's diurnal course.* So far from escaping the *touch* of years she is now undergoing a daily contact with the earth. The use of the solemn Latinism *diurnal,* the only three-syllable word in this mainly monosyllabic poem, completes the contrast. But the final impression the poem leaves is not of two contrasting moods, but of a single mood mounting to a climax in the pantheistic magnificence of the last two lines. How then is the surface conflict reconciled? The metre certainly makes its contribution. The identity of

the metrical pattern in the two verses — which is paralleled by the virtual identity of the word-order (l. 5 repeats l. 1, abstract noun + verb + pronoun + abstract noun, l. 6 repeats l. 2, and l. 8 and l. 4 both have nouns but no verb) — suggests an underlying identity of mood. The gap between the two verses is also bridged by the negatives. There are no less than six negatives in the first six lines. Indeed, as the first line really means "I was not mentally awake," all the sentences are essentially negative propositions, until we reach the tremendous positive of the last two lines. Finally, the description of the living Lucy as a mere *thing* has prepared the transition to the dead Lucy who is passively *rolled*. The rhymes have no special significance, as far as I can see, but the alliterations should not be overlooked. The initial *s*'s in l. 1 do not seem to me of much interest (it is much the weakest line in the poem), though they may ᴕe intentional, but the *r*'s in ll. 7–8 are masterly. There are no less than three initial *r*'s and four internal *r*'s in the last twelve words[1]; and they provide a kind of cohesive cement to the lines. The implication is that the pantheistic universe is solidly *one*. The parallel lines in verse one are without alliteration, and its absence confirms the suggestion of fragility in the living Lucy (a *thing* who can only be described in negative terms).

English Poetry (London, 1950), pp. 33–34

This essay comes from a chapter in which Mr. Bateson has been arguing for "the all-importance of meaning in poetry and the comparative insignificance of sound," hence perhaps his somewhat driving, or no-nonsense, manner.

Logical

The third kind of structure commonly found is **logical structure.** The speaker argues a case, and comes to some sort of conclusion. Probably the most famous example of a poem that moves to a resolution through an argument is Andrew Marvell's "To His Coy Mistress." The speaker begins, "Had we but world

---

[1] The *r*'s *in earth's diurnal course* are not sounded in modern English. Wordsworth, however, certainly sounded them. Hazlitt had found "a strong tincture of the northern *burr*" in his voice when they first met in 1798 (the year before "A slumber did my spirit seal" was written). See Hazlitt's "My First Acquaintance with Poets."

enough, and time" (that is, "if"), and for twenty lines he sets forth
what he might do. At the twenty-first line he says, "But," and he
indicates that the preceding twenty lines, in the subjunctive, are
not a description of a real condition. The real condition (as he sees
it) is that Time oppresses us, and he sets this idea forth in lines
21–32. In line 33 he begins his conclusion, "Now therefore,"
clinching it in line 45 with "Thus."

Here is another example of a poem with a logical structure.

> Mark but this flea, and mark in this
> How little that which thou deniest me is:
> It sucked me first, and now sucks thee,
> And in this flea our two bloods mingled be.
> Thou knowest that this cannot be said   5
> A sin, nor shame, nor loss of maidenhead;
>   Yet this enjoys before it woo,
>   And pampered swells with one blood made of two,
>   And this, alas, is more than we would do.
>
> O stay! Three lives in one flea spare,   10
> Where we almost, yea, more than married are;
> This flea is you and I, and this
> Our marriage bed and marriage temple is.
> Though parents grudge, and you, we're met
> And cloistered in these living walls of jet.   15
>   Though use° make you apt to kill me,   *custom*
>   Let not to that, self-murder added be,
>   And sacrilege, three sins in killing three.
>
> Cruel and sudden! Hast thou since
> Purpled thy nail in blood of innocence?   20
> Wherein could this flea guilty be,
> Except in that drop which it sucked from thee?
> Yet thou triumph'st and saist that thou
> Find'st not thyself, nor me, the weaker now.
>   'Tis true. Then learn how false fears be; 25
>   Just so much honor, when thou yield'st to me,
>   Will waste, as this flea's death took life from thee.
>
>   John Donne, "The Flea"

The speaker is a lover who begins by assuring his mistress that
sexual intercourse is of no more serious consequence than a flea
bite. Between the first and second stanzas the woman has appar-

ently threatened to kill the flea, moving the lover to exclaim in line 10, "O stay! Three lives in one flea spare." In this second stanza he reverses his argument, now insisting on the importance of the flea, arguing that since it has bitten both man and woman it holds some of their lives as well as its own. Unpersuaded of its importance, the woman kills the flea between the second and third stanzas; and the speaker uses her action to reinforce his initial position, when he says, beginning in line 25, that the death of the flea has no serious consequences and her yielding to him will have no worse consequences.

VERBAL IRONY

Among the commonest devices in poems with logical structure (although this device is employed elsewhere too) is **verbal irony.** The speaker's words mean more or less the opposite of what they seem to say. Sometimes it takes the form of **understatement,** as when Andrew Marvell's speaker remarks with cautious wryness, "The grave's a fine and private place, / But none, I think, do there embrace," or when Sylvia Plath sees an intended suicide as "the big strip tease"; sometimes it takes the form of **overstatement,** or **hyperbole,** as when Donne's speaker says that in the flea he and the lady are "more than married." Speaking broadly, intensely emotional contemporary poems, such as those of Plath, often use irony to undercut — and thus make acceptable — the emotion.

PARADOX

Another common device in poems with a logical structure is **paradox:** the assertion of an apparent contradiction, as in "This flea is you and I." But again it must be emphasized that irony and paradox are not limited to poems with a logical structure. In "Auld Lang Syne," for instance, there is the paradox that the remembrance of joy evokes a kind of sadness, and there is understatement in "we've wandered mony a weary fitt," which stands (roughly) for something much bigger, such as "we have had many painful experiences." The student who wishes to see irony and paradox examined as structural principles should consult Cleanth Brooks's *Well-Wrought Urn.*

CONCLUDING REMARKS

If you are going to write about a fairly short poem (say, fewer than thirty lines), it's not a bad idea as pointed out on p. 13, to copy out the poem, double-spaced. By writing it out you will be forced to notice details, down to the punctuation. After you have copied the poem, proofread it carefully against the original. Catching an error — even the addition or omission of a comma — may help you to notice a detail in the original that you might otherwise have overlooked. And of course now that you have the poem with ample space between the lines, you have a worksheet with room for jottings.

A good essay is based on a genuine response to a poem: a response may in part be stimulated first by reading the poem aloud, and then by considering the following questions:

1. Who is the speaker? (Age, sex, personality, frame of mind.) Is the speaker fully aware of what he or she is saying, or does the speaker reveal himself or herself unconsciously? In short, what is the speaker's personality, and what are the moral and intellectual values?

2. To whom is the speaker speaking? What is the situation (including the time and place)?

3. Does the poem proceed in a straightforward way, or at some points does the speaker reverse course altering his or her tone or perception?

4. Is the interest chiefly in character or in meditation — that is, is the poem chiefly psychological or philosophical?

5. Do certain words have rich and relevant associations that relate to other words to help define the theme? What is the role of the figurative language, if any? Does it help to define the speaker or the theme? What is to be taken symbolically, and what literally?

6. What is the role of sounds effects, including repetitions of sound and of entire words, and shifts in versification? If there are off-rhymes, what function do they serve? If there are unexpected stresses or pauses, what functions do they serve?

7. What is the effect of the form — say, quatrains, or blank verse, or pairs of rhyming lines? If the sense overflows the form, running without pause from (for example) one quatrain into the next, what explanation can be offered?

Writing about poetry may seem to be easier than writing about fiction or drama because most poems that students encounter are fairly short. They can usually keep the entire work before their eyes, and they need not be endowed with an exceptional memory. But the brevity may be deceptive. Because most of us are not used to reading poetry, we overlook a good deal of its complexity. Prose (the point will be mentioned again) runs straight on, but poetry is always turning back on itself, complicating its pattern of sound and of meaning.

Of course the prose of fiction is not the prose of a newspaper or a history book; it too is not used merely as a vehicle to give information about something outside of itself; rather, as David Lodge indicates in his essay on *Hard Times,* word by word it builds its own world. (Another way of putting it: The words of newspapers and textbooks aim or should aim, at being inconspicuous. They are a sort of window, or telescope, through which we see things, but generally we do not value them for themselves. We look beyond them. They are road signs, telling us where Boston is, or how to get to the expressway. But the words of a piece of literature, especially of a poem, are among the things we are looking at and looking for.) Still, fiction tells a story, and the story is a major part of its interest. We are not expected to dwell on each word in a story; the narrative line carries us forward. But in poetry we are supposed to delight in the words themselves or, better, in their combinations, as well as in the experience they point to.

Poets assume their readers will enjoy their virtuoso performances with words. Alexander Pope may not have been fully conscious of exactly what he was doing when he wrote "Die and endow a college or a cat," but he probably would have been delighted with F. W. Bateson's perceptive analysis (p. 201) of the line. (Quite likely Pope *was* fully conscious; the man who wrote the lines about Ajax and Camilla — see p. 225–226 — cared about the minutest problems of poetry. In any case, as Robert Frost has said, the poet deserves credit for anything good that is found in the poem.) A poet exploits more fully than does the writer of fiction such devices as alliteration and rhythm; a substantial part of the meaning of the work resides in them. Frost touched on this matter when he defined poetry as "what gets lost in translation." Auden touched on it when he said that his ideal reader notices misprints.

This is not to say that poetry is all sound and no sense but only that the sound plays a larger part in making the sense than it does in expository prose and even in fiction. The so-called musical qualities of poetry are among the hardest to discuss, for two reasons: first, we are not much aware of these resources because few of us write poetry, and we therefore sometimes do not notice them; second, when we do notice them, we are likely to talk wildly about them. Once we have learned that there is such a thing as onomatopoeia (see p. 231), we may too quickly find the sound echoing the sense, even when it does not.

About the only advice one can give is this: Read the poem over and over, aloud at least a couple of times, and try to hear as well as see what is going on. But once you have noticed things, don't believe them until further rereading convinces you that they are really there. Be especially cautious about making large claims for the effect of the sound of a single word. But keep a shrewd eye (and ear) open for the effects of combinations of sounds, such as those pointed out in Pope. Here is the first stanza of Walter Savage Landor's "Past Ruined Ilion," followed by some perceptive comments by Monroe Beardsley on the combinations of sounds. (Ilion is Troy, and Helen is Helen of Troy, whose beauty caused the Trojan War; Alcestis was brought back to life from the land of the dead.)

> Past ruined Ilion Helen lives,
>   Alcestis rises from the shades;
> Verse calls them forth; 'tis verse that gives
>   Immortal youth to mortal maids.

Beardsley says:

The "n" sound in "ruined Ilion Helen" ties them together in a single catastrophe. The "v" of "verse" and the "f" of "forth" bring them together, suggesting that the statement "Verse calls them forth" is naturally true. "Maids" is given irony because its meaning contrasts with the meaning of the two words that are connected with it, "shades" by rhyme and "mortal" by alliteration. The sound-parallelism of "Immortal" and "mortal" reinforces the slight paradox of the claim that the youth of the maid will outlive the maid.

Aesthetics (New York, 1958), pp. 236–237

For example, notice that Beardsley says that "the 'n' sound in 'ruined Ilion Helen' ties them together in a single catastrophe." He does *not* say that the "n" sound is catastrophic or that it is mournful. He notes combinations, relationships between words, and he also relies on the meanings of the words. He can speak of "a single catastrophe" because "ruined" *means* ruined. Ilion (Troy) is a vanished city, and Helen is long dead. He does not make extravagant claims for the inherent meaning of the "n" sound. But he has seen some connections, and he talks plausibly about them.

An explication or an analysis of a single poem will normally require some comment on the sound patterns, but not every essay on poetry need concern itself with such patterns. Good papers can be written on the development of an image or of a motif in a group of poems — for example, Frost's use of woods or stars, or Yeats's use of the legend of Helen of Troy. A paper that traces a recurrent image or motif may reveal a meaning, generated by a group of poems, that is barely perceptible in a single poem. The essayist who takes on such a job is the sort of reader Yeats had in mind when he wrote in one of his prefaces, "I must leave my myths and images to explain themselves as the years go by and one poem lights up another." But whatever the topic and the approach, the essayist's goal is to illuminate.

RHYTHM AND VERSIFICATION: A GLOSSARY

Rhythm (most simply, in English poetry, stresses at regular intervals) has a power of its own. A highly pronounced rhythm is common in such forms of poetry as charms, college yells, and lullabies; all of them are aimed at inducing a special effect magically. It is not surprising that *carmen,* the Latin word for poem or song, is also the Latin word for charm and the word from which "charm" is derived.

In much poetry rhythm is only half heard, but its omnipresence is suggested by the fact that when poetry is printed it is customary to begin each line with a capital letter. Prose (from Latin *prorsus,* "forward," "straight on") keeps running across the paper until the right-hand margin is reached, and then, merely because the paper has given out, the writer or printer starts again at the left, with a small letter. But verse (Latin *versus,* "a turning") often ends well short of the right-hand margin, and the next line begins at the left — usually with a capital — not because paper has run out but because the rhythmic pattern begins again. Lines of poetry are continually reminding us that they have a pattern

Notice that a mechanical, unvarying rhythm may be good to put the baby to sleep, but it can be deadly to readers who wish to keep awake. A poet varies his rhythm according to his purpose; he ought not to be so regular that he is (in W. H. Auden's words) an "accentual pest." In competent hands, rhythm contributes to meaning; it says something. Ezra Pound has a relevant comment: "Rhythm *must* have meaning. It can't be merely a careless dash off, with no grip and no real hold to the words and sense, a tumty tum tumty tum tum ta."

Consider this description of Hell from *Paradise Lost* (stressed syllables are marked by   ; unstressed syllables by   ):

´ ´ ´ ´ ´ ´ ˘ ´ ˘ ´
Rocks, caves, lakes, fens, bogs, dens, and shades of death.

The normal line in *Paradise Lost* is written in iambic feet — alternate unstressed and stressed syllables — but in this line Milton immediately follows one heavy stress with another, helping to communicate the "meaning" — the oppressive monotony of Hell. As a second example, consider the function of the rhythm in two lines by Alexander Pope:

˘ ´ ˘ ´ ˘ ´ ´ ´ ˘ ´
When Ajax strives some rock's vast weight to throw,

˘ ´ ´ ´ ˘ ˘ ˘ ´ ´ ´
The line too labors, and the words move slow.

The stressed syllables do not merely alternate with the unstressed ones; rather, the great weight of the rock is suggested by three consecutive stressed words, "rock's vast weight," and the great effort involved in moving it is suggested by another three consecutive stresses, "line too labors," and by yet another three, "words move slow." Notice, also, the abundant pauses within the lines. In the first line, for example, unless one's speech is slovenly, one must pause at least slightly after "Ajax," "strives," "rock's," "vast," "weight," and "throw." The grating sounds in "Ajax" and "rock's" do their work, too, and so do the explosive *t*'s. When Pope wishes to suggest lightness, he reverses his procedure, and he groups *un-*stressed syllables:

> Not so, when swift Camilla scours the plain,
>
> Flies o'er th' unbending corn, and skims along the main.

This last line has twelve syllables and is thus longer than the line about Ajax, but the addition of "along" helps to communicate lightness and swiftness because in this line (it can be argued) neither syllable of "along" is strongly stressed. If "along" is omitted, the line still makes grammatical sense and becomes more "regular," but it also becomes less imitative of lightness.

The very regularity of a line may be meaningful too. Shakespeare begins a sonnet thus:

> When I do count the clock that tells the time.

This line about a mechanism runs with appropriate regularity. (It is worth noticing, too, that "*c*ount the *c*lock" and "*t*ells the *t*ime" emphasize the regularity by the repetition of sounds and syntax.) But notice what Shakespeare does in the middle of the next line:

> And see the brave day sunk in hideous night.

The technical vocabulary of **prosody** (the study of the principles of verse structure, including meter, rhyme and other sound effects, and stanzaic patterns) is large. An understanding of these terms will not turn anyone into a poet, but it will enable one to discuss some aspects of poetry more efficiently. The following are the chief terms of prosody.

Meter

Most English poetry has a pattern of **stressed** (**accented**) sounds, and this pattern is the **meter** (from the Greek word for "measure"). Although in Old English poetry (poetry written in England before the Norman-French Conquest in 1066) a line may have any number of unstressed syllables in addition to four stressed syllables, most poetry written in England since the Conquest has not only a fixed number of stresses in a line but also a fixed number of unstressed syllables before or after each stressed one. (One really ought not to talk of "unstressed" or "unaccented" syllables, since to utter a syllable — however lightly — is to give it some stress. It is really a matter of *relative* stress, but the fact is that "unstressed" or "unaccented" are parts of the established terminology of versification.)

METRICAL FEET

In a line of poetry the **foot** is the basic unit of measurement. It is on rare occasions a single stressed syllable; but generally a foot consists of two or three syllables, one of which is stressed. The repetition of feet, then, produces a pattern of stresses throughout the poem.

Two cautions:

1. A poem will seldom contain only one kind of foot throughout; significant variations usually occur, but one kind of foot is dominant.

2. In reading a poem, one chiefly pays attention to the sense, not to a presupposed metrical pattern. By paying attetntion to the sense, one often finds (reading aloud is a great help) that the stress falls on a word that according to the metrical pattern would be unstressed. Or a word that according to the pattern would be stressed may be seen to be unstressed. Furthermore, by reading for sense one finds that not all stresses are equally heavy; some are almost as light as unstressed syllables, and sometimes there is a **hovering stress** — that is, the stress is equally distributed over two adjacent syllables. To repeat: One reads for sense, allowing the syntax to help indicate the stresses.

The most common feet in English poetry are:

Iamb (adjective: **iambic**): one unstressed syllable followed by one stressed syllable. The iamb, said to be the most common pattern in English speech, is surely the most common in English poetry. It is called a **rising meter,** the foot rising toward the stress. The following example has five iambic feet:

I saw the sky descend ing black and white.

> Robert Lowell

Trochee (trochaic): one stressed syllable followed by one unstressed; a **falling meter,** the foot falling away from the stress.

Let her live to earn her dinners.

> J. M. Synge

Anapest (anapestic): two unstressed syllables followed by one stressed; a rising meter.

There are man y who say that a dog has his day.

> Dylan Thomas

Dactyl (dactylic): one stressed syllable followed by two unstressed; a falling meter. This trisyllabic foot is common in light verse or verse suggesting joy, but its use is not limited to such material, as Longfellow's *Evangeline* shows. Thomas Hood's sentimental "The Bridge of Sighs" begins:

Take her up tenderly.

Spondee (spondaic): two stressed syllables; most often used as a substitute for an iamb or trochee; it neither rises nor falls.

Smart lad, to slip betimes away.

> A. E. Housman

Pyrrhic: two unstressed syllables; it is often not considered a legitimate foot in English.

METRICAL LINES

A metrical line consists of one or more feet and is named for the number of feet in it. The following names are used:

monometer:	one foot	**pentameter:**	five feet
dimeter:	two feet	**hexameter:**	six feet

| **trimeter:** | three feet | **heptameter:** | seven feet |
| **tetrameter:** | four feet | **octameter:** | eight feet |

A line is scanned for the kind and number of feet in it, and the **scansion** tells you if it is, say, anapestic trimeter (three anapests):

⏑ ⏑ ╱　　⏑ ⏑ ╱　　⏑ ⏑ ╱
As I came　to the edge　of the woods.

    Frost

Another example, this time iambic pentameter:

⏑ ╱　⏑ ╱　⏑ ╱　⏑ ╱　⏑ ╱
Since brass, nor stone, nor earth, nor boundless sea.

    Shakespeare

A line ending with a stress has a **masculine ending;** a line ending with an extra unstressed syllable has a **feminine ending.** The **caesura** (usually indicated by the symbol / /) is a slight pause within the line. It need not be indicated by punctuation, and it does not affect the metrical count:

> Awake, my St. John ! / / leave all meaner things
> To low ambition, / / and the pride of kings.
> Let us / / (since Life can little more supply
> Than just to look about us / / and to die)
> Expatiate free / / o'er all this scene of Man;
> A mighty maze! / / but not without a plan;
> A wild, / / where weeds and flowers promiscuous shoot;
> Or garden, / / tempting with forbidden fruit.
>
>   Pope

The varying position of the caesura helps to give Pope's lines an informality that plays against the formality of the pairs of rhyming lines.

An **end-stopped line** concludes with a distinct syntactical pause, but a **run-on line** has its sense carried over into the next line without syntactical pause. (The running-on of a line is called *enjambment.*) In the following passage, only the first is a run-on line:

> Yet if we look more closely we shall find
> Most have the seeds of judgment in their mind:

Nature affords at least a glimmering light;
The lines, though touched but faintly, are drawn right.

Pope

Meter produces **rhythm,** recurrences at equal intervals, but rhythm (from a Greek word meaning "flow") is usually applied to larger units than feet. Often it depends most obviously on pauses. Thus, a poem with run-on lines will have a different rhythm from a poem with end-stopped lines, even though both are in the same meter. And prose, though it is unmetrical, can thus have rhythm, too. In addition to being affected by syntactical pause, rhythm is affected by pauses due to consonant clusters and the length of words. Polysyllabic words establish a different rhythm from monosyllabic words, even in metrically identical lines. One can say, then, that rhythm is altered by shifts in meter, syntax, and the length and ease of pronunciation. But even with no such shift, even if a line is repeated verbatim, a reader may sense a change in rhythm. The rhythm of the final line of a poem, for example, may well differ from that of the line before, even though in all other respects the lines are identical, as in Frost's "Stopping by Woods on a Snowy Evening," which concludes by repeating "And miles to go before I sleep." One may simply sense that this final line ought to be spoken, say, more slowly and with more stress on "miles."

Patterns of Sounds

Though rhythm is basic to poetry, **rhyme** — the repetition of the identical or similar stressed sound or sounds — is not. It is, presumably, pleasant in itself; it suggests order; and it also may be related to meaning, for it brings two words sharply together, often implying a relationship, as Landor's "shades" and "maids," where death and feminine youth and beauty are linked. **Perfect** or **exact rhymes** occur when differing consonant sounds are followed by identical stressed vowel sounds, and the following sounds, if any, are identical (foe : toe; meet : fleet; buffer : rougher). Notice that perfect rhyme involves identity of sound, not of spelling. "Fix" and "sticks," like "buffer" and "rougher," are perfect rhymes.

In **half rhyme** (or **off rhyme**), only the final consonant sounds of the rhyming words are identical; the stressed vowel sounds as well as the initial consonant sounds, if any, differ (soul : oil; mirth : forth; trolley : bully). **Eye rhyme** is not really rhyme; it merely looks like rhyme (cough : bough). In **masculine rhyme** the final syllables are stressed and, after their differing initial consonant sounds, are identical in sound (stark : mark; support : retort). In **feminine rhyme** (or **double rhyme**) stressed rhyming syllables are followed by identical unstressed syllables (revival : arrival; flatter : batter). **Triple rhyme** is a kind of feminine rhyme in which identical stressed vowel sounds are followed by two identical unstressed syllables (machinery : scenery; tenderly : slenderly). **End rhyme** (or **terminal rhyme**) has the rhyming word at the end of the line. **Internal rhyme** has at least one of the rhyming words within the line (Wilde's "Each narrow *cell* in which we *dwell*").

    Alliteration is sometimes defined as the repetition of initial sounds ("*A*ll the *a*wful *a*uguries" or "*B*ring me my *b*ow of *b*urning gold"), sometimes as the prominent repetition of a consonant ("*a*fter *li*fe's *fi*tful *fe*ver"). **Assonance** is the repetition, in words in proximity, of identical vowel sounds preceded and followed by differing consonant sounds. Whereas "tide" and "hide" are rhymes, "tide" and "mine" are assonantal. **Consonance** is the repetition of identical consonant sounds and differing vowel sounds in words in proximity (fail : feel; rough : roof; pitter : patter). Sometimes consonance is more loosely defined merely as the repetition of a consonant (fai*l* : pee*l*). **Onomatopoeia** is said to occur when the sound of a word echoes or suggests the meaning of a word. "Hiss" and "buzz" are onomatopoetic. There is a mistaken tendency to see onomatopoeia everywhere, for example, in "thunder" and "horror." Many words sometimes thought to be onomatopoetic are not clearly imitative of the thing they denote; they merely contain some sounds that — when we know what the word means — seem to have some resemblance to the thing they denote. Tennyson's lines from "Come down, O maid" are usually cited as an example of onomatopoeia:

> The moan of doves in immemorial elms
> And murmuring of innumerable bees.

Stanzaic Patterns

Lines of poetry are commonly arranged in a rhythmical unit called a *stanza* (from an Italian word meaning a "room" or "stopping-place"). Usually all the stanzas in a poem have the same rhyme pattern. A stanza is sometimes called a **verse,** though "verse" may also mean a single line of poetry. (In discussing stanzas, rhymes are indicated by identical letters. Thus, *a b a b* indicates that the first and third lines rhyme with each other, while the second and fourth lines are linked by a different rhyme. An unrhymed lines is denoted by *x*.) Common stanzaic forms in English poetry are the following:

Couplet: stanza of two lines, usually, but not necessarily, with end rhymes. "Couplet" is also used for a pair of rhyming lines. The **octosyllabic couplet** is iambic or trochaic tetrameter:

Had we but world enough and time,
This coyness, lady, were no crime.

    Marvell

Heroic couplet: a rhyming couplet of iambic pentameter, often "closed," that is, containing a complete thought, with a fairly heavy pause at the end of the first line and a still heavier one at the end of the second. Commonly, there is a parallel or an antithesis within a line, or between the two lines. It is called heroic because in England, especially in the eighteenth century, it was much used for heroic (epic) poems.

Some foreign writers, some our own despise;
The ancients only, or the moderns, prize.

    Pope

Triplet (or **tercet**): a three-line stanza, usually with one rhyme.

Whenas in silks my Julia goes
Then, then (methinks) how sweetly flows
That liquefaction of her clothes.

    Herrick

Quatrain: a four-line stanza, rhymed or unrhymed. The **heroic** (or **elegiac**) **quatrain** is iambic pentameter, rhymming *a b a b.* The **ballad stanza** is a quatrain alternating iambic tetrameter with iambic trimeter lines, usually rhyming *x a x a.* Sometimes it is followed by a **refrain,** a line or lines repeated several times.

Sonnet: a fourteen-line poem, predominantly in iambic pentameter. The rhyme is usually according to one of the two following schemes. The **Italian** (or **Petrarchan**) **sonnet** has two divisions: the first eight lines (rhyming *a b b a   a b b a*) are the **octave,** the last six (rhyming *c d   c d   c d,* or a variant) are the **sestet.** Keats's "On First Looking into Chapman's Homer" (p. 208) is an Italian sonnet. The second kind of sonnet, the **English** (or **Shakespearean**) **sonnet,** is usually arranged into three quatrains and a couplet, rhyming *a b a b c d c d   e f e f   g g.* In many sonnets there is a marked correspondence between the rhyme scheme and the development of the thought. Thus an Italian sonnet may state a generalization in the octave and a specific example in the sestet. Or an English sonnet may give three examples — one in each quatrain — and draw a conclusion in the couplet.

Blank Verse and Free Verse

A good deal of English poetry is unrhymed, much of it in **blank verse,** that is, unrhymed iambic pentameter. Introduced into English poetry by Surrey in the middle of the sixteenth century, late in the century it became the standard medium (especially in the hands of Marlowe and Shakespeare) of English drama. In the seventeenth century, Milton used it for *Paradise Lost,* and it has continued to be used in both dramatic and nondramatic literature. For an example see the passage from Milton on page 200. A passage of blank verse that has a rhetorical unity is sometimes called a **verse paragraph.**

The second kind of unrhymed poetry fairly common in English, especially in the twentieth century, is **free verse** (or **vers libre**): rhythmical lines varying in length, adhering to no fixed metrical pattern and usually unrhymed. The pattern is often largely based on repetition and parallel grammatical structure. Here is a sample of free verse.

When I heard the learn'd astronomer,
When the proofs, the figures, were ranged in columns before me,
When I was shown the charts and diagrams, to add, divide, and
      measure them,
When I sitting heard the astronomer where he lectured with much
      applause in the lecture-room,
How soon unaccountable I became tired and sick,
Till rising and gliding out I wander'd off by myself,
In the mystical moist night-air, and from time to time,
Look'd up in perfect silence at the stars.

>   Walt Whitman, "When I Heard the Learn'd Astronomer"

What can be said about the rhythmic structure of this poem? Rhymes are absent, and the lines vary greatly in the number of syllables, ranging from nine (the first line) to twenty-three (the fourth line), but when we read the poem we sense a rhythmic structure. The first four lines obviously hang together, each beginning with "When"; indeed, three of these four lines begin "When I." We may notice, too, that each of these four lines has more syllables than its predecessor (the numbers are nine, fourteen, eighteen, and twenty-three); this increase in length, like the initial repetition, is a kind of pattern. But then, with the fifth line, which speaks of fatigue and surfeit, there is a shrinkage to fourteen syllables, offering an enormous relief from the previous swollen line with its twenty-three syllables. The second half of the poem — the pattern established by "When" in the first four lines is dropped, and in effect we get a new stanza, also of four lines — does not relentlessly diminish the number of syllables in each succeeding line, but it *almost* does so: fourteen, fourteen, thirteen, ten.

The second half of Whitman's poem thus has a pattern too, and this pattern is more or less the reverse of the first half of the poem. We may notice too that the last line (in which the poet, now released from the oppressive lecture hall, is in communion with nature) is very close to an iambic pentameter line, that is, the poem concludes with a metrical form said to be the most natural in English. The effect of naturalness or ease in this final line, moreover, is increased by the absence of repetitions (e.g., not only of "When I," but even of such syntactic repetitions as "charts and diagrams," "tired and sick," "rising and gliding") that characterize most of the previous lines. But of course this final effect of naturalness is part of a carefully constructed pattern in which rhythmic structure is part of meaning. Though at first glance free verse may appear unrestrained, as T. S. Eliot (a practitioner) said, "No *vers* is *libre* for the man who wants to do a good job" — or for the woman who wants to do a good job.

In recent years poets who write what earlier would have been called "free verse" have characterized their writing as **open form.** Poets such as Charles Olson, Robert Duncan, and Denise Levertov reject the "closed form" of the traditional, highly patterned poem, preferring instead a form that seems spontaneous or exploratory. To some readers the unit seems to be the phrase or the line rather than the group of lines, but Denise Levertov insists that the true writer of open-form poetry must have a "form sense"; she compares such a writer to "a sort of helicopter scout flying over the field of the poem, taking aerial photos and reporting on the state of the forest and its creatures — or over the sea to watch for the schools of herring and direct the fishing fleet toward them."★ And, Levertov again, "Form is never more than a *revelation* of content."

Sample Essay on Rhythm

Here is an excellent analysis by a student. Notice that she quotes the poem and indicates the metrical pattern, and that she proceeds chiefly by explaining the effect of the variations or departures from the norm, in the order in which they occur.

```
        Sound and Sense in Housman's ''Eight O'Clock''

    Before trying to analyze the effects of sounds and

rhythms in Housman's ''Eight O'Clock,'' it will be

useful to quote the poem and to indicate which sylla-

bles are stressed and which are unstressed. It must be

understood, however, that the following scansion is
```

★"Some Notes on Organic Form," reprinted in *The Poetics of the New American Poetry,* ed. Donald M. Allen and Warren Tallman (New York, 1973), pp. 316–317.

relatively crude, because it falsely suggests that all
stressed syllables (marked ´) are equally stressed,
but of course they are not: in reading the poem aloud,
one would stress some of them relatively heavily, and
one would stress others only a trifle more than the
unstressed syllables. It should be understood, too,
that in the discussion that follows the poem some
other possible scansions will be proposed.

> He stood, | and heard | the steeple
>   Sprinkle | the quar | ters on | the mor | ning
> town.
> One, two, | three, four, | to mar | ket-place | and
> people
>   It tossed | them down.
> Strapped, noosed, | nighing | his hour,
>   He stood | and coun | ted them | and cursed | his
> luck;
> And then | the clock | collec | ted in | the tower
>   Its strength, | and struck.

As the first line of the second stanza makes especially clear, the poem is about a hanging — at eight
o'clock, according to the title. Housman couid have
written about the man's thoughts on the justice or
injustice of his fate, or about the reasons for the
execution, but he did not. Except for the second line
of the second stanza – ''He stood and counted them and
cursed his luck'' – he seems to tell us little about

the man's thoughts. But the poem is not merely a narrative of an event; the sound effects in the poem help
to convey an idea as well as a story.

The first line establishes an iambic pattern. The
second line begins with a trochee (''Sprínkle''), not
an iamb, and later in the line possibly ''on'' should
not be stressed even though I marked it with a stress
and made it part of an iambic foot, but still the line
is mainly iambic. The poem so far is a fairly jingling
description of someone hearing the church clock chim-
ing at each quarter of the hour. Certainly, even
though the second line begins with a stress, there is
nothing threatening in ''Sprinkle,'' a word in which
we almost hear a tinkle.

But the second half of the first stanza surprises
us, and maybe even jolts us. In ''One, two, three,
four'' we get four consecutive heavy stresses. These
stresses are especially emphatic because there is a
pause, indicated by a comma, after each of them. Time
is not just passing to the chimes of a clock; this is
a countdown, and we sense that it may lead to something significant. Moreover, the third line, which is
longer than the two previous lines, does not end with
a pause. This long line (eleven syllables) runs on
into the next line, almost as though once the countdown has begun there is no stopping it. But then we do
stop suddenly, because the last line of the stanza has
only four syllables —— far fewer than we would have
expected. In other words, this line stops unexpectedly

because it has only two feet. The first line had three feet, and the second and third lines had five feet. Furthermore, this short, final line of the stanza ends with a heavy stress in contrast to the previous line, which ends with an unstressed syllable, ''péople.'' As we will see, the sudden stopping at the end is a sort of preview of a life cut short. Perhaps it is also a preview of a man dropping through a trapdoor and then suddenly stopping when the slack in the hangman's rope has been taken up.

In the first line of the second stanza the situation is made clear, and it is also made emphatic by three consecutive stresses: ''Strapped, noosed, nigh-ing his hour.'' The pauses before each of these stresses make the words especially emphatic. And though I have marked the first two words of the next line ''He stood,'' possibly ''He'' should be stressed too. In any case even if ''He'' is not heavily stressed, it is certainly stressed more than the other unstressed syllables, ''and,'' ''-ed'' (in ''counted''), and ''his.'' Similarly in the third line of the stanza an effective reading might even stress the first word as well as the second, thus: ''And then.'' And although normal speech would stress only the second syllable in ''collected,'' in this poem the word appears after ''clock,'' and so one must pause after the <u>k</u> sound in ''clock'' (one simply can't say ''clock collected'' without pausing briefly between the two words), and the effect is to put more than

usual stress on the first syllable, almost turning it
into ''collécted.'' And so this line really can reasonably be scanned like this:

And then the clock collected in the tower.

And again the third line of the stanza runs over into
the fourth, propelling us onward. The final line
surely begins with a stress, even though ''Its'' is
not a word usually stressed, and so in the final line
we begin with two strong stresses, ''Its strength.''
This line, like the last line of the first stanza, is
unusually short, and it too ends with a heavy stress.
The total effect, then, of the last two lines of this
stanza is of a clock striking, not just sprinkling
music but forcefully and emphatically and decisively
striking. The pause after ''strength'' is almost like
the suspenseful pause of a man collecting his strength
before he strikes a blow, and that is what the clock
does:

And then the clock collected in the tower

Its strength, and struck,

If ''clock collected'' has in its <u>k</u> sounds a sort of
ticktock effect, the clock at the end shows its force,
for when it strikes the hour, the man dies.

I said near the beginning of this essay that Housman did not write about the man's thought about the
justice or injustice of the sentence, and I think this

is more or less true, but if we take into account the sound effects in the poem we can see that in part the poem is about the man's thoughts: he sees himself as the victim not only of his ''luck'' but of this ma-chine, this ticking, unstoppable contraption that strikes not only the hours but a man's life.

SAMPLE ESSAYS

Each of these two essays on poetry looks closely at a short poem. Neither essay has an adequately focused title, but the fault is mine, not Van Doren's or Hall's; both essays were untitled comments in anthologies, and I have given them unobtrusive titles.

Van Doren seeks to demonstrate that although Words-worth's "The Solitary Reaper" is "not equally good in all of its parts" it is nevertheless an admirable poem. In short, he an-nounces his thesis at the outset, and he tries to demonstrate the truth of this twofold assertion by pointing out weaknesses and also by pointing out admirable strengths. After an initial paragraph on the origin of the poem and a second paragraph on the motif of solitude, he moves forward stanza by stanza. Part of the excel-lence of this essay is in the judicious balancing of praise and blame. It is easy to write an attack but hard to keep the reader from won-dering why you are bothering to write about something you dis-like, and it is hard to avoid sounding supercilious. Van Doren, even while commenting adversely, keeps us aware of his respect for the work; he never allows us to think that he believes he is superior to the work he is discussing. He wisely ends his essay by saying that although the last stanza is the weakest, the excellence of the first stanza "makes the entire work admirable."

Donald Hall's essay is taken from a textbook, and Hall is a teacher as well as a poet; but, as I have several times suggested, when you write you too are a teacher. Hall begins by naming the subject "in a general way," and he then (still in his opening para-graph) offers a "quick paraphrase." But this, of course, is Hall's way of preparing for the rest of his essay; we see that a more careful examination is needed, and Hall then goes on to provide it. He takes a close look at the poem and tells us what he sees. He also tells us something about what he feels ("my favorite part of the poem," "for me the unforgettable, untranslatable, nearly unmentionable beauty"), and we are grateful for these revelations because even his references to his responses to the poem help us to experience the poem more fully. Notice, too, that Hall's organization is simple but effective; after his introductory paragraph he moves through the poem in an orderly way, beginning at the beginning — the title, too often neglected by essayists — and he works his way through to the end. Simple, but clear and helpful.

Wordsworth's "The Solitary Reaper" ★
Mark Van Doren

Behold her, single in the field,
  Yon solitary Highland lass!
Reaping and singing by herself;
  Stop here, or gently pass!
Alone she cuts and binds the grain,   4
And sings a melancholy strain;
O listen! for the vale profound
Is overflowing with the sound.   8

No nightingale did ever chaunt
  More welcome notes to weary bands
Of travelers in some shady haunt,
  Among Arabian sands:
A voice so thrilling ne'er was heard   12
In spring-time from the cuckoo-bird,
Breaking the silence of the seas
Among the farthest Hebrides.   16

Will no one tell me what she sings? —
  Perhaps the plaintive numbers flow
For old, unhappy, far-off things,
  And battles long ago:
Or is it some more humble lay,   20
Familiar matter of today?

★The title of this essay is the editor's.

Some natural sorrow, loss, or pain,
That has been, and may be again?   24

Whate'er the theme, the maidens sang
   As if her song could have no ending;
I saw her singing at her work,
   And o'er the sickle bending; —   28
I listened, motionless and still;
And, as I mounted up the hill,
The music in my heart I bore,
Long after it was heard no more.   32

   William Wordsworth, "The Solitary Reaper"

The fact that this poem is not equally good in all of its parts
does not mean that it is unadmirable. Perhaps no poem is perfect
or could be; and perhaps an appearance of perfection is the most
suspicious appearance a poem can put up. At any rate, here is a famous poem that deserves its fame, and yet each stanza is inferior to
the one before it. The first, which is the best, has none before it,
and in fact contains or expresses the whole of the impulse that was
moving Wordsworth as he wrote. Not as he saw this Highland girl,
for he never saw her. He read about her in a prose book of travels,
Thomas Wilkinson's *Tour in Scotland*. Wilkinson saw the solitary
lass, and wrote a sentence about her which made Wordsworth in
effect see her too — made him, that is, see her as a poet. Many great
poems have come thus out of books: most commonly, out of prose
books. Prose discovers the matter and leaves it clear; after which
the poet has only to write his poem as if the matter of it were his
own, as indeed it comes to be.

Wordsworth is most deeply interested in the fact that this girl
in his mind's eye inhabits a solitude. . . . There are many soli-
tudes, and the present one is Wordsworth's own of which he always wrote so well. He puts the reaper into it and makes her belong there, a figure undefined except by the fact that she stands alone
in a world which has no content other than her thought and feeling. Her mood at the moment is melancholy in the sweet way that
Wordsworth understood so well. Good and healthy persons, in
harmony with their surroundings, are both sad and happy there.
They do not comprehend their universe as it weighs upon them,
but they love it and can therefore bear its weight — gravely, because it is so huge and old, but joyfully too because they feel their
strength as they do so.

The first eight lines say all that Wordsworth really has to say about this, and about the girl who is his symbol. "Behold her, single in the field." She is single; she is solitary; she is by herself; she is alone — we are told four times, in five lines, that this is true, as if nothing else matters, and nothing does for Wordsworth. Also, she is singing. She is a peasant girl, and she is singing as her kind is disposed to do, sadly, sweetly, and powerfully to herself. The folk knows, if civilized men do not, how the weight of the world is borne by those whose turn has come to be alive in it. Such is Wordsworth's deepest conviction as in his imagination he watches the girl. The eight lines put her clearly before us, bending gracefully as she sings some song of which he says only that it is melancholy, and that it is loud enough to fill a whole valley.

> O listen! for the vale profound
> Is overflowing with the sound.

If these are the best lines in the poem, the reason is their mysterious power to create the thing they mention. The deep valley fills with music as we listen; and overflows. This is partly a matter of onomatopoeia in the lines themselves, and partly a matter of their rhythmical relation to the six lines above. The eight-line stanza Wordsworth has decided to use — perhaps he is deciding only now — consists of a quatrain and two couplets. To point this out is not to explain the force we feel in the series as Wordsworth manages it. Few poems have begun more happily, or so rapidly achieved so much momentum. The initial quatrain, tetrameter except for its short fourth line that so sensibly halts us for a scrutiny of the thing, the person to be seen — the girl herself, bending down and rising up, reaping and soliloquizing — is followed, once we have checked our progress and stopped a gaze, by two melodious pairs of lines whose rhymes flow into one another as if by magic, producing in us a lively sense of the music that takes its rise in the maiden, fills the valley around her, keeps on filling it, and overflows. The two couplets are in a sense one sound, drawn out indefinitely and continuing in our ears, so that the remainder of the poem, no matter what it may say, will be assured of an accompaniment, a ground harmony, a remembered song that hums in the mind long after its occasion has ceased.

Having done this much — and it was a great thing to do — Wordsworth henceforth is reduced to conscious reflection upon his subject. The reflections are fine and the poem as a whole is fine, but nothing in it, not even the second stanza, quite matches that opening section in which the subject was created — all at once created, by no effort that could be observed, and by no means that we may be altogether sure of naming rightly.

The first reflection takes the form of a comparison. The song we heard was beautiful and strong; there is no doubt of that; but Wordsworth must suspect us of doubt, or he would not tell us how much better it was than something else. Than the voice of the Arabian nightingale; or the voice of the cuckoo in spring, among the farthest Hebrides. South or north, he insists, there is nothing to compare; and yet the comparison proceeds. The fact that it is a double comparison does not help to justify it. The girl's song is said to be more exciting than either of two distant sounds; and we believe this, yet are left thinking of those distant sounds, which replace hers. The second of them in particular is rendered with genius. The two compound words in line 14, "spring-time" and "cuckoo-bird," reinforce each other so freshly that one of them seems to spring out of the other as a rocket springs out of itself, bounding off with redoubled speed and joy. In two strokes of its wings the line mounts high and flies away, taking us with it to remote and moveless seas which nevertheless tremble when this sound arrives. "Breaking" is the word. It creates the very silence it shatters, softly and far away.

The stanza is noble, yet less so than the one that rendered it unnecessary. And the rest of the poem goes steadily downhill. The third stanza is of all things a rhetorical question, or worse yet, a pair of them. "Will no one tell me what she sings?" Certainly no one will, for Wordsworth is the authority. He does not understand these Highland words, or the girl is too far away for them to be heard, but that is no matter. The net meaning of the song is his to know if anybody is to know it, and he should not be asking for assistance. Lines 18–20 are agreeably suggestive of a romantic burden that the words may bear; and as such they are preferable to the couplets (21–24) he dutifully writes because he remembers his own theory that great poetry comes out of familiar and domestic things as well as out of battles long ago; it is not a useful theory at the moment, but he jogs on through it, finishing the stanza at last. He has long since lost contact with his subject in its purity. The quatrain of this stanza was intrinsically better than its couplets; but it was in the quatrain that he strayed away, farther even than he had gone in the magnificent stanza about the sands of Arabia and the Hebridean seas.

The last stanza recovers a fragment of the magic that is gone, but only a fragment. "Whate'er the theme" — it begins prosaically, still reflecting upon a very unimportant topic. It moves then into a series of lines whose function is to fix in us a sense of the song's immortality. We had that sense at the end of the first stanza, and noted it then. There is no object to our being reminded of it at the end of the poem — the poem, Wordsworth seems to be saying, will end but the song will not — and yet there is little chance that we shall be excited by learning something we already know. Wordsworth throws his discourse into the past tense —"I saw her," "I listened" — but this is a mere device of syntax. "I listened, motionless and still." That is better, for it suspends both him and us in a state of listening where it is possible to lose ourselves. This had been, however, our original state, which the sound and third stanzas interrupted; and perhaps it is not available to us again. Indeed it is not, or to Wordsworth either, judging by the pious assurance he gives us in the last three lines that he will not forget an unforgettable experience. The experience, in fact, is dead; though we can always revive it by returning and rereading stanza one. That is the contribution of the poem, and it alone makes the entire work admirable.

Hardy's "Transformations"
Donald Hall

Portion of this yew
Is a man my grandsire knew.
Bosomed here at its foot:
This branch may be his wife,
A ruddy human life
Now turned to a green shoot.   5

These grasses must be made
Of her who often prayed,
Last century, for repose;
And the fair girl long ago   10
Whom I often tried to know
May be entering this rose.

So, they are not underground,
But as nerves and veins abound
In the growths of upper air,   15
And they feel the sun and rain,

And the energy again
That made them what they were!

Thomas Hardy, "Transformations"

Taking the poem as a whole, it is easy to name the subject —
in a general way. Hardy is talking about how people endure after
their deaths as their bodies (molecules from their bodies) become
parts of plant life. All right. But this general sense is mere commonplace — *everybody* has talked about turning into grass or flowers after death — and the pleasures of poetry always lie in the particulars, not in the generalized content. My quick paraphrase of this
poem is neither complicated nor moving, but the poem itself is another matter.

The title is "Transformations." A lot of people, first reading
the poem, think that Hardy is talking about the *cycle* of life. But I
suggest that to talk about a cycle, in this poem, is not to use words
carefully. (One of the uses of poetry is that it teaches us to use words
carefully.) A cycle is a complete circle, and implies a motion from
human being back to human being. People have written such poems,
with their flavor of cannibalism, and Hardy could have done so if
he had meant to; the girl could have been entering a fruit tree, and
he could eat the fruit, and therefore the girl would be part of human life again. But Hardy is talking about *transformation,* the motion of matter from one sort of object to another. In this case, though
it would not be necessary, the people are transformed into trees,
grass, and flowers.

Let us look at the first two lines of the poem. "Portion of this
yew / Is a man my grandsire knew. . . ." These lines have three
beats each, iambic largely but with soft syllables missing and added
(they scan /ᴗ / ᴗ/ᴗ ᴗ/ ᴗ/ᴗ/) and they rhyme nicely: direct rhyme
of a noun and a verb that we would not normally connect, but that
come together without strain, with an effect of plainness. If we read
carefully, trying to be sensitive to the insides of words, we know a
good deal. The sentence is simple and declarative. How does Hardy
know that a portion (some part) of this yew is a man his grandsire
knew? ("My grandsire" knew him, so presumably "I" did not. This
presumption seems to put the dead man far back in time.) The answer is simple, providing we use a little common sense. Also, it
helps to know that a yew tree, an evergreen, commonly grows in
graveyards. Hardy (I won't call him "the speaker of the poem") is
walking in a graveyard. He either sees a stone, or remembers where
someone was buried. Maybe his grandsire told him — but that is

not the sort of thing we *know,* or that is is even useful to speculate on. The grave is next to a yew tree; it is common sense, then, to say that, "Portion of this yew / Is a man. . . ."

The third line gives some readers trouble. Because of the word "Bosomed," and also because of the later information about the dead man's wife, they think that the line refers to a woman. But this is not sensible. Hardy's punctuation — as a glance at a few poems will tell you — is conventional, and he would never join two complete sentences with a comma, or break the second sentence with the heavy stop of a colon. Readers who make this mistake are not looking closely. They are racing through the words as if they were reading a newspaper, grabbing at whatever sense can seem approximate or immediate.

No, the "portion" of "the man" is "Bosomed here at its foot." Hardy is talking about the hump of a grave, which could be *like* a bosom, but which could also be held to the tree as a child is held at the bosom of his mother. I think either reading or both readings work in the poem. It is also true that a yew tree characteristically has little knobs or bumps on it, rather harsh facsimiles of bosoms. I think this last reading of the line is far-fetched, but may be someone else can see more in it than I can.

The rhyme word of the third line, which is also three feet long, stands out by itself, ready to be picked up by the sixth line, which unifies the stanza. Glancing at the poem as a whole again, we can see that it has three stanzas — the third a summation or conclusion based on data collected in the first two; each of the three stanzas is divided into two parts, at the third line. This structural consistency is another, small reason why a sensible reader will reject the thought that "Bosomed" in line three goes with "wife" in line four.

In the fourth line, the situation of the poet walking in the graveyard is reinforced. Husbands and wives tend to be buried next to each other. Noticing the hump of the husband's grave, Hardy naturally notices or remembers the grave of the wife, which is also near the yew. But the verb "is" changes to the verb "may be"; he knows, when he talks of a person becoming a green shoot — a *particular* part of the tree — that he is being fanciful, and his "may be" is his modest acknowledgment of his fancifulness. It was easy to assert, with fair certainty, that "Portion of this yew / Is a man. . . ."

"A ruddy human life / Now turned to a green shoot." Having expressed his fancy as fancy, Hardy fleshes it out in the fifth and sixth lines as if it were fact; his imagination seizes on it and develops it. "Ruddy" means red-cheeked and healthy. The word can be

slang in England, a euphemism for "bloody" or "God-awful."
Anyone who, having consulted a dictionary, thinks Hardy could
have meant "god-awful" is not being very sensitive. The "green"
of "green shoot" heightens the red of "ruddy." Blood and chlorophyll, the two great life sustainers, stand in colorful contrast. "Human," of course, contrasts with "shoot," and "turned" is the action
that creates "transformation." Having imagined a possibility, based
on an original probability, Hardy's imagination takes off. Eventually we will want to wonder whether the movement toward greater
and greater fancifulness is part of the inner speech of this simple
poem.

The second stanza extends the fancy, though it continues the
scheme of the poem by talking of two more buried people. "These
grasses" (moving away from the yew, we turn to cemetery grass —
perhaps the grass of a particular grave his eyes moves toward) "must
be made / Of her who often prayed, / Last century, for repose."
First we may notice that "must be" is a different sort of verb from
"is" or "may be." It could mean, "these grasses absolutely incon-
trovertibly have to be," but this sense of "must be" would violate
the attitude of modest fancy that Hardy has set up. He is not being
that extravagant. Fortunately, there is an idiomatic sense of "must
be" which roughly means "stands to reason that." Returned to a
built-up area we knew as a child, we say, "The baseball field must
have been over there," and we are talking about a probability, not
a fact.

The woman prayed, and therefore bent over as grass does in
the wind, or kept low to the ground like grass — as opposed to
yew trees. She prayed "Last century," which does not logically have
to mean a long time ago, but otherwise why would Hardy say so?
We begin to have the sense that Hardy writes as an old man. The
irony of praying for repose, and getting it as grass (in the poet's
fancy), is clear enough, and the verbally similar (but differently
spelled) rhymes of "made" and "prayed" are satisfying.

The last half of the second stanza is the most fanciful, and I
think it is probably my favorite part of the poem. "And the fair girl
long ago" seems to confirm the speaker's age: He is looking at the
grave of someone he "long ago" wished to court. Hardy remembers the girl "Whom I often tried to know" as fair and imagines
her becoming a beautiful flower. He recalls that he failed to know
her; here we have a small nostalgic romantic story.

I said that Hardy imagined her becoming a beautiful flower.
What he wrote was not my prosaic paraphrase but, "May be en-

tering this rose." Here is a rose growing in the graveyard, presumably near the grave of this remembered girl. Hardy reverts to "May be" with its acknowledgment of fantasy. But here it is part of a verb compound, and not the whole verb — she "May be entering" at this moment. The implication of the present tense (implication only, not statement) is that she has died more recently, an old lady who had long ago been a fair girl.

But for me the unforgettable, untranslatable, nearly unmentionable beauty lies in the strange verb "entering." Her molecules rise up the green stem as if they were going inside a house — or as if, most strangely, they were a man entering a woman. This brings me to a level of the poem which is tenuous, which is perhaps not even there — but it seems consistent. I refer to the way in which sexes seem to change or switch. We do not distinguish between male and female daisies, but usually with people, we think of male in male terms and female in female terms. In this poem, the first man we meet is "bosomed" at the root of the yew, and though this can mean only that he is clutched to the mother's bosom, I suggest that there is a way in which the word grants him bosoms also, changes his sex. When his wife is fancifully reincarnated, she becomes a phallic "shoot." I see no sexual change in the next woman. The young girl "May be entering this rose."

The final stanza changes tactics. Instead of talking about the individual dead it generalizes, referring to "they" — all the dead. And it moves by false logic, saying, "So," as if the generalizations followed from the particulars. Clearly they do not. Hardy knows that because of his fancies ("may be"), he has not proved that the dead, for instance, "feel" things again. Hardy is *intending* his illogic. . . . Both the illogic and the fantastic image serve the same purpose: They express the poet's feeling.

In reading "Transformations," I think it is important that we keep our intelligence alert and register Hardy's illogic — in order to follow the track of his feeling. The second line of the last stanza is another brilliant mixture of real observations with (more importantly) emotional distortions. We do not think of a plant as having nerves in the same way that a human does. We do think of leaves as having veins, and of stems as having little capillaries along which chlorophyll, like blood, might travel. So "nerves" is fancy and "veins" has the reality of leaf-veins that are analogous to human veins. But there is also a visual level to the line. A tree or bush without leaves, against the sky, can look like an anatomical diagram of human nerves and veins. This distant visual background gives more weight to Hardy's fantastic assertion that these people live again, even in their feelings.

"Abound" is a lively, fruitful word, expressive in its denial of death. "In the growths of upper air" effectively removes the old corpses from claustrophobic coffins and liberates them into oxygen. "Growths," literally applied to trees, grass, and the rosebush, carries energy like "abound." It is another denial of death.

The final three-line portion is the most unrealistic and the most ecstatic of the poem. "And they feel the sun and rain" — well, we can *imagine* plants feeling sun and rain, because we can see their reaction to drought and damp, but we only assert when we say that they feel, we do not know it. Suddenly the emotional necessity behind this poem becomes clear — if it had not become clear earlier. An old man walks in the graveyard which is populated with dead whom he knew or knew of. He begins to imagine their survival — scientifically feasible — as molecules of vegetable matter. Then suddenly he insists on their survival as sentient objects, insists on the denial of death. The old man is expressing, by means of the distortion of his illogic, his moving desire to endure, to survive death, to feel "the energy again" that makes him what he is. Notice that he does not say that the plants feel the energy that makes them what they *are*; rather, "That made them what they *were!*" It is the human state that the old man wants. So Hardy makes a poem that starts with a realistic commonplace and ends with scientific falsities which represent a common and deep emotion: We wish to survive our deaths.

7
Writing about Film

This chapter offers some comments about the nature of film, some definitions of indispensable technical terms, a few suggestions about topics, a sample essay by a student, a list of questions that you may want to ask yourself as you begin to think about writing on a film, and, finally, two published essays on films.

FILM AS A MEDIUM

Perhaps one's first thought is that a film (excluding cartoons, documentaries, newsreels, and so on) is rather like a play: a story is presented by means of actors. The film, of course, regularly uses some techniques not possible in the playhouse, such as close-ups and rapid changes of scene, but even these techniques can usually be approximated in the playhouse, for example by means of lighting. It may seem, then, that one can experience a film as though it were a photographic record of a play. And indeed some films are nothing more than film records of plays.

There are, however, crucial distinctions between film and drama. First, though drama uses such visual matters as gestures, tableaux effects, and scenery, the plays that we value most highly are *literature:* the word dominates, the visual component is subordinate. One need not be a film fanatic who believes that the invention of the sound track was an impediment to film in order to realize that a film is more a matter of pictures than of words. The camera usually roves, giving us crowded streets, empty skies, rainy nights, or close-ups of filled ashtrays and chipped coffee cups. A critic has aptly said that in Ingmar Bergman's *Smiles of a Summer Night* "the almost unbearably ornate crystal goblets, by their aspect and their positioning in the image, convey the oppressive luxuriousness of the diners' lives in purely and uniquely filmic terms." In the words of the Swiss director Eric Rohmer, "the cinema is the description of man and his surroundings."★

Some of the greatest sequences in cinema, such as the battle scene in Orson Welles's *Falstaff* (also titled *Chimes at Midnight*), or parts of the search for Anna in Michelangelo Antonioni's *L'Avventura,* have no dialogue but concentrate on purely visual matters. In *L'Avventura* a group of rich and bored Italians go on a yachting excursion and visit a volcanic island off the coast of Sicily, where one member of the party — Anna — disappears. Anna's fiancé, Sandro, and Anna's best friend, Claudia, search for her, but during the search they find that they are attracted to each other and they become lovers; Claudia later discovers that Sandro is unfaithful to her — but she and Sandro both were unfaithful to Anna, and the implication is that Claudia and Sandro will (in their way) remain weary partners. During the film's two hours there are long sequences when, in a conventional sense, little "happens" — for example, there are shots of the sea, or of a character, far from the camera, walking on the island during bad weather. But of course in this film the setting itself is an important part of the story, the barren and crumbling island being symbolic of the decadent people who walk on it and symbolic also of the vast inhospitable universe in which these figures — rendered small by their distance from the camera — aimlessly move. The long silences (there are epi-

★Films made for televison, however, in contrast to the films under discussion, are, for the most part, close to drama. They are usually in essence a play recorded on film, showing people talking and moving on a stage but conveying no sense of a large world and no sense of details, offering nothing to look at. This is not surprising: television technology is still primitive, and (unlike film) television cannot clearly portray a distant object (for example, a horseman on the skyline), nor can it sharply portray fine detail even of an object close to the camera. Perhaps one should add here, however, that in the middle 1960s some directors, especially Jean-Luc Godard, rejected the idea that cinema is primarily a visual medium. Godard's characters sit around (they scarcely seem to *act*), talking about politics and their emotions.

sodes without dialogue or background music) are as important as what is said, and what is seen is more important than what is said.

In short, the speaker in a film does not usually dominate. In a play the speaker normally holds the spectator's attention, but in a film when a character speaks, the camera often gives us a **reaction shot,** focusing not on the speaker, but on the face or gestures of a character who is affected by the speech, thus giving the spectator a visual interpretation of the words. In Truffaut's *400 Blows,* for example, we hear a reform school official verbally assault a boy, but we see the uncomfortable boy, not the official. Even when the camera does focus on the speaker, it is likely to offer an interpretation. An extreme example is a scene from *Brief Encounter:* a gossip is talking, and the camera gives us a close-up of her jabbering mouth which monstrously fills the screen.

This distance between film and drama can be put in another way: a film is more like a novel than a play, the action being presented not directly by actors but by a camera, which, like a novelist's point of view, comments on the story while telling it. A novelist may, like a dramatist, convey information about a character through dialogue and gesture, but she may also simply tell us about the character's state of mind. Similarly, a film-maker may use her camera to inform us about unspoken thought. In Murnau's *Last Laugh,* when the hotel doorman reads a note firing him, the camera blurs; when he gets drunk, the camera spins so that the room seems to revolve. Somewhat similarly, Antonioni's *Red Desert* occasionally uses out-of-focus shots to convey Giuliana's view of the world; when she is more at ease, for example with her husband, the shots are in proper focus. In Bertolucci's *Conformist,* a shot of a chase through the woods is filmed with a hand-held camera whose shaky images convey to us the agitated emotions of the chase. At the end of *Bonnie and Clyde,* when Clyde is riddled with bullets, because his collapse is shot in slow motion he seems endowed not only with unusual grace but also with almost superhuman powers of endurance.

Even the choice of the kind of emulsion-coated celluloid is part of the comment. A highly sensitive or "fast" film requires less light to catch an image than a "slow" film does, but it is usually grainier. Perhaps because newsreels commonly use fast film a grainy quality is often associated with realism. Moreover, because fast film shows less subtle gradations from black to white than slow film does, its harsh contrasts make it especially suitable for the harsh, unromantic *Battle of Algiers.* Different film stocks may be used within a single motion picture. In *Wild Strawberries,* for instance, Bergman uses high-contrast stock for the nightmare sequence though elsewhere in the film the contrasts are subtle.

The medium, as everyone knows, is part of the message; Laurence Olivier made Shakespeare's *Henry V* in color but *Hamlet* in black and white because these media say different things. Peter Brook's film of *King Lear* is also in black and white, with an emphasis on an icy whiteness that catches the play's spirit of old age and desolation; a *Lear* in color probably would have an opulence that would work against the lovelessness and desolation of much of the play. John Houseman said that he produced *Julius Caesar* in black and white because he wanted "intensity" rather than "grandeur," and because black and white evoked newsreels of Hitler and thus helped to establish the connection between Shakespeare's play and relatively recent politics. Peter Ustinov said that he made *Billy Budd* in black and white because he wanted it to seem real; and Richard Brooks's *In Cold Blood,* also in black and white, tried to look like a documentary. Similarly, although by 1971 most fiction films were being made in color, Peter Bogdanovich made *The Last Picture Show* in black and white, partly to convey a sense of the unexciting life of a small town in America in the 1950s, and partly to evoke the films of the fifties. When a film is made in color, however, the colors may be symbolic (or at least suggestive) as well as realistic. In *A Clockwork Orange,* for example, hot colors (oranges and reds) conveying vitality and aggressiveness in the first half of the film are displaced in the second half by cool colors (blues and greens) when the emphasis turns to "clockwork," i.e., to mechanization.

The kind of lens used also helps to determine what the viewer sees. In *The Graduate* Benjamin runs toward the camera (he is trying to reach a church before his girl marries another man) but he seems to make no progress because a telephoto lens was used and thus his size does not increase as it normally would. The lens, that is, helps to communicate his desperate sense of frustration. Conversely, a wide-angle lens makes a character approach the camera with menacing rapidity; he quickly looms into the foreground. But of course a film-maker, though he resembles a novelist in offering pervasive indirect comment, is not a novelist any more than he is a playwright or director of a play; his medium has its own techniques, and he works with them, not with the novel's or the drama's. The wife who came out of the movie theater saying to her husband "What a disappointment; it was exactly like the book" knew what a film ought to be.

FILM TECHNIQUES

At this point it may be well to suspend generalizations temporarily and to look more methodically at some techniques of filmmaking. What follows is a brief grammar and dictionary of film, naming and explaining the cinematic devices that help filmmakers embody their vision in a work of art. An essay on film will probably discuss some of these devices, but there is no merit in mechanically trotting them all out.

Shots

A **shot** is what is recorded between the time a camera starts and the time it stops, that is, between the director's call for "action" and his call to "cut." Perhaps the average shot is about ten seconds (very rarely a fraction of a second, and usually not more than fifteen or so seconds). The average film is about an hour and a half, with about 600 shots, but Hitchcock's *Birds* uses 1,360 shots. Three common shots are (1) a **long shot** or **establishing shot,** showing the main object at a considerable distance from the camera and thus presenting it in relation to its general surroundings (for example, captured soldiers, seen across a prison yard, entering the yard); (2) a **medium shot,** showing the object in relation to its immediate surroundings (a couple of soldiers, from the knees up, with the yard's wall behind them); (3) a **close-up,** showing only the main object, or, more often, only a part of it (a soldier's face, or his bleeding feet).

In the outside world we can narrow our vision to the detail that interests us by moving our head and by focusing our eyes, ignoring what is not of immediate interest. The close-up is the movie director's chief way of directing our vision and of emphasizing a detail. (Another way is to focus sharply on the significant image, leaving the rest of the image in soft focus.) The close-up, a way of getting emphasis, has been heavily used in recent years, not always successfully. As Dwight Macdonald said of *Midnight Cowboy* and *Getting Straight,* "a movie told in close-ups is like a comic book, or like a novel composed in punchy one-sentence paragraphs and set throughout in large caps. How refreshing is a long or middle shot, a glimpse of the real world, so lovely and so *far away,* in the midst of those interminable processions of [a] hairy ogre face."

While taking a shot, the camera can move: it can swing to the right or left while its base remains fixed (a **pan shot**), up or down while fixed on its axis (a **tilt shot**), forward or backward (a **traveling shot**), or in and out and up and down fastened to a crane (a **crane shot**). The fairly recent invention of the **zoom** lens enables the camera to change its focus fluidly, so that it can approach a detail — as a traveling shot does — while remaining fixed in place. Much will depend on the angle (high or low) from which the shots are made. If the camera is high (a **high-angle shot**), looking down on figures, it usually will dwarf them, perhaps even reduce them to crawling insects, making them vulnerable, pitiful, or contemptible. The higher the angle, the more likely it is to suggest a God's-eye view of entrapped people. If the camera is low (a **low-angle shot**), close to the ground and looking up, thereby showing figures against the sky, it probably will give them added dignity. In Murnau's *Last Laugh,* we first get low angle shots of the self-confident doorman, communicating his grand view of himself; later, when he loses his strength and is reduced to working as a lavatory attendant, we see him from above, and he seems dwarfed. But these are not invariable principles. A shot in *Citizen Kane,* for example, shows Kane from above, but it does not dwarf him; rather, it shows him dominating his wife and then in effect obliterating her by casting a shadow over her. Similarly, a low-angle shot does not always add dignity: films in which children play important parts often have lots of low-angle shots showing adults as menacing giants; and in *Dr. Strangelove* Stanley Kubrick regularly photographed Colonel Jack D. Ripper from low angles, thus emphasizing the colonel's power. In *Citizen Kane,* Kane is often photographed from floor level, similarly emphasizing his power, but some low-angle shots late in the film, showing him in his cavernous mansion, help to convey his loneliness. In short, by its distance from the subject, its height from the ground, and its angle of elevation, the camera comments on or interprets what happens. It seems to record reality, but it offers its own version. It is only a slight exaggeration to say that the camera always lies, that is, gives a personal vision of reality.

Sequences

A group of related scenes — such as the three scenes of soldiers mentioned earlier — is a **sequence,** though a sequence is more likely to have thirty scenes than three. A sequence corresponds roughly to a chapter in a novel, the shots being sentences and the scenes being paragraphs. Within a sequence there may be an **intercut,** a switch to another action that, for example, provides an ironic comment on the main action of the sequence. If intercuts are so abundant in a sequence that, in effect, two or more sequences are going at once (for example, shots of the villain about to ravish the heroine alternating with shots of the hero riding to her rescue), we have a **cross-cut.** In the example just given, probably the tempo would increase, the shots being progressively shorter as we get to the rescue. Though often a sequence will early have an establishing shot, it need not. Sometimes an establishing shot is especially effective if delayed, as in Dreyer's *Day of Wrath,* where scenes of a witch tied to the top rungs of a ladder lead to a long shot of the context: the witch has been tied to the top of a tall ladder near a great heap of burning faggots. Still at a distance, the next shot shows the soldiers tilting the ladder up into the air and onto the pyre.

Transitions

Within a sequence, the transitions normally are made by **straight cuts** — a strip of film is spliced to another, resulting in an instantaneous transfer from one scene to the next. Usually an audience is scarcely (if at all) conscious of transitions from, say, a long shot of a character to a medium shot of him, or from a close-up of a speaker to a close-up of his auditor. But sometimes the director wants the audience to be fully aware of the change, as an author may emphasize a change by beginning a new paragraph or, even more sharply, by beginning a new chapter. Two older, and now rather unfashionable, relatively conspicuous transitions are sometimes still used, usually between sequences rather than within a sequence. These are the **dissolve** (the scene dissolves while a new scene appears to emerge from beneath it, there being a moment when we get a blur of both scenes), and the **fade** (in the fade-out the screen grows darker until black; in the **fade-in** the screen grows lighter until the new scene is fully visible). In effect the camera is saying "Let us now leave X and turn to Y," or "Two weeks later." In *2001* a prehistoric apelike creature discovers that he can use a bone as a tool, and he destroys a skeleton with it. Then he throws the bone triumphantly into the air, where it dissolves into a spaceship of the year 2001. The point is that the spaceship is the latest of ours weapons, and progress is linked with destructiveness. Two older methods, even less in favor today than the dissolve and the fade but used in many excellent old films and in some modern films that seek an archaic effect, are the **wipe** (a sort of windshield wiper crosses the screen, wiping off the first scene and revealing the next), and the **iris** (in an **iris-in,** the new scene first appears in the center of the previous scene and then this circle expands until it fills the screen; an **iris-out** shows the new scene first appearing along the perimeter and then the circle closes in on the previous scene). Chaplin more than once ended a scene with an iris-out of the tramp walking jauntily toward the horizon. Fairly recently François Truffaut used iris shots in *The Wild Child,* suggesting by the encircling darkness the boy's isolation from most of the world surrounding him as he concentrated on a single object before him. In Kurosawa's *High and Low* a wipe is used with no archaic effect: an industrialist, trying to decide whether to pay an enormous ranson to free a child, has been told to toss the money from a train; the scene showing him arriving at his decision in his luxurious home is wiped off by a train that rushes across the screen. He has decided to pay.

Editing

A film, no less than a poem or a play or a picture or a palace, is something made, and it is not made by simply exposing some footage. Shots — often taken at widely separated times and places — must be appropriately joined. For example, we see a man look off to the right; then we get a shot of what he is looking at, and then a shot of his reaction. Until the shots are assembled, we don't have a film — we merely have the footage. V. I. Pudovkin put it this way: "The film is not *shot,* but built, built up from the separate strips of celluloid that are its raw material." This building-up is the process of **editing.** In *Film Technique* Pudovkin gives some examples of editing:

1. In the simplest kind of editing, the film tells a story from the best viewpoints, that is, sometimes from long shots, sometimes from medium shots, sometimes from close-ups.

2. Simultaneous actions, occurring in different places, can be narrated by cutting back and forth from one to the other.

3. Relationships can be conveyed by contrast (shots of starvation cut in with shots of gluttony), by symbolism (in Pudovkin's *Mother,* shots of an ice floe melting are cut into shots of a procession of workers, thereby suggesting that the workers' movement is a natural force coming to new life), and by *leitmotif* (that is, repetition of the same shot to emphasize a recurring theme).

More than a story can be told, of course; something of the appropriate emotion can be communicated by juxtaposing, say, a medium-long shot of a group of impassively advancing soldiers against a close-up of a single terrified victim. Similarly, emotion can be communicated by the duration of the shots (quick shots suggest haste; prolonged shots suggest slowness) and by the lighting (progressively darker shots can suggest melancholy; progressively lighter shots can suggest hope or joy). The Russian theorists of film called this process of building by quick cuts **montage.** The theory held that shots, when placed together, add up to more than the sum of the parts. Montage, for them, was what made a film a work of art and not a mere replica of reality. American writers commonly use the term merely to denote quick cutting, and French writers use it merely in the sense of cutting.★

All this talk about ingenious shots and their arrangement, then, assumes that the camera is a sort of pen, carefully setting forth images and thus at every point guiding the perceiver. The director (through the actors, camera technicians, cutters, and a host of others) makes an artifact, rather as a novelist makes a book or a sculptor makes a statue, and this artifact is a sort of elaborate contraption that manipulates the spectators by telling them at every second exactly how they ought to feel. But recently there has been a reaction against such artistry, a feeling that although the elaborate editing of, say, Eisenstein and the other Russians is an esthetic triumph, it is also a moral failure because by its insistent tricky commentary it seems to deny the inherent worth of the event in itself as it happens. Moreover, just as the nineteenth-century narrator in the novel, who continually guided the reader ("Do not fear, gentle reader, for even at this moment plans were being laid . . .") was in the twentieth-century novel sloughed off, forcing the readers in large measure to deduce the story for themselves, so too some contemporary film-makers emphasize improvisation, fully aware that the film thus made will not at every point guide or dominate the viewer. Rather, the viewers of such a film become something of creators themselves, making the work of art by sorting out the relevant from the irrelevant images. Norman Mailer, in an essay on his film *Maidstone,* calls attention to the fact that in making this sort of film the camera, expecting an interesting bit of acting, may zoom in on what later turns out to be dull, but the scene is not deleted or shot again. The dull parts, the mistakes, are kept, and what was missed is not reenacted. In *Maidstone,* Mailer says, "When significant movement was captured, it was now doubly significant because one could not take it for granted. Watching film became an act of interpretation and restoration for what was missed."

★ You don't have to be in Hollywood, or in Russia or France, to write a script. You may find it challenging and entertaining to recall either some incident you were involved in, or a scene from a novel, and then to recast it as a script, indicating shots, camera angles, lighting, and sound track.

THEME

It is time now to point out an obvious fact; mastery of technique, though necessary to good film-making, will not in itself make a good film. A good film is not a bag of cinematic devices, but the embodiment, through cinematic devices, of a vision, an underlying **theme**. What is this theme or vision? Well, it is a film-maker's perception of some aspect of existence that he thinks is worthy of our interest. Normally this perception involves characters and a plot. Though recent American films, relying heavily on color, rock music in stereophonic sound, quick cutting, and the wide screen, have tended to emphasize the emotional experience and deemphasize narrative, still most of the best cinema is concerned with what people do, that is, with character and plot. Character is what people are, plot is what happens, but the line between character and plot fades, for what people are is in large measure what they do, and what is done is in large measure the result of what people are.

Character and plot, then, finally are inseparable; in a good film, everything hangs together. Harold Lloyd said that he had idea men who suggested numerous bits of comic business, and then he chose "the ones that [he] thought would be most appropriate to the particular film we were doing." The operative words are "most appropriate." A very funny bit of business might not be appropriate — might somehow not seem to fit — in a particular film because it was not in harmony with the underlying theme or vision or idea, the "clothes rack" (Lloyd's term) on which the funny bits (the clothes) were hung. In *The Freshman,* Lloyd said, the underlying idea or theme was the student's enormous desire for popularity, and everything in the film had to further this theme. Or, to take the comments of a more recent film-maker, we can listen to Truffaut on the themes of *The 400 Blows* and *Jules and Jim,* and on the disastrous lack of a theme in *Shoot the Piano Player:*

> In *400 Blows,* I was guided by the desire to portray a child as honestly as possible, and to invest his actions with a moral significance. Similarly, with *Jules and Jim,* my desire to keep the film from seeming either pornographic, indelicate, or conventional guided me. The

trouble with *Shoot the Piano Player* was that I was able to do anything — that the subject itself didn't impose its own form. . . . As it stands, there are some nice bits in the film, but it can't be said: this is the best work on this particular theme. There isn't any theme.

(It does not follow, of course, that the artist is fully aware of his theme from the start. Antonioni mentions that "it often happens that I experience fragmentary feelings before the experiences themselves take hold." But if they do not finally take hold, the film will probably arouse the sort of response that Truffaut mentions in his comments on *Shoot the Piano Player*.)

And so we come back to the idea of a vision, or, in a less exalted word, a theme. Some critics, we recall, have argued that the concept of theme is meaningless: a film is only a detailed presentation of certain imaginary people in imaginary situations, not a statement about an aspect of life. Susan Sontag, in a challenging essay in *Against Interpretation,* argues that our tendency to seek a meaning in what we perceive is a manifestation of a desire to control the work of art by reducing its rich particulars to manageable categories. But Sontag's view itself is reductive. If we read in a newspaper about a marriage or a business failure or a baseball game, we take it only as a particular happening of some interest, and we do not assume that it implies much if anything beyond itself. It tells of something that has happened, but it does not tell what ought to happen or what usually happens; that is, it does not imply anything about the ways of people in general. When, however, we read a novel, or see on the stage or screen a happening, we inevitably feel — if only because we are asked to give the event an hour or more of our attention — that it is offered to us as noteworthy, an example not of what *happened* (it didn't happen; it's fictional) but an example of what *happens.* The characters in the fictional work are (like the characters in newspaper items) individuals, not mere abstractions, but (unlike those in newspaper items) they are significant individuals, in some measure revealing to us a whole class of people or a way of life. An artist gives us a representation that can be thought about.

Sometimes we sense that a film has an arguable thesis. Stanley Kubrick, for example, has said that *A Clockwork Orange* "warns against the new psychedelic fascism — the eye-popping, multimedia, quadrasonic, drug-oriented conditioning of human beings by other human beings — which many believe will usher in the forfeiture of human citizenship and the beginning of zombie-dom." A film-maker, however, need not argue a thesis that is subject to verification (for example, that the older generation seeks to repress the younger generaton); it is enough if he sees in the human experience something worth our contemplation (for example, the conflict between generations) and embodies it on film. A theme can usually be named by an abstract noun or phrase (the quest for happiness, the difficulty of achieving self-knowledge, the fragility of love) and though we recognize that any such formula is not the whole life, it is nonetheless important. Adequately embodied in a film (or in any other kind of art) this exploration of experience alters our experience of life, including our experience of ourselves. Let Truffaut have the last word on this topic:

> I also believe that every film must contain some degree of "planned violence" upon its audience. In a good film, people must be made to see something that they don't want to see: they must be made to approve of someone of whom they had disapproved, they must be forced to look where they had refused to look.

GETTING READY TO WRITE

Mastery of terminology does not make anyone a perceptive film critic, but it helps writers to communicate their perceptions to their readers. Probably an essay on a film will not be primarily about the use of establishing shots or of wipes, or of any such matters, but rather it will be about some of the reasons why a particular film pleases or displeases, succeeds or fails, seems significant or insigifnicicant, and in discussing these large matters it is sometimes necessary (or at least economical) to use the commonest technical terms. Large matters are often determined in part by such seemingly small matters as the distance of the camera from its subject, or the way in which transitions are made, and one may as well use the conventional terms. But it is also true that a film-maker's technique and technology alone cannot make a first-rate film. There has to be an idea, a personal vision, a theme (see pp. 261–263) that is embodied in all that is flashed on the screen.

Writing an essay about a film presents difficulties not encountered in writing about stories, plays, and poems. Because we experience film in a darkened room, we cannot easily take notes, and because the film may be shown only once, we cannot always take another look at passages that puzzle us. But some brief notes can be taken even in the dark; it is best to amplify them as soon as light is available, while one still knows what the scrawls mean. If you can see the film more than once, do so; and, of course, if the script has been published, study it. Draft your paper as soon as possible after your first viewing, and then see the film again. You can sometimes check hazy memories of certain scenes and techniques with fellow viewers. But even with multiple viewings and the aid of friends, it is almost impossible to get the details right; it is best for the writer to be humble and for the reader to be tolerant.

Sample Essay on Visual Symbols

Printed here is a student's essay on a film. Because it is on a version of *Macbeth,* it is in some degree a comparison between a film and a play, but it does not keep shifting back and forth nor does it make the obvious point that there are many differences. Rather, it fairly quickly announces that it will be concerned with one kind of difference — the use of visual symbols that the camera can effectively render — and it then examines four such symbols.

Here is the skeleton of the essay, "A Japanese *Macbeth,*" paragraph by paragraph:

> The Japanese film of *Macbeth* is not a film of a stage-performance; it is a cinematic version.

> The film sometimes changes Shakespeare's plot, but this essay will be concerned only with the changes that are visual symbols: the fog, the castle, the forest, the horses.

> The fog, the castle, and the forest can be treated briefly. The fog shows nature blinding man; the castle shows man's brief attempt to impose his will on the natural landscape; the forest shows nature entrapping man.

> The nervous, active horses — which could not be actually shown on the Elizabethan stage — suggest man's fierce, destructive passions.

> The film, though literally false to the play, is artistically true.

This is a solid organization: the title, though not especially imaginative, at least catches our interest and gives a good idea of the general topic; the first paragraph introduces a significant point, and the second narrows it and announces precisely what the essay will cover. The third paragraph studies three of the four symbols announced in the second paragraph, and the fourth paragraph studies the fourth, more complicated symbol. The concluding paragraph in a way reaffirms the opening paragraph, but it does so now in the light of concrete evidence that has been offered. Organizing the essay, of course, is only part of the job. The writer of this essay has done more than work out an acceptable organization; he has some perceptions to offer, and he has found the right details and provided neat transitions so that the reader can move through the essay with pleasure.

A Japanese Macbeth

Essayist's general position, and implicit thesis, is clear from the start.

A Japanese movie-version of Macbeth sounds like a bad idea—until one sees Kurosawa's film, Throne of Blood, in which Toshiro Mifune plays Macbeth. It is a much more satisfying film than, say, Olivier's Othello, largely because it is not merely a filmed version of a play as it might be performed on a stage, but rather it is a freely re-created version that is designed for the camera. The very fact that it is in Japanese is probably a great help to Westerners. If it were in English, we would be upset at the way some speeches are cut, but because it is in Japanese, we do not compare the words to Shakespeare's, and we concentrate on the visual aspects of the film.

As the paragraph proceeds, it zooms in on the topic.

There are several differences in the plots of the two works. Among the alterations are such things as these: Shakespeare's three witches are reduced to one; Lady Macbeth has a miscarriage; Macbeth is killed by his own troops and not by Macduff. But this paper will discuss another sort of change, the introduction of visual symbols, which the camera is adept at rendering, and which play an important part in the film. The four chief visual symbols are the fog, the castle, the forest, and the horses.

Essayist tells us exactly what will be covered in the rest of the essay.

The fog, the castle, and the forest, though highly effective, can be dealt with rather briefly. When the film begins we get a slow panoramic view of the ruined castle seen through the fog. The film ends with a similar panoramic view. These two scenes end with a dissolve, though almost all of the other scenes end abruptly with sharp cuts, and so the effect is that of lingering sorrow at the transience of human creations, and awe at the permanence of the mysterious natural world, whose mist slowly drifts across what once was a mighty castle built by a great chief. The castle itself, when we come to see it in its original condition, is not a particularly graceful Japanese building. Rather, it is a low, strong building, appropriate for an energetic warrior. The interior scenes show low, oppressive ceilings, with great exposed beams that almost seem to crush the people within

Transition (through repetition of part of previous sentence) and helpful forecast.

Analysis, not mere plot-telling.

the rooms. It represents man's achievement in the center of the misty tangled forest of the mysterious world, but it also suggests, de-

Thoughtful interpretation.

spite its strength, how stifling that achievement is, in comparison with the floating mists and endless woods. The woods, rainy and misty, consist of curiously gnarled trees and vines, and suggest a labyrinth that has entrapped man, even though for a while man thinks he is secure in his castle. Early in the film we see Macbeth riding through the woods, in and out of mists, and behind a maze of twisted trees that periodically hide him from our sight.

Further interpretation. Maybe it is not too fanciful to suggest that the branches through which we glimpse him blindly riding in the fog are a sort of net that entangles him. The trees and the mist are the vast unfathomable universe; man can build his castle, can make his plans, but he cannot subdue nature for long. He cannot have his way forever; death will ultimately catch him, de-

Essayist moves chro-nologically.

spite his strength. One later scene of the forest must be mentioned. Near the end of the film, when the forest moves (the soldiers are holding up leafy boughs to camouflage them-selves), we get a spectacular shot; Shake-

Summary leads, at the end of the paragraph, to interpretation.

speare talks of the forst moving, but in the film we see it. Suddenly the forest seems to give a shudder and to be alive, crawling as though it is a vast horde of ants. Nature is seen to rise up against Macbeth's crimes.

The first half of this paragraph is a well-handled comparison.

Shakespeare's stage could do very little about such an effect as the fog, though his poetry can call it to mind, and it could do even less about the forest. Kurosawa did not feel bound to the text of the play: he made a movie, and he took advantage of the camera's ability to present impressive and significant scenic effects. Similarly, he made much use of horses, which, though mentioned in Shakespeare's play, could not be shown on the Elizabethan stage. In fact, in <u>Macbeth</u> (III.iii.12—13) Shakespeare more or less apologizes for the absence of horses when one murderer explains to the other that when horsemen approach the palace it is customary for them to leave their horses and to walk the rest of

A reminder of a point made earlier, but now developed at length.

the way. But the film gives us plenty of horses, not only at the start, when Macbeth is galloping in the terrifying forest, but throughout the film, and they are used to suggest the terror of existence, and the evil passions in Macbeth's heart. Shakespeare provided a hint. After King Duncan is murdered, Shakespeare tells us that Duncan's horses ''Turned wild in nature, broke their stalls,'' and even that they ate each other (II.iv.16—18). In the film, when Macbeth and his wife plot the murder of their lord, we see the

panic—struck horses running around the courtyard of the castle—a sort of parallel to the
scene of Macbeth chaotically riding in and out
of the fog near the beginning of the movie.
The horses in the courtyard apparently have
sensed man's villainous plots, or perhaps they
are visual equivalents of the fierce emotions
in the minds of Macbeth and his wife. Later,
when Macbeth is planning to murder Banquo, we
see Banquo's white horse kicking at his attendants. Banquo saddles the horse, preparing to
ride into the hands of his assassins. Then Kurosawa cuts to a long shot of the courtyard at
night, where Banquo's attendants are nervously
waiting for him to return. Then we hear the
sound of a galloping horse, and suddenly the
white horse comes running in, riderless. Yet
another use of this motif is when we cut to a
wild horse, after Macbeth's wife has said that
she is pregnant. In the film the wife has a
miscarriage, and here again the horse is a visual symbol of the disorder engendered within
her (the child would be the heir to the
usurped throne), as the other horses were symbols for the disorder in her mind and in Mac-

Thoughtful generali-
zation.

beth's. All of these cuts to the horses are
abrupt, contributing to the sense of violence
that the unrestrained horses themselves embody. Moreover, almost the only close-ups in

the film are some shots of horses, seen from a
low angle, emphasizing their powerful, oppressive brutality.

Conclusion is chiefly a
restatement but the
last sentence gives it
an interesting twist.

Throne of Blood is not Shakespeare's Mac-
beth--but even a filmed version of a staged
version of the play would not be Shakespeare's
Macbeth either, for the effect of a film is
simply not identical with the effect of a play
with live actors on the stage. But Throne of
Blood is a fine translation of Macbeth into an
approximate equivalent. Despite its lack of
faithfulness to the literal text, it is in a
higher way faithful. It is a work of art, like
its original.

CONCLUDING REMARKS

These questions may help to bring impressions out into the
open and may with some reworking provide topics for essays.

1. If the film is adapted from fiction or drama, does it slav-
ishly follow its original and neglect the potentialities of the camera?
Or does it so revel in cinematic devices that it distorts the original
work? If visual symbols are used, are they used effectively?

2. If the film is adapted from fiction or drama, does it do
violence to the theme of the original? Is the film better than its
source? Are the additions or omissions due to the medium or to a
crude or faulty interpretation of the original? Is the film *Coma* more
sensational or less than the book? In what ways can it be said that
the film is different from the book?

3. Can film deal as effectively with inner action — mental
processes — as with external, physical action? In a given film, how
is the inner action conveyed?

4. Are shots and sequences adequately developed or do they seem jerky? (Sometimes, of course, jerkiness may be desirable.)

5. Are the characters believable?

6. Are the actors appropriately cast? (Wasn't it a mistake to cast Robert Redford as Gatsby? Audrey Hepburn as Liza Doolittle? Nureyev as Valentino?)

7. Does the sound track offer more than realistic dialogue? Is the music appropriate and functional? (Music may, among other things, imitate natural sounds, give a sense of locale or of ethnic group, suggest states of mind, provide ironic commentary, or — by repeated melodies — help to establish connections.) Are ume, tempo, and pitch — whether of music or of such sounds as the wind blowing or cars moving — used to stimulate emotions?

8. All works of art are contrivances, of course, but (as a Roman saying puts it) the art is to conceal art. Does the film seem arty, a mere *tour de force,* or does it have the effect of inevitability, the effect of rightness, conveying a sense that a vision has been honestly expressed? Are characters or scenes clumsily dragged in? Are unusual effects significant? Does the whole add up to something? Do we get scenes or characters or techniques that at first hold us by their novelty but then have nothing further to offer?

9. Is the title significant? Are the newspaper or television advertisements appropriate?

Some final advice: Early in the essay it is usually desirable to sketch enough of the plot to give the readers an idea of what happenes. (In the previous essay the student does not sketch the plot, but he says it is a version of *Macbeth,* and thus gives the necessary information.) But do not try to recount everything that happens: it can't be done, and the attempt will frustrate you and bore your readers. Once you introduce the main characters and devote a few sentences to the plot, thus giving the readers a comfortable seat, get down to the job of convincing them that you have something interesting to say about the film — that the plot is trivial, or that the hero is not really cool but cruel, or that the plot and the characters are fine achievements but the camera work is sometimes needlessly tricksy, or that all is well.

Incidentally, a convenient way to give an actor's name in your essay is to put it in parentheses after the character's name or role, thus: "The detective (Humphrey Bogart) finds a clue. . . ." Then, as you go on to talk about the film, use the names of the characters or the roles, not the names of the actors, except of course when you are talking about the actors themselves, as in "Bogart is exactly right for the part."

SAMPLE ESSAYS

First, notice that these two essays are critical essays, not reviews. A critical essay normally aims at helping readers to understand better a work with which they are already familiar, though it usually assumes that their familiarity is a bit faded and therefore it briefly reminds them of the plot, relationships between characters, and so forth. But a review normally aims at describing and evaluating a work so that the readers can decide whether or not they wish to know it at first hand. (For a more detailed discussion of a review, see pp. 87–91 and pp. 181–185.

Stanley Solomon's discussion of *The Maltese Falcon* (1941) concentrates not on film techniques such as lighting or cuts but on the genre or type. And in discussing the genre he concentrates not so much on the plot as on what the plot adds up to, the moral vision embodied in the story. He presents his thesis in his first paragraph — a sure-fire strategy: *The Maltese Falcon* set the pattern for the private detective film, a form in which the hero confronts irredeemable evil and reveals the truth about his experiences. Notice that Solomon begins the paragraph by speaking of "the private detective film," and then, as the paragraph goes on, moves toward a clear and helpful description of the moral gist of such a film by telling us of the hero's aim. Notice, too, that Solomon's second paragraph (on the hero) grows easily out of his first. In short, his essay is clearly organized. Finally, notice that we never lose sight of the writer's thesis — the moral sense in *The Maltese Falcon* that defines the genre — and that when bits of plot are summarized they are summarized in order to support the thesis. The last paragraph glances at "post-*Falcon*" movies, but the last sentence brings us back to the central topic, *The Maltese Falcon*.

The selection by David Bordwell is part of an essay originally entitled "The Dual Cinematic Tradition in *Citizen Kane*." In the earlier part, not reprinted here, Bordwell asserts his thesis: *Citizen Kane* unites two cinematic traditions, cinema as objective realism and cinema as subjective vision. The first of these traditions was established at the end of the nineteenth century by the Lumière brothers, whose films, such as *The Train Arriving at the Station,* reproduced external reality. (The film showed exactly what the title announced.) The second of the two cinematic traditions, subjective vision, was established at the turn of the century by the films of Georges Méliès, a professional magician who produced films full of trickery and fantasy, such as *A Trip to the Moon.* In the extract printed here, Bordwell closely examines the union of these two traditions in the first few minutes of Welles's *Citizen Kane* (1941). Notice that he does not merely tell the plot; when he tells us that the camera shows us a "No Trespassing" sign, he adds that "It is a tingling moment," and he explains why: "The driving force of cinema is to trespass." Throughout his essay Bordwell calls attention to the *ways* in which the film establishes its meanings.

The Detective as Moralist: The Maltese Falcon★

Stanley J. Solomon

No other classic of the American cinema has so decidedly lent its form to a genre as *The Maltese Falcon* did to the private detective film. Many earlier films helped establish the essential motifs and iconography still noticeable in recent examples, but until Sam Spade found his way through the intricate paths of *The Maltese Falcon* the crucial moral terrain of the genre had not been mapped. There were some very good detective films before this, especially the Thin Man series and a couple of the Sherlock Holmes films. But the strengths of such films reflected the genial or eccentric traits and quirks of their heroes encountering complicated puzzles that they would proceed to solve, not as an activity of professional or moral responsibility but as an expression of their skills or style of life. The two earlier versions of Spade's adventure, *Dangerous Female* (also called *The Maltese Falcon*), directed by Roy Del Ruth in 1931, and *Satan*

★The essay has been retitled.

Met a Lady, directed by William Dieterle in 1936, were within that format and now seem trivial. What John Huston, Humphrey Bogart, and a brilliant supporting cast brought to the genre in 1941 was the dark side of human nature, the confrontation with irredeemable evil, and the determination of the hero, no matter what the cost, to disclose the truth about the sordid experiences he has endured.

Most of the moral burden of the private detective film is placed on the hero, who functions in this regard as a source of moral awareness. His frequent professional experience with the criminal world prior to the beginning of any film in this genre makes the detective both suspicious of all relationships and cynical about human motivation. Typically, the detective adopts the mannerisms of the criminal characters he works among, and to judge by appearance alone we would associate Sam Spade with the worst of the type. Sophisticated criminals such as Gutman and Cairo attempt to hire Spade because they sense that his superb detective skills serve only his self-interest and can be readily diverted to illegal activities. The police, who also admire him, believe him capable of murder. Aside from his secretary, no one trusts him or suspects that his inner nature aspires to the knowledge of moral truth. The detective from then on was destined to work from a position of inner isolation to the establishment of a socially acceptable moral order in the world around him.

To imbue a whole genre with a moral sense required a model with the dramatic persuasiveness to make questions of morality seem inevitable to the narrative fabric. When at the end of *The Maltese Falcon* Spade declares his intention of turning over to the police the murderess, Brigid, with whom he has fallen in love, he presents a number of reasons for his decision, some of which he himself apparently regards as unimportant. But one reason, by its basic logic, firmly ties in to a code of ethics Spade argues for as operating within the entire value system of his profession. "When a man's partner is killed, he's supposed to do something about it," he states vehemently, speaking to the woman he loves but will send to prison for killing a man he disliked. To let her go, merely on personal grounds, would be "bad all around, bad for every detective everywhere." Spade does not suggest that such a code is simply a matter of personal belief, though as far as the cinema goes, he may indeed have invented it; rather, he indicates that the moral issue relates primarily to the nature of his profession, and in order to remain a professional he must follow the code to its logical conclusion — in this instance, sacrificing the women he loves. Spade presents this imperative so forcefully that there seems no alternative, and it is this inevitability, the film's premises carried to their ultimate extension, that came to define the genre's moral dimension.

The issue of integrity that from then on was present in private detective films (usually dramatized by the attempt of one or more characters to "buy off" the detective) dovetailed with the development of the genre's premise that the true investigator is committed to his professional life above any other concerns — income, safety, or love. The cynical Spade seems the most unlikely of characters, at first, to create this generic concept of integrity; his literary antecedents come from the Dashiell Hammett–Raymond Chandler "hard-boiled school" of the 1920s. Yet his evident surface toughness, his disdain for his late partner's wife, with whom he has had an affair, his lack of illusions, and his contempt for certain characters do not in any real way contradict his inner drive toward an almost spiritual goal. His higher aims lead him ultimately to ignore money, which everyone assumes he eagerly covets — the one thousand dollars he turns over to the police in the end may be tainted in that it was given to him by a criminal, but it was legally earned and belongs to Spade. Similarly, measuring his professional code against his personal feelings, he abandons Brigid.

From the premise of integrity stem other chief qualities of the genre associated with this particular film, perhaps most apparent in the hero's descent into the nether world of criminal life. The assorted criminals and perverts populating detective films prior to *The Maltese Falcon,* who commit isolated crimes for greed or revenge — motives common to the genre before 1941 — suggest infrequent deviations from the normal world. The post-*Falcon* criminals have come to inhabit the total visual environment of the film, suggesting that the hero's descent occurs in a generally corrupt and decadent world (an allegorical dramatization of the real world) in which he himself symbolizes the main bulwark against depravity. The eccentric criminal types encountered by Spade — Brigid, Gutman, Cairo, and Wilmer — have long since been absorbed into the classic tradition of the cinema and have now become more lovable than sinister; but we must not forget Spade's own obvious disgust for their moral failure. All along he intends to bring them to justice, but equally apparent is his design to humiliate them as well, to make certain that no lingering claims can be made by some witness or participant to the equality of evil with the moral sense that Spade represents. Yet while manipulating events so as to provide demonstrations of the futility of evil, he often puts himself in grave danger. In the last sequence of the film Spade telephones the police to pick up the three male villains, explicitly warning them about the gunman Wilmer. Up to that moment, Spade has treated Wilmer as a teenage version of a 1930s James Cagney-type gangster, but Spade's handling of Wilmer is an act intended merely to dramatize the normal world's view of the despicable criminal; in reality, Spade is aware of the possibility that Wilmer might kill him. The point is that the detective-hero's descent into the nether world is based not on mere curiosity or casual involvement in a case, but on his hatred of evil and his desire to track it to its source, eventually to eradicate it, and thereby to cleanse the polluted environment of the film.

Therefore, the profession of the private investigator seems very much the equivalent of a calling to a life of self-sacrifice and commitment, resembling the life style of the medieval knight-errant. To perform well in his pursuits, the detective often adopts the disguise of one or another form of corruption for the purpose of gaining information or deluding the enemy, as Spade himself notes at the end. No matter what role he temporarily plays, the detective retains his identification with the moral order of the outside world he represents. Little is seen of this outside — presumably better — world in *The Maltese Falcon* or in any of the genre's major films, but its spirit is symbolized by the private eye's conviction that the discovery of truth is of ultimate value.

The Dual Cinematic Tradition in the Beginning of Citizen Kane★

David Bordwell

The opening twelve minutes of *Citzen Kane* capsulize its approach and scope. At the very start, Welles uses a basic property of film to establish *Kane*'s method and pays homage to the two founts of cinema — the fantasy of Méliès and the reportage of Lumière.

The camera glides slowly up a fence. "No Trespassing," warns a sign. Immediately, the camera proceeds to trespass. It is a tingling

★ As page 273 explains a bit more fully, the two traditions are realism and fantasy or (to put it differently) objectivity and subjectivity.

moment, because the driving force of cinema is to trespass, to relentlessly investigate, to peel back what conceals and confront what reveals. "The camera," writes Pudovkin, "as it were, forces itself, ever striving, into the profoundest deeps of life; it strives thither to penetrate, whither the average spectator never reaches as he glances casually around him. The camera goes deeper." Cinema is a perfecting of vision because the eye of the camera, unlike that of the spectator, cannot be held back by fences or walls or signs; if anything interferes with the steady progress into the heart of a scene, we know it is an artificial and temporary obstacle. Thus it is this forward-cleaving movement, begun in *Kane*'s first scene, that is completed at the climatic track-in to the Rosebud sled.

Immediately, the imagery becomes dreamlike: a castle, a light snapped out and mysteriously glowing back to life, a man's lips, eerily sifting snow, a shattered crystal, a tiny cottage. Dissolves languidly link huge close-ups; space is obliterated; the paperweight smashes but makes no sound; a nurse enters, distorted in the reflection. We then see the deathbed dark against an arched window, and the shot fades out. The sequence is a reprise of the dream-structure of the European avant-garde films, especially *Caligari, Un Chien Andalou,* and *Blood of a Poet.* Welles celebrates the magic of Méliès and stresses, in both the content and the juxtaposition of the images, the subjective side of cinema.

But suddenly, in one of the most brilliant strokes in film, the "News on the March" sequence bursts on our eyes, history fills the screen, and we are confronted with the Lumière side of cinema, reality apparently unmanipulated. The stentorian announcer, the corny sensationalism, the *Time* style, and the histrionic music announce the newsreel's affinity with the popular "March of Time" shorts. (It is still the funniest parody of mass-media vulgarity ever filmed.) Furthermore, since each shot looks like period footage, "News on the March" virtually recapitulates the technical development of cinema from 1890 to 1941. Scratches on the emulsion, jerky movement, jump cuts, overexposures, handheld camerawork, insertion of authentic newsreel clips, the use of different filmstocks and cameras — each frame is historically persuasive. Glimpses of Chamberlain, Teddy Roosevelt, and Hitler are immediately and indelibly convincing. Thus as the first sequence had given us a private, poetic image of Kane, so this sequence supplies the public, documentary side of him. In clashing the two together, Welles immediately establishes the basic tension of *Kane* (and cinema itself): objective fact versus subjective vision, clearness and superficiality versus obscurity and profundity, newsreel versus dream. By making us question the very nature of experience, this clash of forms and styles produces the tension between reality and imagination that is the film's theme.

"News on the March" does more, though. Jumping, skittery, grainy, the sequence is the narrative hub of the film, the Argument of the story, simultaneously running through Kane's life and outlining the story we are about to see. It builds our curiosity, plants a handful of clues, establishes the film's leaping, elliptical form, and, anticipating a major tendency of contemporary films, reminds the audience that it is an audience and that it is watching a film.

Appendixes

APPENDIX A:
WRITING ABOUT
NONFICTIONAL PROSE

Style as Meaning

As David Lodge shows in his analysis (p. 145) of a short chapter from Dickens's *Hard Times,* an analysis of prose need not be much different from an analysis of poetry. Novelists, like poets, are often attentive to connotations, to figurative language, to irony — in short, they use words in the ways that we expect imaginative writers to use them. They also exploit, of course, the humbler devices that we all use, such as parallel constructions, repetition, and subordination, and other matters discussed in the first part of Chapter 2, "Style and Format." But something more should be said about the relationship between prose style (whether in fiction or nonfiction) and meaning.

Suppose, to begin indirectly, we take a page of handwriting, or even a signature. We need not believe that graphology is an exact science to believe that the shape of the ink lines on paper (apart from the meaning of the words) often tells us something about the writer. We look at a large, ornate signature and we sense that the writer is confident; or we look at a tiny signature written with the finest of pens, and we wonder why anyone is so self-effacing.

More surely than handwriting, the writer's style reveals, among other things, his attitude toward himself, toward his reader, and toward his subject. The writer's attitudes are reflected in what is usually called tone. It is difficult to distinguish between style and tone, but we can try. Most discussions of style concentrate on what might be thought of as ornament: figurative language ("a sea of troubles"), inversion ("A leader he is not"), repetition and parallelism ("government of the people, by the people, for the people"), balance and antithesis ("It was the best of times, it was the worst of times"). Indeed, for centuries style has been called "the dress of thought," implying that the thought is something separate from the expression; the thought, in this view, is dressed up in stylistic devices. But in most of the writing that we read with interest and pleasure the stylistic devices are not ornamental and occasional but integral and pervasive. When we talk about wit, sincerity, tentativeness, self-assurance, aggressiveness, objectivity, and so forth, we can say we are talking about style, but we should recognize that style now is not a matter of ornamental devices that dress up some idea but part of the idea itself. And "the idea itself" includes the writer's unified yet appropriately varied tone of voice. To take a brief example: the famous English translation of Caesar's report of a victory, "I came, I saw, I conquered," might be paraphrased thus: "After getting to the scene of the battle I studied the situation. Then I devised a strategy that won the battle." But this paraphrase loses much of Caesar's message; the brevity and the parallelism of the famous version, as well as the alliteration (came, conquered) convey tight-lipped self-assurance — convey, that is, the tone that reveals Caesar to us. And this tone is a large part of Caesar's message. Caesar is really telling us not only about what he did, but about what sort of person he is. (The Latin original is even more tight-lipped and more alliterative: *veni, vidi, vici*.)

Short and Long Sentences

We have just seen the effect of brevity in Caesar's "I came, I saw, I conquered," but more should be said about the effect of the length of a sentence. Of course a succession of short sentences, or of sentences built out of short independent clauses, may be merely choppy and tedious rather than tight-lipped, but let's consider an effective example, taken from a book review. The passage describes the methods by which George Jackson, in prison, resisted efforts to destroy his spirit:

> He trains himself to sleep only three hours a night. He studies Swahili, Chinese, Arabic and Spanish. He does pushups to control his sexual urge and to train his body. Sometimes he does a thousand a day. He eats only one meal a day. And, always, he is reading and thinking.
>
> Julius Lester, *New York Times Book Review* (20 Nov. 1970), 12–14

That the author is capable of writing longer, more complicated sentences is evident in the next paragraph:

> Yet, when his contact with the outside world is extended beyond his family to include Angela Davis, Joan, a woman who works with the Soledad defense committee, and his attorney, he is able to find within himself feelings of love and tenderness.

Can we account for the success of the passage describing Jackson's prison routine? First, the short sentences, with their repeated commonplace form (subject, verb, object) in some degree imitate Jackson's experience: they are almost monotonously disciplined, almost as regular as the pushups the confined Jackson does. Later, when Jackson makes contact with Angela Davis and others, the long sentence helps to suggest the expansion of his world. Second, the brevity of the sentences suggests their enormous importance, certainly to Jackson and to Julius Lester and, Lester hopes, to the reader.

The effect of a short or long sentence largely depends on the content and the context; brevity does not always suggest confinement, and length does not always suggest expansion. But good writers do set forth their meaning in part through such things as the length of a sentence and the kind of syntax. Take, for example, these two long sentences. The first (from Dr. Johnson's *Life of Dryden*) is a periodic sentence — that is, the syntax remains incomplete until late; or, to put it a little differently, it creates mild suspense because the meaning is not revealed until the end.

> To search his plays for vigorous sallies and sententious elegances, or to fix the dates of any little pieces which he wrote by chance or by solicitation, were labor too tedious and minute.

Johnson's sentence, by holding the full meaning suspended until the end, and by using parallel or balanced clauses and phrases ("to search" and "to fix"; "vigorous sallies" and "sententious elegances"), suggests an assured speaker who from the start knows where he is going. This assurance harmonizes with and thus contributes to the faintly ironic point of the sentence.

But now consider a different sort of long sentence, one that states the main idea first, and then adds modifications in unparallel clauses. It suggests a speaker in the process of improvising his thoughts. The author is John Donne.

> We study health, and we deliberate upon our meats and drink and air and exercises, and we hew and we polish every stone that goes to that building; and so our health is a long and regular work.

Now Donne's sentence is no less artful than Johnson's, especially in its interesting figure of the body as a carefully constructed building — but we feel that we see Donne hewing his sentence as he speaks, and he takes us along with him, step by step.

Diction

Much of the tone will depend on the diction, the writer's selection of words. Of course all writers (and speakers) share many words, such as "the," "and," "walk," "sky," "book," and countless others. But some words are used only by certain speakers in certain situations. For the sake of simplicity, we can distinguish three levels of diction: high or formal, middle or informal, and low or vulgar or popular. Examples of a word on each level might be *umbilicus, navel,* and *belly button.* It's not that one word is right and the others wrong; each is right in the right context. A lecturer in a medical school will probably speak of the umbilicus, a physician talking to an adult patient will probably speak of the navel, and ordinary folks on fairly intimate terms will probably speak of the belly button. If you or I, in talking to a friend, were to speak of our umbilicus, the friend would probably regard us as stuffy, unless of course we used the word as a joke.

Remember, too, Lincoln's diction in the beginning of the Gettysburg Address. "Four score and seven years ago" is one way of saying "eighty-seven years ago." Why, then, didn't Lincoln say "eighty-seven"? Probably part of the answer is that "four score and seven" is the language of the Bible; Lincoln appropriately wished to evoke the Bible in this speech dedicating a cemetery to men who had died in a nation that lives "under God." And as President, speaking on a solemn occasion, Lincoln appropriately chose diction that is more formal than the diction of our (or his) ordinary life.

Although "diction" refers chiefly to the choice of words, as between "umbilicus" and "belly button," it can also refer to the arrangement of words. Thus, when the philosopher Bertrand Russell says,

> Brief and powerless is Man's life,

his diction (by the order of the words) is unusual, or at least different from the diction in

> Man's life is brief and powerless,

where the subject, as usual, comes before the predicate. Presumably Russell departs from the ordinary sequence of words not only because he is talking about a great issue but also because he is presenting himself very seriously as the High Priest of Wisdom. Here is more of the same, from an essay entitled "A Free Man's Worship," first published in 1903.

> Brief and powerless is Man's life; on him and all his race the slow, sure doom falls pitiless and dark. Blind to good and evil, reckless of destruction, omnipotent matter rolls on its relentless way; for Man, condemned today to lose his dearest, tomorrow himself to pass through the gate of darkness, it remains only to cherish, ere yet the blow falls, the lofty thoughts that ennoble his little day; disdaining the coward terrors of the slave of Fate, to worship at the shrine his own hands have built; undismayed by the empire of chance, to preserve a mind free from the wanton tyranny that rules his outward life; proudly defiant of the irresistible forces that tolerate, for a moment, his knowledge and his condemnation, to sustain alone, a weary but unyielding Atlas, the world that his own ideals have fashioned despite the trampling march of unconscious power.
>
> *Mysticism and Logic* (London, 1918), pp. 56–57

This passage doubtless is meant to be lofty, but doesn't it ring false? Instead of impressing us with its ideas about man's fate and man's nobility, it evokes unpleasant reflections about Russell's attempt to be eloquent. Biblical diction (as in "Brief and powerless is Man's life," and "ere") suits a modern philosopher less well than it suited Lincoln at Gettysburg, and the use of "Man" instead of "man" seems merely pretentious. Much of the diction, in fact, is that of an orator or melodramatist rather than that of a thinker: "rolls on its relentless way," "the gate of darkness," "the blow falls," "lofty thoughts," "the slave of Fate," "proudly defiant," "irresistible forces," "weary but unyielding." Surely these are not shrewd perceptions; rather they are clichés, canned expressions that have long been on the shelf and that now are dumped into the stew. Finally, the passage is too insistently rhythmic in its iambics, too consciously "poetic." Here are a few examples:

⏑ ⁄ ⏑ ⁄ ⏑ ⁄
on him and all his race

⏑ ⁄ ⏑ ⁄ ⏑ ⁄
for Man, condemned today

⏑ ⁄ ⏑ ⁄ ⏑ ⁄⏑ ⁄
the lofty thought . . . his little day

⏑ ⁄ ⏑ ⁄
his outward life

⏑ ⁄ ⏑ ⁄
the trampling march.

No rule says that prose must never contain metrical passages — indeed, shortly we will see Thoreau effectively using a few metrical feet in prose — but Russell's passage gives the effect of mindless prose trying to impress us by becoming a mouth-filling chant.

It must be added that Russell did not usually write like this. Most of his essays are delightful, partly because although he spoke authoritatively he did not speak solemnly and he did not lose touch with daily life. Here is a brief example, from an essay on the relation of work to happiness.

> Every man who has acquired some unusual skill enjoys exercising it until it has become a matter of course, or until he can no longer improve himself. This motive to activity begins in early childhood: a boy who can stand on his head becomes reluctant to stand on his feet. A great deal of work gives the same pleasure that is to be derived from games of skill. The work of a lawyer or a politician must contain in a more delectable form a great deal of the same pleasure that is to be derived from playing bridge.
>
> *The Conquest of Happiness* (New York, 1930), p. 212

Let's look now at a short passage from the second chapter of Thoreau's *Walden*. Thoreau moved to Walden Pond in 1845, not to escape from life but (in his words) "to live deliberately, to front only the essential facts of life, and see if I could not learn what it had to teach, and not, when I came to die, discover that I had not lived." As the following passage will make clear, he argues that his contemporaries are enslaved by trivial concerns, especially by the products of a technology whose most obvious symbol is the railroad.

> Our life is like a German Confederacy, made up of petty states, with its boundary forever fluctuating, so that even a German cannot tell you how it is bounded at any moment. The nation itself, with all its so-called internal improvements, which, by the way are all external and superficial, is just such an unwieldy and overgrown establishment, cluttered with furniture and tripped up by its own traps, ruined by luxury and heedless expense, by want of calculation, and a worthy aim, as the million households in the land; and the only cure for it as for them is in a rigid economy, a stern and more than Spartan simplicity of life and elevation of purpose. It lives too fast. Men think that it is essential that the *Nation* have commerce, and export ice, and talk through a telegraph, and ride thirty miles an hour, without a doubt, whether *they* do or not; but whether we should live like baboons or like men, is a little uncertain. If we do not get out sleepers, and forge rails, and devote days and nights to the work, but go to tinkering upon our *lives* to improve *them,* who will build railroads? And if railroads are not built, how shall we get to heaven in season? But if we stay at home and mind our business, who will want railroads? We do not ride on the railroad; it rides upon us. Did you ever think what those sleepers are that underlie the railroad? Each one is a man, an Irishman, or a Yankee man. The rails are laid on them, and they are covered with sand, and the cars run smoothly over them. They are sound sleepers, I assure you. And every few years a new lot is laid down and run over; so that, if some have the pleasure of riding on a rail, others have the misfortune to be ridden upon. And when they run over a man that is walking in his sleep, a supernumerary sleeper in the wrong position, and wake him up, they suddenly stop the cars, and make a hue and cry about it, as if this were an exception. I am glad to know that it takes a gang of men for every five miles to keep the sleepers down and level in their beds as it is, for this is a sign that they may sometime get up again.

What are some of the things we might call attention to in this witty, abusive, but ultimately compassionate extract? First, we might note that it makes little use of words that provide logical connections. We do not find expressions such as "More important, . . . most important of all," or "if . . . then," or "either . . . or"; the chief connective is merely "and," which scarcely implies the exact relationship between what precedes and follows it. In fact, Thoreau delights in puzzling us and then unpuzzling us, challenging us with strange or outrageous utterances and then ingeniously resolving them. He is a sort of magician or escape-artist; during one moment we don't quite know what he is up to, and then in the next moment we see him triumphant. Thoreau holds our attention and persuades us, but chiefly through devices that we can call imaginative rather than logical.

The passage begins with a riddling comparison: "Our life is like a German Confederacy." A moment later we understand that he is comparing the individual's inner instability to the messy political situation in the mid-nineteenth century. The belittling implications are immediately emphasized by "petty" and "even a German cannot tell you." Our lives, Thoreau insists, are meaninglessly fragmented, always in motion but going nowhere. But what of the nation's "internal improvements"? Thoreau takes the word "internal" and plays with it — or, better, looks hard at it; in the context of course it means "within the nation," but for Thoreau "internal" thus really means "external," external to the individual man and therefore unimportant. When Thoreau calls these internal improvements mere "furniture," and says that the nation is "cluttered with furniture," he uses another pejorative figure of speech, diminishing the nation to a room filled with junk. This clutter of furniture leads easily and immediately to Thoreau's assertion, emphasized by alliteration, that we are "*tr*ipped by our own *tr*aps." There is a pun here. "Traps" means "personal belongings," "trappings," and also, of course, "snares"; the furniture that should serve us now ensnares us. Most of the remainder of this long denunciatory sentence is somewhat more abstract and less witty in its indictment, but it ends affirmatively, calling (again with the aid of alliteration for emphasis) for "a *s*tern and more than *S*partan simplicity of life and elevation of purpose." The juxtaposition of "*s*tern" and "*S*partan" is wit enough, calling attention through the resemblance in sound to the resemblance in meaning; more wit in this sentence might suggest frivolity, playfulness without seriousness.

The first sentence is moderately long, thirty-two words, and the second is extremely long, a torrent of eighty-four words, but these sentences are followed by a sentence of only four little words, "It lives too fast," a brief and weighty observation that not only looks back to the ceaseless fluctuation mentioned in the first sentence but also looks forward to the rest of the passage. This short sentence may seem clear enough, but in fact it is metaphoric and it needs clarification. Exactly what does it mean to say that a nation "lives too fast"? And what is the connection between our "furniture" and our "traps" and living "too fast"? Thoreau goes on to explain: we are concerned with exporting ice, talking through a telegraph, and riding (on the railroad) at the astounding speed of thirty miles an hour. Even those men who do not do these things think it is essential that these things be done, by someone, anyone. And then, "but whether we should live like baboons or like men, is a little uncertain." Here again, with "baboons," is the diminishing simile — a common weapon in the satirist's arsenal — and there is also, in "a little uncertain," a nice touch of ironic understatement, another common satiric weapon.

The remainder of the passage is concerned with the railroad, here literally referring to our passion for speed, and also symbolizing technology. More precisely, the remainder of the passage is concerned with the disastrous effects of technology on human beings. Mocking those who see in technology the salvation of the nation, Thoreau sarcastically asks, "And if railroads are not built, how shall we get to heaven in season?" Again we get an incantatory yet meaningful playing with the sounds of words ("we do not *ride* on the *rail*road"), and with the meaning of words: "it rides upon us." Next, a pun on "sleeper," the old word for a crosstie:

> Did you ever think what those sleepers are that underlie the railroad? Each one is a man, an Irishman, or a Yankee man. The rails are laid on them, and they are covered with sand, and the cars run smoothly over them.

Possibly in these three sentences, with the repeated *m*'s and *n*'s, and *r*'s and *l*'s, and especially with the three approximately equal clauses in the last sentence, we are meant to hear or at least to be reminded of a train rolling along. And this last sentence, with its clauses linked by "and," faintly echoes the style of many passages in the King James version of the Bible. This biblical echo gives his utterance an air not only of authority but of eternity. As an example, compare that sentence with this line from Ecclesiastes: "The sun also ariseth, and the sun goeth down, and hasteneth to his place where he arose." Probably, too. Thoreau's dactyls (a stressed syllable followed by two unstressed syllables) and anapests (two unstressed syllables followed by a stressed syllable), for example,

$$\acute{\cup}\ \cup\qquad \acute{}\ \cup\ \cup\qquad \acute{}\ \cup\cup\qquad \cup\ \cup\ \acute{}\qquad \cup\cup\ \acute{}$$
"Irishman," "Yankee man," "underlie," "and the cars," "is a man,"

owe something to the cadences of the Bible, where such a rhythm as

$$\cup\ \cup\quad \acute{}\cup\ \cup\quad \acute{}\cup\ \cup\quad \acute{}$$
all the rivers run into the sea

is common. But Thoreau, unlike Bertrand Russell in the passage from "A Free Man's Worship," does not let the meter take over the prose, and he does not abandon close observation and serious thinking. We never feel, as we read this passage, that the sound has triumphed over the sense.

To return to Thoreau's metaphor: the trains do not, of course, literally run over the workmen who built the tracks, but metaphorically they do; the railroad was built at a cost of life, at the cost of dehumanizing men by brute, mindless labor. We are prepared, then, to accept the truth of Thoreau's elegantly stated but damning paradox: "if some have the pleasure of riding on a rail, others have the misfortune to be ridden on." Further, the statement is not only true metaphorically, but also literally:

> And when they run over a man that is walking in his sleep, a supernumerary sleeper in the wrong position, and wake him up, they suddenly stop the cars, and make a hue and cry about it, as if this were an exception.

True, the language is still metaphoric as well as literal here, for Thoreau calls the luckless victim (who was unaware until struck down by the train) a "supernumerary sleeper in the wrong position"; this "sleeper," when he is run over, is awakened — that is, he is jolted out of the unthinking slumber that characterizes his usual life. But Thoreau's chief point here, of course, is that the great "hue and cry" is superficial (by using a cliché or ready-made phrase he implies that the fuss is a mindless reaction, a mere knee-jerk), for the literal running-over of a person is only a rare and crude manifestation of the widespread but for the most part unnoticed destruction that the building of railroads wreaks on the human spirit.

The last sentence of the passage begins by returning to the literal, to the fact that railroad ties shift in their place, but Thoreau ends by interpreting this physical fact symbolically: "this is a sign that they may sometimes get up again." He thus hints at a sort of regeneration or resurrection. If much in the passage as a whole has been witty, aggressive, revolutionary, and (from the point of view of conventional thought) destructive, this ending introduces a quieter yet slightly elevated note. The words are commonplace, for example, "I am glad to know that it takes a gang of men for every five miles," but the sentence contains a touch of prophecy — without oppressive solemnity — a revelation that in the long run mankind may blessedly survive even its newest fads.

A Sample Analysis

Enough has already been said to indicate that a passage of nonfiction does not merely offer some facts or observations; if the writing is good it holds our attention and persuades us in part by its style, and indeed sometimes the subtlest meanings are conveyed through the style rather than through the paraphrasable content. Let's look at E. B. White's "Education," and then we will further consider the relation between style and meaning.

Education ★

E. B. White

I have an increasing admiration for the teacher in the country school where we have a third-grade scholar in attendance. She not

★ *One Man's Meat* (New York, 1942).

only undertakes to instruct her charges in all the subjects of the first three grades, but she manages to function quietly and effectively as a guardian of their health, their clothes, their habits, their mothers, and their snowball engagements. She has been doing this sort of Augean task for twenty years, and is both kind and wise. She cooks for the children on the stove that heats the room, and she can cool their passions or warm their soup with equal competence. She conceives their costumes, cleans up their messes, and shares their confidences. My boy already regards his teacher as his great friend, and I think tells her a great deal more than he tells us.

The shift from city school to country school was something we worried about quietly all last summer. I have always rather favored public school over private school, if only because in public school you meet a greater variety of children. This bias of mine, I suspect, is partly an attempt to justify my own past (I never knew anything but public schools) and partly an involuntary defense against getting kicked in the shins by a young ceramist on his way to the kiln. My wife was unacquainted with public schools, never having been exposed (in her early life) to anything more public than the washroom of Miss Winsor's. Regardless of our backgrounds, we both knew that the change in schools was something that concerned not us but the scholar himself. We hoped it would work out all right. In New York our son went to a medium-priced private institution with semi-progressive ideas of education, and modern plumbing. He learned fast, kept well, and we were satisfied. It was an electric, colorful, regimented existence with moments of pleasurable pause and giddy incident. The day the Christmas angel fainted and had to be carried out by one of the Wise Men was educational in the highest sense of the term. Our scholar gave imitations of it around the house for weeks afterward, and I doubt if it ever goes completely out of his mind.

His days were rich in formal experience. Wearing overalls and an old sweater (the accepted uniform of the private seminary), he sallied forth at morn accompanied by a nurse or a parent and walked (or was pulled) two blocks to a corner where the school bus made a flag stop. This flashy vehicle was as punctual as death: seeing us waiting at the cold curb, it would sweep to a halt, open its mouth, suck the boy in, and spring away with an angry growl. It was a good deal like a train picking up a bag of mail. At school the scholar was worked on for six or seven hours by half a dozen teachers and a nurse, and was revived on orange juice in mid-morning. In a cinder court he played games supervised by an athletic instructor, and in a cafeteria he ate lunch worked out by a dietitian. He soon learned to read with gratifying facility and discernment and to make Indian weapons of a semideadly nature. Whenever one of his classmates fell low of a fever the news was put on the wires and there were breathless phone calls to physicians, discussing periods of incubation and allied magic.

In the country all one can say is that the situation is different, and somehow more casual. Dressed in corduroys, sweatshirt, and short rubber boots, and carrying a tin dinner-pail, our scholar departs at crack of dawn for the village school, two and a half miles down the road, next to the cemetery. When the road is open and the car will start, he makes the journey by motor, courtesy of his old man. When the snow is deep or the motor is dead or both, he makes it on the hoof. In the afternoons he walks or hitches all or part of the way home in fair weather, gets transported in foul. The schoolhouse is a two-room frame building, bungalow type, shingles stained a burnt brown with weather-resistant stain. It has a chemical toilet in the basement and two teachers above stairs. One takes the first three grades, the other the fourth, fifth, and sixth. They have little or no time for individual instruction, and no time at all for the esoteric. They teach what they know themselves, just as fast and as hard as they can manage. The pupils sit still at their desks in class, and do their milling around outdoors during recess.

There is no supervised play. They play cops and robbers (only they call it "Jail") and throw things at one another — snowballs in winter, rose hips in fall. It seems to satisfy them. They also construct darts, pinwheels, and "pick-up sticks" (jackstraws), and the school itself does a brisk trade in penny candy, which is for sale right in the classroom and which contains "surprises." The most highly prized surprise is a fake cigarette, made of cardboard, fiendishly lifelike.

The memory of how apprehensive we were at the beginning is still strong. The boy was nervous about the change too. The tension, on that first fair morning in September when we drove him to school, almost blew the windows out of the sedan. And when later we picked him up on the road, wandering along with his little blue lunch-pail, and got his laconic report "All right" in answer to our inquiry about how the day had gone, our relief was vast. Now, after almost a year of it, the only difference we can discover in the two school experiences is that in the country he sleeps better at night — and *that* probably is more the air than the education. When grilled on the subject of school-in-country *vs.* school-in-city, he replied that the chief difference is that the day seems to go so much quicker in the country. "Just like lightning," he reported.

White entertainingly compares two schools, one private and one public, but he does not explicitly tell us which school is better. In fact, in the final paragraph he claims that after almost a year in the country "the only difference we can discover in the two school experiences is that in the country he sleeps better at night — and *that* probably is more the air than the education." On the whole, White offers scarcely anything that can be called an argument, a discourse in which certain statements are offered as *reasons* for other statements. And yet, when we have finished reading his essay we somehow share his admitted "bias" in favor of public education. Why?

Partly, of course, because of the organization of the essay. At the beginning (an emphatic position) he praises the teacher in the country school, and at the end (an even more emphatic position) he quotes the schoolboy's characterization of how the schooldays go in the country: " 'Just like lightning,' he reported." We might look at these passages even more closely, and say that the praise in the opening paragraph is especially emphatic partly because it compares the teacher's tasks to Hercules' magnificent cleaning of the long-uncleaned stable of King Augeus, and partly because (aside from this playful mythological allusion) it is so insistent in its simplicity: "She has been doing," "She cooks," "she can," "She conceives. . . ." And the end of the final paragraph is especially emphatic partly because it comes from an unexpected but unimpeachable source, and partly because the last sentence is so brief, its brevity being further emphasized by the fact that it is preceded by a sentence about six times as long. But White's praise of the teacher, and his presentation of the boy's comment, would not in themselves allow us to say that White prefers the country school; yet it is clear that he does, and he conveys this preference chiefly through connotations and metaphors and tone.

First, some remarks about the connotations and metaphors. White says, in the beginning of the third paragraph, that when the boy attended the private school he wore "overalls and an old sweater (the accepted uniform of the private seminary)." The word "uniform" is of course playful, but it reinforces ideas already suggested in *"regimented existence"* and *"formal* experience." Here, again, is the first half of the paragraph, with some key words italicized, not because they need emphasis but merely because once they are noticed they scarcely require any further comment.

> His days were rich in formal experience. Wearing overalls and an old sweater (the accepted uniform of the private seminary), he sallied forth at morn accompanied by a *nurse* or a parent and walked (or *was pulled*) two blocks to a corner where the school bus made a flag stop. This *flashy* vehicle was as *punctual as death:* seeing us waiting at the *cold* curb, it would sweep to a *halt, open its mouth, suck the boy in,* and spring away with *an angry growl.* It was a good deal like a train *picking up a bag of mail.* At school the scholar was *worked on* for six or seven hours by half a dozen teachers and a nurse, and was *revived* on orange juice in mid-morning.

Now, in the passage on the country school we can also find words that might seem to have unfavorable associations ("cemetery," "dead") but we don't connect these words with the school itself, as we do connect with the school the "vehicle punctual as death" which would "'suck the boy in" and depart with "an angry growl."

Next, some words on tone. Of course the whole essay is playful. The third-grader is from the outset called a "scholar," he makes weapons "of a semi-deadly nature," and so forth. But the faintly comic diction is most apparent in the paragraph on the private school, where such expressions as "sallied forth at morn," "revived on orange juice," and "breathless phone calls" are amusing because they are a shade too lofty for the relatively trivial subject. This gentle mockery makes the school — which evidently takes itself terribly seriously — a trifle ridiculous. White follows this highly metaphoric and inappropriately lofty (and therefore comic and deflating) paragraph with a sentence that could scarcely be any closer to common speech: "In the country all one can say is that the situation is different, and somehow more casual." Here White is not playing around; rather, he sounds earnest and even at a loss for words. Apparently the public school is not so easily summed up, not so easily (we might say) put in its place. The rest of the paragraph is not so spare; we hear a playful voice in such expressions as "courtesy of his old man" and "makes it on the hoof," and there is a mischievous hint of an equation when he says that the public school "has a chemical toilet in the basement and two teachers above stairs," but on the whole the paragraph about the country school seems plain and unvarnished — natural — compared to the paragraph about the private school. We can put it this way: when White is writing about the zippy private school, he writes a zippy paragraph that gently mocks the school; when he writes about the no-frills public school, he writes a no-frills paragraph that by the apparent simplicity of the writing convinces us of the school's unspectacular but real worth. This simplicity of course is artful, just as artful as (to return to a point made earlier) the organization of the essay, which gives the boy the last word, almost explicitly confirming a presence that White has kept implicit but has nevertheless made clear.

APPENDIX B

A Rose for Emily
William Faulkner

I

When Miss Emily Grierson died, our whole town went to her funeral: the men through a sort of respectful affection for a fallen monument, the women mostly out of curiosity to see the inside of her house, which no one save an old manservant — a combined gardener and cook — had seen in at least ten years.

It was a big, squarish frame house that had once been white, decorated with cupolas and spires and scrolled balconies in the heavily lightsome style of the seventies, set on what had once been our most select street. But garages and cotton gins had encroached and obliterated even the august names of that neighborhood; only Miss Emily's house was left, lifting its stubborn and coquettish decay above the cotton wagons and the gas line pumps — an eyesore among eyesores. And now Miss Emily had gone to join the representatives of those august names where they lay in the cedar-bemused cemetery among the ranked and anonymous graves of Union and Confederate soldiers who fell at the battle of Jefferson.

Alive, Miss Emily had been a tradition, a duty, and a care; a sort of hereditary obligation upon the town, dating from that day in 1894 when Colonel Sartoris, the mayor — he who fathered the edict that no Negro woman should appear on the streets without an apron — remitted her taxes, the dispensation dating from the death of her father on into perpetuity. Not that Miss Emily would have accepted charity. Colonel Sartoris invented an involved tale to the effect that Miss Emily's father had loaned money to the town, which the town, as a matter of business, preferred this way of repaying. Only a man of Colonel Sartoris' generation and thought could have invented it, and only a woman could have believed it.

When the next generation, with its more modern ideas, became mayors and aldermen, this arrangement created some little dissatisfaction. On the first of the year they mailed her a tax notice. February came, and there was no reply. They wrote her a formal letter, asking her to call at the sheriff's office at her convenience. A week later the mayor wrote her himself, offering to call or to send his car for her, and received in reply a note on paper of an archaic shape, in a thin, flowing calligraphy in faded ink, to the effect that she no longer went out at all. The tax notice was also enclosed, without comment.

They called a special meeting of the Board of Aldermen. A deputation waited upon her, knocked at the door through which no visitor had passed since she ceased giving china-painting lessons eight or ten years earlier. They were admitted by the old Negro into a dim hall from which a staircase mounted into still more shadow. It smelled of dust and disuse — a close, dank smell. The Negro led them into the parlor. It was furnished in heavy, leather-covered furniture. When the Negro opened the blinds of one window, a faint dust rose sluggishly about their thighs, spinning with slow motes in the single sun-ray. On a tarnished gilt easel before the fireplace stood a crayon portrait of Miss Emily's father.

They rose when she entered — a small, fat woman in black, with a thin gold chain descending to her waist and vanishing into her belt, leaning on an ebony cane with a tarnished gold head. Her skeleton was small and spare; perhaps that was why what would have been merely plumpness in another was obesity in her. She looked bloated, like a body long submerged in motionless water, and of that pallid hue. Her eyes, lost in the fatty ridges of her face, looked like two small pieces of coal pressed into a lump of dough as they moved from one face to another while the visitors stated their errand.

She did not ask them to sit. She just stood in the door and listened quietly until the spokesman came to a stumbling halt. Then they could hear the invisible watch ticking at the end of the gold chain.

Her voice was dry and cold. "I have no taxes in Jefferson. Colonel Sartoris explained it to me. Perhaps one of you can gain access to the city records and satisfy yourselves."

"But we have. We are the city authorities, Miss Emily. Didn't you get a notice from the sheriff, signed by him?"

"I received a paper, yes," Miss Emily said. "Perhaps he considers himself the sheriff. . . . I have no taxes in Jefferson."

"But there is nothing on the books to show that, you see. We must go by the —"

"See Colonel Sartoris. I have no taxes in Jefferson."

"But, Miss Emily —"

"See Colonel Sartoris." (Colonel Sartoris had been dead almost ten years.) "I have no taxes in Jefferson. Tobe!" The Negro appeared. "Show these gentlemen out."

II

So she vanquished them, horse and foot, just as she had vanquished their fathers thirty years before about the smell. That was two years after her father's death and a short time after her sweetheart — the one we believed would marry her — had deserted her. After her father's death she went out very little; after her sweetheart went away, people hardly saw her at all. A few of the ladies had the termerity to call, but were not received, and the only sign of life about the place was the Negro man — a young man then — going in and out with a market basket.

"Just as if a man — any man — could keep a kitchen properly," the ladies said; so they were not surprised when the smell developed. It was another link between the gross, teeming world and the high and mighty Griersons.

A neighbor, a woman, complained to the mayor, Judge Stevens, eighty years old.

"But what will you have me do about it, madam?" he said.

"Why, send her word to stop it," the woman said. "Isn't there a law?"

"I'm sure that won't be necessary," Judge Stevens said. "It's probably just a snake or a rat that nigger of hers killed in the yard. I'll speak to him about it."

The next day he received two more complaints, one from a

man who came in diffident deprecation. "We really must do something about it, Judge. I'd be the last one in the world to bother Miss
Emily, but we've got to do something." That night the Board of
Aldermen met — three gray-beards and one younger man, a member of the rising generation.

"It's simple enough," he said. "Send her word to have her place
cleaned up. Give her a certain time to do it in, and if she don't . . ."

"Dammit, sir," Judge Stevens said, "will you accuse a lady to
her face of smelling bad?"

So the next night, after midnight, four men crossed Miss Emily's lawn and slunk about the house like burglars, sniffing along
the base of the brickwork and at the cellar openings while one of
them performed a regular sowing motion with his hand out of a
sack slung from his shoulder. They broke open the cellar door and
sprinkled lime there, and in all the out-buildings. As they recrossed
the lawn, a window that had been dark was lighted and Miss Emily
sat in it, the light behind her, and her upright torso motionless as
that of an idol. They crept quietly across the lawn and into the
shadow of the locusts that lined the street. After a week or two the
smell went away.

That was when people had begun to feel really sorry for her.
People in our town remembering how old lady Wyatt, her great-
aunt, had gone completely crazy at last, believed that the Griersons
held themselves a little too high for what they really were. None
of the young men were quite good enough for Miss Emily and such.
We had long thought of them as a tableau; Miss Emily a slender
figure in white in the background, her father a spraddled silhouette
in the foreground, his back to her and clutching a horsewhip, the
two of them framed by the back-flung front door. So when she got
to be thirty and was still single, we were not pleased exactly, but
vindicated; even with insanity in the family she wouldn't have turned
down all of her chances if they had really materialized.

When her father died, it got about that the house was all that
was left to her; and in a way, people were glad. At last they could
pity Miss Emily. Being left alone, and a pauper, she had become
humanized. Now she too would know the old thrill and the old
despair of a penny more or less.

The day after his death all the ladies prepared to call at the house
and offer condolence and aid, as is our custom. Miss Emily met
them at the door, dressed as usual and with no trace of grief on her
face. She told them that her father was not dead. She did that for
three days, with the ministers calling on her, and the doctors, trying

to persuade her to let them dispose of the body. Just as they were about to resort to law and force, she broke down, and they buried her father quickly.

We did not say she was crazy then. We believed she had to do that. We remembered all the young men her father had driven away, and we knew that with nothing left, she would have to cling to that which had robbed her, as people will.

III

She was sick for a long time. When we saw her again, her hair was cut short, making her look like a girl, with a vague resemblance to those angels in colored church windows — sort of tragic and serene.

The town had just let the contracts for paving the sidewalks, and in the summer after her father's death they began to work. The construction company came with niggers and mules and machinery, and a foreman named Homer Barron, a Yankee — a big, dark, ready man, with a big voice and eyes lighter than his face. The little boys would follow in groups to hear him cuss the niggers, and the niggers singing in time to the rise and fall of picks. Pretty soon he knew everybody in town. Whenever you heard a lot of laughing anywhere about the square, Homer Barron would be in the center of the group. Presently we began to see him and Miss Emily on Sunday afternoons driving in the yellow-wheeled buggy and the matched team of bays from the livery stable.

At first we were glad that Miss Emily would have an interest, because the ladies all said, "Of course a Grierson would not think seriously of a Northerner, a day laborer." But there were still others, older people, who said that even grief could not cause a real lady to forget *noblesse oblige* — without calling it *noblesse oblige.* They just said, "Poor Emily. Her kinsfolk should come to her." She had some kin in Alabama; but years ago her father had fallen out with them over the estate of old lady Wyatt, the crazy woman, and there was no communication between the two families. They had not even been represented at the funeral.

And as soon as the old people said, "Poor Emily," the whispering began. "Do you suppose it's really so?" they said to one another. "Of course it is. What else could . . ." This behind their hands; rustling of craned silk and satin behind jalousies closed upon the sun of Sunday afternoon as the thin, swift clop-clop-clop of the matched team passed: "Poor Emily."

She carried her head high enough — even when we believed

that she was fallen. It was as if she demanded more than ever the recognition of her dignity as the last Grierson; as if it had wanted that touch of earthiness to reaffirm her imperviousness. Like when she bought the rat poison, the arsenic. That was over a year after they had begun to say "Poor Emily," and while the two female cousins were visiting her.

"I want some poison," she said to the druggist. She was over thirty then, still a slight woman, though thinner than usual, with cold, haughty black eyes in a face the flesh of which was strained across the temples and about the eyesockets as you imagine a light-house-keeper's face ought to look. "I want some poison," she said.

"Yes, Miss Emily. What kind? For rats and such? I'd recom —"

"I want the best you have. I don't care what kind."

The druggist named several. "They'll kill anything up to an elephant. But what you want is —"

"Arsenic," Miss Emily said. "Is that a good one?"

"Is . . . arsenic? Yes ma'am. But what you want —"

"I want arsenic."

The druggist looked down at her. She looked back at him, erect, her face like a strained flag. "Why, of course," the druggist said. "If that's what you want. But the law requires you to tell what you are going to use it for."

Miss Emily just stared at him, her head tilted back in order to look him eye for eye, until he looked away and went and got the arsenic and wrapped it up. The Negro delivery boy brought her the package; the druggist didn't come back. When she opened the package at home there was written on the box, under the skull and bones: "For rats."

IV

So the next day we all said, "She will kill herself"; and we said it would be the best thing. When she had first begun to be seen with Homer Barron, we had said, "She will marry him." Then we said, "She will persuade him yet," because Homer himself had remarked — he liked men, and it was known that he drank with the younger men in the Elk's Club — that he was not a marrying man. Later we said, "Poor Emily," behind the jalousies as they passed on Sunday afternoon in the glittering buggy, Miss Emily with her head high and Homer Barron with his hat cocked and a cigar in his teeth, reins and whip in a yellow glove.

Then some of the ladies began to say that it was a disgrace to the town and a bad example to the young people. The men did not want to interfere, but at last the ladies forced the Baptist minister — Miss Emily's people were Episcopal — to call upon her. He would never divulge what happened during that interview, but he refused to go back again. The next Sunday, they again drove about the streets, and the following day the minister's wife wrote to Miss Emily's relations in Alabama.

So she had blood-kin under her roof again and we sat back to watch developments. At first nothing happened. Then we were sure that they were to be married. We learned that Miss Emily had been to the jeweler's and ordered a man's toilet set in silver, with the letters H.B. on each piece. Two days later we learned that she had bought a complete outfit of men's clothing, including a nightshirt, and we said, "They are married." We were really glad. We were glad because the two female cousins were even more Grierson than Miss Emily had ever been.

So we were surprised when Homer Barron — the streets had been finished some time since — was gone. We were a little disappointed that there was not a public blowing-off, but we believed that he had gone on to prepare for Miss Emily's coming, or to give a chance to get rid of the cousins. (By that time it was a cabal, and we were all Miss Emily's allies to help circumvent the cousins.) Sure enough, after another week they departed. And, as we had expected all along, within three days Homer Barron was back in town. A neighbor saw the Negro man admit him at the kitchen door at dusk one evening.

And that was the last we saw of Homer Barron. And of Miss Emily for some time. The Negro man went in and out with the market basket, but the front door remained closed. Now and then we would see her at a window for a moment, as the men did that night when they sprinkled the lime, but for almost six months she did not appear on the streets. Then we knew that this was to be expected too; as if that quality of her father which had thwarted her woman's life so many times had been too virulent and too furious to die.

When we next saw Miss Emily, she had grown fat and her hair was turning gray. During the next few years it grew grayer and grayer until it attained an even pepper-and-salt iron-gray, when it ceased turning. Up to the day of her death at seventy-four it was still that vigorous iron-gray, like the hair of an active man.

From that time on her front door remained closed, save for a period of six or seven years, when she was about forty, during which she gave lessons in china-painting. She fitted up a studio in one of the downstairs rooms, where the daughters and grand-daughters of Colonel Sartoris' contemporaries were sent to her with the same regularity and in the same spirit that they were sent on Sundays with a twenty-five cent piece for the collection plate. Meanwhile her taxes had been remitted.

Then the newer generation became the backbone and the spirit of the town, and the painting pupils grew up and fell away and did not send their children to her with boxes of color and tedious brushes and pictures cut from the ladies' magazines. The front door closed upon the last one and remained closed for good. When the town got free postal delivery Miss Emily alone refused to let them fasten the metal numbers above her door and attach a mailbox to it. She would not listen to them.

Daily, monthly, yearly we watched the Negro grow grayer and more stooped, going in and out with the market basket. Each December we sent her a tax notice, which would be returned by the post office a week later, unclaimed. Now and then we would see her in one of the downstairs windows — she had evidently shut up the top floor of the house — like the carven torso of an idol in a niche, looking or not looking at us, we could never tell which. Thus she passed from generation to generation — dear, inescapable, impervious, tranquil, and perverse.

And so she died. Fell ill in the house filled with dust and shadows, with only a doddering Negro man to wait on her. We did not even know she was sick; we had long since given up trying to get any information from the Negro. He talked to no one, probably not even to her, for his voice had grown harsh and rusty, as if from disuse.

She died in one of the downstairs rooms, in a heavy walnut bed with a curtain, her gray head propped on a pillow yellow and moldy with age and lack of sunlight.

V

The Negro met the first of the ladies at the front door and let them in, with their hushed, sibilant voices and their quick, curious glances, and then he disappeared. He walked right through the house and out the back and was not seen again.

The two female cousins came at once. They held the funeral on the second day, with the town coming to look at Miss Emily beneath a mass of bought flowers, with the crayon face of her father musing profoundly above the bier and the ladies sibilant and macabre; and the very old men — some in their brushed Confederate uniforms — on the porch and the lawn, talking of Miss Emily as if she had been a contemporary of theirs, believing that they had danced with her and courted her perhaps, confusing time with its mathematical progression, as the old do, to whom all the past is not a diminishing road, but, instead, a huge meadow which no winter ever quite touches, divided from them now by the narrow bottleneck of the most recent decade of years.

Already we knew that there was one room in that region above stairs which no one had seen in forty years, and which would have to be forced. They waited until Miss Emily was decently in the ground before they opened it.

The violence of breaking down the door seemed to fill this room with pervading dust. A thin, acrid pall as of the tomb seemed to lie everywhere upon this room decked and furnished as for a bridal: upon the valance curtains of faded rose color, upon the rose-shaded lights, upon the dressing table, upon the delicate array of crystal and the man's toilet things backed with tarnished silver, silver so tarnished that the monogram was obscured. Among them lay a collar and tie, as if they had just been removed, which, lifted, left upon the surface a pale crescent in the dust. Upon a chair hung the suit, carefully folded; beneath it the two mute shoes and the discarded socks.

The man himself lay in the bed.

For a long while we just stood there, looking down at the profound and fleshless grin. The body had apparently once lain in the attitude of an embrace, but now the long sleep that outlasts love, that conquers even the grimace of love, had cuckolded him. What was left of him, rotted beneath what was left of the nightshirt, had become inextricable from the bed in which he lay; and upon him and upon the pillow beside him lay that even coating of the patient and biding dust.

Then we noticed that in the second pillow was the indentation of a head. One of us lifted something from it, and leaning forward, that faint and invisible dust dry and acrid in the nostrils, we saw a long strand of iron-gray hair.

Index

Symbols Commonly Used in Marking Papers

All instructors have their own techniques for commenting on essays, but many make substantial use of the following symbols. When instructors use a symbol, they assume that the student will carefully read the marked passage and will see the error or will check the appropriate reference.

agr	faulty agreement between subject and verb
awk (K)	awkward
cap	use a capital letter
cf	comma fault
choppy	too many short sentences; subordinate; see pp. 54–55
diction	inappropriate word; see p. 46
emph	emphasis is obscured
frag	fragmentary sentence
id	unidiomatic expression
ital	underline to indicate italics; see p. 72
k	awkward
l	logic; this does not follow
lc	use lower case, not capitals
mm	misplaced modifier
¶	new paragraph
pass	weak use of the passive; see p. 53
ref	reference of pronoun vague or misleading